TEACHING STRESS MANAGEMENT

Activities for Children and Young Adults

Nanette E. Tummers

Eastern Connecticut State University

Human Kinetics

Library of Congress Cataloging-in-Publication Data

Tummers, Nanette.
  Teaching stress management : activities for children and young adults / Nanette Tummers.
      p. cm.
  Includes bibliographical references.
  ISBN-13: 978-0-7360-9336-1 (soft cover)
  ISBN-10: 0-7360-9336-2 (soft cover)
  1. Students--Mental health. 2. Stress in children. 3. Stress in youth. 4. Stress management--
Study and teaching. I. Title.
  LB3430.T86 2011
  155.9'042--dc22

                          2011009242

ISBN-10: 0-7360-9336-2 (print)
ISBN-13: 978-0-7360-9336-1 (print)

Copyright © 2011 by Nanette E. Tummers

The web addresses cited in this text were current as of March 2011, unless otherwise noted.

Acquisitions Editor: Cheri Scott; **Developmental Editor:** Ragen E. Sanner; **Assistant Editors:** Anne Rumery and Derek Campbell; **Copyeditor:** Tom Tiller; **Permission Manager:** Dalene Reeder; **Graphic Designer:** Fred Starbird; **Graphic Artist:** Denise Lowry; **Cover Designer:** Keith Blomberg; **Photographer (cover):** Photodisc; **Photographer (interior):** Mountain photo used in design courtesy of Daniel W. Sanner; sunflower, clouds, and gosling photos used in design courtesy of Ragen E. Sanner; all others © Human Kinetics, unless otherwise noted; **Art Manager:** Kelly Hendren; **Associate Art Manager:** Alan L. Wilborn; **Illustrator:** © Human Kinetics; **Printer:** United Graphics

Printed in the United States of America   10 9 8 7 6 5 4 3 2 1

The paper in this book is certified under a sustainable forestry program.

Human Kinetics
Web site: www.HumanKinetics.com

United States: Human Kinetics, P.O. Box 5076, Champaign, IL 61825-5076
800-747-4457
e-mail: humank@hkusa.com

Canada: Human Kinetics, 475 Devonshire Road Unit 100, Windsor, ON N8Y 2L5
800-465-7301 (in Canada only)
e-mail: info@hkcanada.com

Europe: Human Kinetics, 107 Bradford Road, Stanningley, Leeds LS28 6AT, United Kingdom
+44 (0) 113 255 5665
e-mail: hk@hkeurope.com

Australia: Human Kinetics, 57A Price Avenue, Lower Mitcham, South Australia 5062
08 8372 0999
e-mail: info@hkaustralia.com

New Zealand: Human Kinetics, P.O. Box 80, Torrens Park, South Australia 5062
0800 222 062
e-mail: info@hknewzealand.com

E5141

This book is dedicated to my best
stress management tools: the girls
(Becky, Carol, Dorothy, Jane, Kathy, Lee, Leslie,
Lisa, Lucy, Lynda, Jackie, Jessica, Peggy, Sara,
Sarah, and Greg and Gus)!

Contents

Activity Finder

Activity	Page	Concept	Early childhood	Elementary	Middle school	Young adult	Reproducible available in appendix A
CHAPTER 4 *(continued)*							
Hardiness Discussion and Writing Exercises	53	Hardiness			x	x	Hardiness Discussion and Writing Exercises, page 201
What Habits Do Successful Students Practice?	53	Hardiness			x	x	
Stress Detective	55	Social and Emotional Learning		x	x	x	Stress Detective Log, page 202
Wellness Brainstorm	55	Social and Emotional Learning			x	x	Wellness Brainstorm, page 203
Wellness Magazine	56	Social and Emotional Learning			x	x	
Gratitude Journal	57	Social and Emotional Learning	x	x	x	x	Gratitude Journal, page 205
Scaffold Meditations	58	Social and Emotional Learning		x	x	x	
Loving Kindness	58	Social and Emotional Learning		x	x	x	
A Beam of Kindness	59	Social and Emotional Learning	x	x	x	x	
Practicing Random Acts of Kindness	60	Social and Emotional Learning	x	x	x	x	
Wise Owl Speaks	61	Social and Emotional Learning		x	x		Wise Owl Checklist, page 206
What Pushes Your Angry Buttons?	62	Social and Emotional Learning		x	x	x	What Pushes Your Angry Buttons?, page 207
Dealing With Difficult Situations	62	Social and Emotional Learning		x	x	x	Dealing With Difficult Situations, page 208
Count to 10	63	Social and Emotional Learning	x	x	x	x	
Talking About Feelings	64	Social and Emotional Learning	x	x	x		
Understanding Strong Feelings	64	Facing Fierce Feelings	x	x	x		
Stop, Drop, and Be Calm Tool	65	Facing Fierce Feelings	x	x	x		Stop, Drop, and Be Calm, page 209
Stop, Breathe, and Act Smart Tool	66	Facing Fierce Feelings	x	x			Stop, Breathe, and Act Smart, page 210
Facing Feelings Step-by-Step Tool	67	Facing Fierce Feelings			x	x	
Logging Strong Feelings	68	Facing Fierce Feelings	x	x	x	x	Strong Feelings Log, page 211
Problem Diary	68	Facing Fierce Feelings		x	x	x	Problem Diary, page 212

(continued)

Activity	Page	Concept	Early childhood	Elementary	Middle school	Young adult	Reproducible available in appendix A
CHAPTER 4 (continued)							
Hitting the Pause Button	89	Heart Smart		x	x	x	
This Is My Happy Place	90	Happiness	x	x	x	x	
It's Raining Healthy Habits!	91	Healthy Lifestyle		x	x	x	Mind Map, page 223
Better Sleep Habits Checklist	92	Healthy Lifestyle		x	x	x	
Physical Activity Challenge	93	Physical Activity	x	x	x	x	Physical Activity Challenge Calendar, page 224
Repeat to Delete Stress	94	Physical Activity		x	x	x	
Eat for the Health of It	95	Healthy Eating		x	x	x	
Sizing Up the Ads	96	Healthy Eating		x	x	x	
CHAPTER 5							
Belly Breaths	99	Breathing Tools	x	x	x	x	
Open-the-Throat Breath	99	Breathing Tools	x	x	x	x	
"My Name Is . . ."	100	Breathing Tools	x	x			
Wild Kingdom Breath	101	Breathing Tools	x	x			
Stretching Out the Breath	101	Breathing Tools		x	x	x	
Mask Breath	102	Breathing Tools	x	x	x		
Breathe In, Breathe Out	102	Breathing Tools		x	x	x	
ABC Breath	103	Breathing Tools	x	x			
Whole-Body Breathing	103	Breathing Tools		x	x	x	
Quiet Down	104	Breathing Tools		x	x	x	
Breathing In Cool Air, Breathing Out Warm Air	105	Meditation		x	x	x	
Sign of Peace	106	Meditation		x	x	x	
My Favorite Things	107	Meditation		x	x	x	
Taking a Test	108	Meditation		x	x	x	
Blueprint	108	Meditation		x	x	x	
Shake It Up!	109	Meditation		x	x		
Spirit, Mind, and Body Scan	110	Meditation		x	x		
Sound Meditation	111	Meditation	x	x	x	x	
Walking Meditation	112	Meditation		x	x	x	
Outdoor Walking Meditation	112	Meditation		x	x	x	
Neck Stretch	113	Stretching		x	x	x	
Save That Pose!	114	Yoga Movement	x	x			
Freeze It!	115	Yoga Movement	x	x	x		

(continued)

Activity	Page	Concept	Early childhood	Elementary	Middle school	Young adult	Reproducible available in appendix A
CHAPTER 5 (continued)							
Tree and Leaf Game	116	Yoga Movement	x	x	x		
Sun Salutations	117	Yoga Movement		x	x	x	
Diamond Breath	119	Qigong		x	x	x	
Playing With Energy	119	Qigong		x	x	x	
Birds in Flight	121	Guided Creative Imagination		x	x	x	
Floating Bubbles	122	Guided Creative Imagination		x	x	x	
Kick It to the Curb	122	Guided Creative Imagination		x	x	x	
Glitter Jars	123	Guided Creative Imagination		x	x		
Paint a Picture	124	Guided Creative Imagination		x	x		
A Few of My Favorite Things	124	Guided Creative Imagination	x	x			
Brain Scan	125	Guided Creative Imagination		x	x	x	
Spring Cleaning	126	Guided Creative Imagination			x	x	
Superhero	128	Guided Creative Imagination	x	x			
Rainbow Adventure	128	Guided Creative Imagination	x	x			
Energizing With the Colors of the Rainbow	129	Guided Creative Imagination			x	x	
Flower Power Shower	130	Guided Creative Imagination		x	x		
Wise Sage	131	Guided Creative Imagination		x	x	x	
Ordering a Pizza	131	Guided Creative Imagination		x	x		
Take a Hike in Soothing Nature	132	Guided Creative Imagination			x	x	
Progressive Relaxation Short Script	133	Relaxation	x	x	x		
Pay Attention to Me!	135	Relaxation	x	x	x		
Autogenics	136	Relaxation	x	x	x	x	
Quick Minute of Autogenics	137	Relaxation	x	x	x	x	
Ball of Warmth	137	Relaxation		x	x	x	
Using Stress Balls	138	Relaxation		x	x	x	

Activity	Page	Concept	Early childhood	Elementary	Middle school	Young adult	Reproducible available in appendix A
CHAPTER 5 (continued)							
Three-Minute Checkup	138	Relaxation		x	x	x	
Beach Wave	139	Relaxation		x	x	x	
Nature's Colors	140	Relaxation		x	x		
Relaxation With Beanie Babies	140	Relaxation	x	x			
Starfish	141	Relaxation	x	x			
Magic Freeze Wand	142	Relaxation	x	x			
Bat Ears	142	Music Therapy	x	x	x	x	
Copycat	143	Music Therapy	x	x	x	x	
Drumming	144	Music Therapy	x	x	x	x	
Puppets	145	Expressive Art Therapy	x	x	x		
Jewelry	146	Expressive Art Therapy		x	x	x	
Dealer's Choice	146	Expressive Art Therapy		x	x	x	
This Is My Life!	147	Journaling		x	x	x	
Unsent Letters	148	Journaling		x	x	x	
My Dreams	148	Journaling		x	x	x	
Fill in the Blank!	149	Journaling		x	x	x	Fill in the Blank!, page 225
My Accomplishments	150	Journaling		x	x	x	My Accomplishments, page 226
A Reflection on the Serenity Prayer	150	Journaling		x	x	x	My Reflection on the Serenity Prayer, page 227
An Expansion of the Serenity Prayer	151	Journaling			x	x	
Sharing My Stress Strategies	152	Journaling		x	x	x	Sharing My Stress Strategies, page 228
My Favorite Ways to De-Stress	152	Journaling		x	x	x	
Brief Grief	153	Journaling		x	x	x	Steps for Goal Setting, page 229
Retelling a Story From a New Perspective	154	Storytelling		x	x	x	
Stress Management Heroes	155	Storytelling		x	x	x	
Humor Scrapbook	156	Humor		x	x	x	Tickle My Funny Bone, page 230
Joke of the Day or Week	156	Humor		x	x	x	
Stand Up for Humor	157	Humor		x	x	x	
A Funny Thing Happened on the Way to . . .	157	Humor		x	x	x	
Silly Movie Fest	158	Humor		x	x	x	

(continued)

Activity	Page	Concept	Early childhood	Elementary	Middle school	Young adult	Reproducible available in appendix A
CHAPTER 6 (continued)							
Genevieve's Happy Teachers Retreat Day	183	Curriculum Infusion	x	x	x	x	
Tokens of Appreciation	184	Curriculum Infusion	x	x	x		
Circle of Respect	184	Curriculum Infusion		x	x	x	
Zany Scavenger Hunt	185	Team Building			x	x	
Making a Cup of Hot Chocolate	186	Team Building		x	x	x	
Color Me Awesome	186	Team Building	x	x	x	x	
Team Architects	187	Team Building		x	x	x	
Supreme Team Challenge	187	Team Building		x	x	x	
Air Traffic Control	188	Team Building	x	x			
Dream Team Newspaper or Web Page	188	Team Building		x	x	x	
News 24-7	189	Team Building		x	x		
Team Video	189	Team Building		x	x		
Meaningful Mobiles	190	Team Building		x	x	x	
Take Your Little Brother or Sister to School Day	191	Mentoring		x	x	x	
Dear Little Sibling	191	Mentoring				x	Dear Little Sibling, page 236
Peer Problem Solving	192	Peer Mentoring		x	x	x	
Service Project for Stress Management	194	Service Learning				x	
Greeting to Know Each Other	195	After-School Program	x	x	x	x	

Preface

The Centers for Disease Control and Prevention (CDC) is a federal agency that provides the United States with information and tools intended to protect and enhance people's health. The CDC (2008a) has identified six critical categories of health risk behavior among U.S. students: injury and violence; inactivity; poor nutrition; tobacco use; use of alcohol and drugs; and sexual behavior that contributes to unplanned pregnancy, infection with HIV, or infection with other sexually transmitted diseases. Although stress is not currently listed among these leading categories of risk, we (as administrators, educators, parents, professionals, and others involved with students) know that stress is pervasive in students' lives and that it is entwined with many of the risk behaviors that students exhibit. Indeed, the CDC (2009a) identifies stress among youth as a quickly emerging risk factor that may contribute to many of the six listed categories of risky behavior.

Despite the urgent need to address the influence of stress in student's lives, the current literature does not cover stress management for students in a manner that is pedagogically sound, practical, and comprehensive. In order to fill that gap, this book provides a resource for understanding stress among today's young people. The book honors your willingness and passion to provide engaging, experiential stress management activities for students by means of student-centered learning endeavors and a belief in the importance of high-quality activities that support healthy and balanced living. This volume offers you numerous insights into the vital role that stress management can play in the lives of students from pre-K through the 12th grade in a developmentally sound fashion. The book speaks both to parents and to professionals who work with students in a wide variety of school and nonschool settings (e.g., afterschool and high-risk programs). The main purpose of the book is to offer pragmatic methods for integrating stress management into any environment—for example, into an academic class as an activity or a short "stressless" break during recess.

Teaching Stress Management provides an effective and practical approach that is aligned with the National Health Education Standards (Joint Committee 2007). The information presented in part I of the book is based on applied research and on evidence from best practices in our schools. The activities described in part II can be used by schools at little or no cost to help students deal proactively with their stress. This book offers you the best research and practical application from the positive psychology movement, including the emerging focus areas of optimism, social support, resiliency, right-brain engagement, mindfulness, emotional intelligence, and the responsive classroom. These approaches can enhance our students' health and happiness by helping them develop the skills needed to meet NHES standard 7: "Students will demonstrate the ability to practice health-enhancing behaviors and avoid or reduce health risks" (Joint Committee 2007).

It is increasingly apparent that our students suffer mounting consequences from the stress they experience. As concerned teachers, parents, and community members, we must all commit to serve as advocates who teach our students how to reduce and manage their stress. The following chapters provide simple, cost-effective, and engaging tools to help our student learn to navigate and thrive in the stressful world in which they live and as they become productive citizens with the lifelong skillset of stress management.

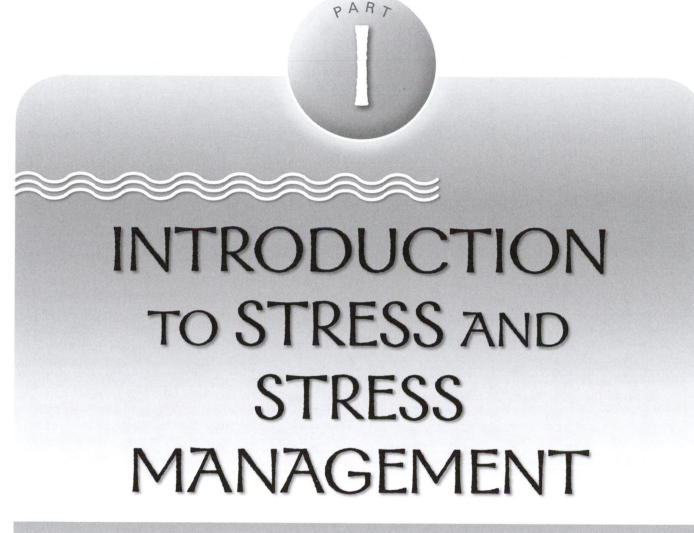

PART

I

INTRODUCTION TO STRESS AND STRESS MANAGEMENT

© Photodisc

Stress in Our Schools Today

HAL: I honestly think you ought to calm down; take a stress pill and think things over.

2001: A Space Odyssey

This chapter will help you develop your understanding both of stress in students' lives and of the critical need to help students develop their ability to prevent and proactively manage stress. Because stress management is a lifelong skill, we must provide students with as many opportunities as possible to practice using stress management tools throughout their school years. The National Health Education Standards (NHES) lay out expectations "for what students should know and be able to do . . . [in order] to promote personal, family, and community health" (Joint Committee 2007). Of the eight standards, only the first one covers content—basic facts and core concepts of health—whereas the remaining seven address skill development. Similarly, this book emphasizes the need for students to practice and enhance their stress management skills. The standards are listed in the accompanying sidebar, and they are referred to in this book by means of the abbreviated titles given in parentheses after each standard in the sidebar list.

Never before have educators had to deal with the breadth and depth of the stress and mental health problems currently experienced by students. In fact, the mental health issues facing our students, and consequently our teachers, are fast becoming an educational crisis (Middlebrooks & Audage 2008). This chapter provides the information necessary for you to understand the reality of stress in our students' lives—and how it affects their health and happiness. It is important for instructors to understand the national standards in order to provide students with the necessary practices needed to meet the cognitive, interpersonal, and physical health goals set forth in the standards. Each standard builds on others; for example, students need to understand what influences their stress (NHES 2, analyzing influences) in order to practice health-enhancing behaviors (NHES 7).

Addressing Stress in the Classroom

It is critical for stressed students to be helped by supportive adults who care for them, and this need is in fact the reason that this book exists. As you will find out, stress plays a decisive role in the current and future health of our students. In addition, anyone who works with students must develop his or her own stress management skills, and students need to see adults who model lifelong stress management, provide creative and engaging methods for practicing these skills, and advocate for the importance of stress management in the curriculum.

The National Health Education Standards

- **Standard 1**—Students will comprehend concepts related to health promotion and disease prevention to enhance health. (core concepts)

- **Standard 2**—Students will analyze the influence of family, peers, culture, media, technology, and other factors on health behaviors. (analyzing influences)

- **Standard 3**—Students will demonstrate the ability to access valid information, products, and services to enhance health. (accessing information)

- **Standard 4**—Students will demonstrate the ability to use interpersonal communication skills to enhance health and avoid or reduce health risks. (interpersonal communication)

- **Standard 5**—Students will demonstrate the ability to use decision-making skills to enhance health. (decision making)

- **Standard 6**—Students will demonstrate the ability to use goal-setting skills to enhance health. (goal setting)

- **Standard 7**—Students will demonstrate the ability to practice health-enhancing behaviors and avoid or reduce health risks. (practicing health-enhancing behaviors)

- **Standard 8**—Students will demonstrate the ability to advocate for personal, family, and community health. (advocacy)

Reprinted from NHES.

According to the Office of the Surgeon General (1999), mental health problems collectively account for more than 15 percent of the overall burden of disease from all other causes, and a growing body of evidence suggests that many chronic diseases are rooted in a mental health issue. In the past, cancer was not spoken about and was considered a social stigma; now, mental health is not talked about and is often excluded from school curriculums. Thus it is imperative that we realize the importance and urgency of treating and preventing mental illness and promoting mental wellness, especially given the amount of time that public school students spend in school and after-school programs.

Much of the research on stress has focused on adults or college students by necessity because it is difficult to conduct research using children as human subjects. In turning our attention to children, it is important that we not view them merely as mini adults. Children's physical, psychological, and social growth—as well as their environments—are constantly changing to a much greater extent than is true for adults, whose lives tend to settle into a certain stability. In contrast, children can change rapidly. Do you remember your own growth spurts as a child? Have you witnessed how quickly a child's mood can change? In addition, research suggests (Jensen 2005) that children have not fully developed the part of the brain responsible for making sound health choices; in fact, that part of the brain is not fully matured until the early 20s.

What Is Stress?

Defining stress can be a complicated matter because the word itself can indicate a cause, a symptom, or a response; the meaning depends on the context. Stress can indicate a force or strain requiring change (stressors are the people, events, and situations that cause stress). Stress can also refer to a generalized mental state, as in feeling "stressed out" or distressed, or to a bodily reaction, as in the fight-or-flight response (Rutter 1983). If you asked a child, a teacher, a parent, or a colleague to define stress, each would likely offer a

different interpretation. Stress is a subjective and individualized occurrence. How the stress is perceived depends on a variety of factors, such as a child's age, temperament, gender, environment, and support (Trad & Greenblatt 1990).

The term stress is a fairly new addition to the American vernacular, yet it currently seems ubiquitous, and most everyone seems to be feeling stressed by the constraints, problems, and concerns of the 21st century. In contrast, the word was rarely used at the turn of the previous century, when people died mostly from infectious diseases. Now, however, with the introduction of vaccines and immunization, death is most often caused by lifestyle diseases, and many of the risk factors that contribute to these illnesses arise in early childhood—for example, inactivity, overeating, smoking, and unmanaged stress. Therefore, it is crucial that a child's education begin as early as possible to help the child recognize sources of stress, understand and manage symptoms of stress, and engage in planning and behaviors to prevent and manage the detrimental effects of stress.

This book uses the concept of stress put forth by James Humphrey in *Stress Management for Elementary Schools* (1993). In this view, the *perception* of stress involves any external or internal factor that makes it difficult for the student to adapt and thus forces the student to exert increased effort in order to come into equilibrium or balance. Perception is critical. Very few things are universally or inherently stressful to every person; rather, it

© Julie Eydman/fotolia.com

The perception of stress resides in the eye of the student. You may not yet know all of the individual stressors that a student is trying to cope with, so try to remember that the student's perspective of stress defines the situation.

is the individual's perception that makes something a stressor. Thus, in the school context, no two children react in the same way to the same potential stressor.

In order to help you understand the nature of perception, here is a short lesson in brain physiology. The amygdala, which is part of the brain's limbic system, is located in the brain stem. Its role is to regulate emotions; it generates and stores them and connects emotions to situations. In stressful situations, the amygdala can quickly override the brain's ability to think things through; instead, it allows emotions to rule over facts. Our goal here, then, is to help students develop the ability to prevent the amygdala from taking over—that is, to make a conscious, deliberate choice to stop during the "almost moment" that occurs just before the amygdala takes over. Dr. Amy Saltzman uses the term "almost moment" in working with children in underserved schools in the San Francisco Bay Area (Saltzman 2010). The skills we teach students can help them use the almost moment—that critical juncture where intervention is possible—to switch out of emotion mode into thinking mode. In stress management, then, students learn to respond effectively to difficult thoughts and feelings rather than merely reacting when these thoughts and feelings have taken over.

Types of Stress

Students may be surprised to learn that stress doesn't always mean something bad; in fact, stress is necessary for motivation and growth. Stress is perceived as negative when the accumulation of stressors becomes overwhelming or when the source of stress lies beyond our control.

Eustress

Though often viewed as negative, stress can involve challenge that is constructive or positive, and this form of stress is known as eustress, or good stress (Selye 1974). Eustress involves a challenge that motivates and energizes the student without the resultant negative cascade of stress-related symptoms. Think of a bodybuilder who does the same weight routine for years without change or challenge; the bodybuilder will not get stronger or build bigger muscles. The same goes for learning how to do math or ride a skateboard. We crave challenge, and the body and mind can actually get a boost from facing challenge—we feel pumped up! In such situations, the body releases a hormone called epinephrine (also called adrenaline), which causes the body to become stronger and muster the energy to meet the challenge. This process is beneficial in the short run, but if it continues too long the body will be unable to keep up with the demands.

Distress

Distress involves the perception of stress as negative. It can include daily hassles such as being late, forgetting one's homework or lunch, or waiting one's turn in a long line. Acute distress is intense but short-lived, as when you almost hit a pothole while riding your bike. Chronic or long-term stress, also called toxic stress (Middlebrooks & Audage 2008), persists over a longer period of time and may involve a combination of stressors (e.g., difficult schoolwork, trouble at home, and bullying by a classmate). The word toxic here is appropriate. This form of stress can be extremely detrimental to our students in the areas of brain development, immune system function, learning and memory, overreactivity to stress, and, ultimately, long-term health problems.

Emerging research estimates that 70 percent to 80 percent of illnesses and diseases are connected in some way to stress (Seaward 2006). The number one killer of Americans is heart disease, and prolonged or chronic stress is related to high blood pressure, elevated heart rate, abnormal blood lipids and blood sugar levels, and inflammation—which all contribute to heart attacks and strokes. Stress has also been found to be a factor in migraines and headaches and in digestive disorders such as irritable bowel syndrome, ulcers, and colitis. Another disease facing many Americans is cancer. Stress may affect the body's ability to correctly replicate healthy cells and may encourage abnormal cell growth. In addition, when the body and mind are continually engaged in reaction to perceived stress, the body releases emergency hormones including epinephrine and cortisol, which can interfere with restful sleep and cause sleep deprivation, which denies our bodies the ability to explore feelings and situations from the different perspective that deep, restful dream states enable.

Fight or Flight

Stress sets off the fight-or-flight system that allows the body to access resources that enable one to fight or flee. This system was designed to adapt and protect us in cases of acute, life-threatening stressors, but in the case of unrelenting chronic stress the system becomes overloaded and unable to recover. *This is the critical concept in understanding modern-day stress*: Our bodies do not get the time to rebuild and recover all the resources expended in trying to meet the demands of constant stressors. Therefore, the individual may react not by fighting or fleeing but by freezing, denying, lying, hiding, avoiding, procrastinating—or just giving up!

Children Under Stress

According to a report (Middlebrooks & Audage 2008) by the Centers for Disease Control and Prevention (CDC), stress can exert major influence on brain development during early childhood. Childhood stress has been linked to risky behaviors and health problems in adulthood. Categories of risk include the physical (e.g., accidents, bullying), the chemical (e.g., fetal alcohol syndrome, secondary or sidestream smoke), the biological (e.g., malnutrition, genetics), the psychological (e.g., sexual abuse, neglect, emotional abuse, divorce), and the socioeconomic or cultural (e.g., competition, discrimination, poverty) (Middlebrooks & Audage 2008; Arnold 1990).

It is difficult to pinpoint the percentage of our students who are stressed at any given time. The American Academy of Family Physicians estimates that 75 percent to 90 percent of visits to physicians are stress related. At most schools, for example, it would be fairly easy to identify when testing is being done by the increase in student visits to the school nurse or by days missed due to illness.

According to a national survey conducted by the National Institute of Mental Health, our children and teens face significant mental health challenges (Merikangas et al. 2010). Here are some key findings from the survey of more than 10,000 young people ranging in age from 13 to 18 years old:

- 11 percent reported being severely impaired by a mood disorder (e.g., depression or bipolar disorder).
- 10 percent reported being severely impaired by a behavior disorder such as attention deficit/hyperactivity disorder.
- 8 percent reported being severely impaired by at least one type of anxiety disorder.

Adapted from Merikangas et al. 2010.

The Youth Risk Behavior Surveillance System (YRBSS) is a national school-based survey of ninth and twelfth graders (Centers for Disease Control 2010c). According to the 2009 Youth Risk Behavior Survey (YRBS), conducted by the CDC over a 12-month period, 26.1 percent of ninth graders nationwide reported that they had "felt so sad or hopeless almost every day for two or more weeks in a row that they [had] stopped doing some usual activities" (Centers for Disease Control 2010).

A major retrospective study of 17,000 adults examined the link between childhood stress and health problems in adulthood (Middlebrooks & Audage 2008). Two-thirds of adults reported at least one adverse childhood experience, such as abuse or exposure to violence, and 20 percent reported three or more such experiences. These experiences were related to participating in risky behaviors as youth, including getting pregnant, engaging in various risky sexual practices, abusing alcohol or drugs, and attempting suicide.

It is estimated that five percent of children have attention deficit/hyperactive disorder (ADHD) without a learning disability and another four percent have ADHD with a learning disability according to the National Health Interview Survey, making ADHD the most common behavior disorder (Pastor & Reuben 2008). Gonzalez and Sellers (2002) found that students who used problem solving and other strategies to manage their emotional reactions to stress were able to improve their academic and social functioning. In another approach, meditation was found to reduce ADHD symptoms of stress and anxiety in children of ages 11 to 17 (Grosswald, Stixrud, Travis, & Bateh 2008).

Obviously, then, children are facing a great deal of distress, but parents may be unaware of this reality. According to a survey conducted by the American Psychological Association titled *Stress in America* (Munsey 2010), parents often don't know what is stressing their children. One-third of students reported having a headache, but only 13 percent of parents reported that their children had headaches related to stress. Nearly half of students reported sleep difficulty, but only 13 percent of parents perceived their children as having difficulty sleeping. The most widely studied symptoms are recurrent abdominal pain and headaches (Sharrer & Ryan-Wenger 2002). These findings have been replicated in other studies indicating that children perceive higher levels of stress in their own experience than do their parents (Bagdi

& Pfister 2006). Here are some common signs and symptoms of stress exhibited by students:

- Avoiding school or activities
- Bed-wetting
- Confrontational behavior (e.g., picking on others)
- Crying
- Depression
- Disturbed eating patterns
- Disturbed sleep patterns
- Headache
- Lashing out and anger
- Stomachache
- Vomiting
- Withdrawal, extreme shyness

Cleary, there is a disconnect between what students are experiencing and what parents are perceiving. With that in mind, chapter 3 offers ways to help parents understand the seriousness of stress and stress-related symptoms in their children's lives.

Causes of Stress for Students

Traumatic events are common experiences among children. In a study of 1,420 children, more than two-thirds reported experiencing at least one traumatic event (Copeland, Keeler, Angold, & Costello 2007). About 13 percent of the two-thirds who reported a traumatic event reported developing short-term symptoms of post-traumatic stress. Students who experienced numerous events were more vulnerable to depression, anxiety, and other stress-related issues.

Stressful issues challenging students today also include:

- Changing family patterns—This category of stressors includes abuse, divorce, job loss, military deployment, and the illness of a parent or sibling.

- Loss—Threat of the loss of a parent or caretaker is a nearly universal risk factor for stress among children (Rutter 1983). A special report in the *New England Journal of Medicine* found that after the 9/11 terrorist attacks, 34 percent of children experienced at least one stress symptoms, and 47 percent reported worrying about their safety and that of their loved ones (Schuster et al. 2001).

- Economic concerns—The National Association of School Psychologists (2008) suggests that economic uncertainty is a critical source of stress for many families. The stress on the family can be unsettling and confusing and can easily be transferred to children. It is important for children in such situations to feel in control.

- Puberty and sexuality concerns including sexual orientation (Desrochers, Cowan, and Christner 2009).

- Typical academic issues—School provides various stressors, including overscheduling, adjustment such as transitioning from elementary to middle school, competition, testing, gender differences in learning and achievement, being held back, homework load, and accessibility concerns for students with disabilities.

- Bullying—School bullying (whether physical, verbal, relational, or cyber) has become a source of stress for many students. In a National Institutes of Health study surveying more than 7,500 students in the sixth through tenth grades, about 21 percent of students reported being bullied physically at least once in the previous 2 months, 54 percent reported being bullied verbally, 51 socially, and 14 percent electronically (Wang, Iannotti, & Nansel 2009). Friendship generally played a protective role against bullying but not in the case of cyberbullying.

- Technology—New ways of using technology are not always healthy for our children, and the potential problems include excessive consumerism, sex texting (or "sexting," i.e., sending sexually explicit photos and words via digital communication), sedentary hours spent playing video games instead of engaging in physical activity, exposure to violence, pressure from social networking, and serious violations of privacy as students can be videotaped and broadcasted without their knowledge or permission. Research suggests that childhood exposure to violence portrayed in the media (TV, film, and video) may lead to more aggressive and antisocial behavior as children grow older (Christakis & Zimmerman 2007; Huesmann 2007). There is also a digital divide. Some students lack access to the Internet either at home or (due to limited transportation options) at the library and thus may be unable to research a topic in the same way that other students can.

- Pressure to excel—Gifted students may also experience excessive stress (Bradley 2006). In addition to the normal stressors experienced by their peers, gifted students are also subject to the stressors of overscheduling, high expectations, competition, perfectionism, difficulty in relating to peers, and lack of constructive challenge.

It is clear that students today contend with an enormous depth and breadth of daily stressors. Young students are less cognitively and emotionally developed than adults, yet many are often left without guidance on how to deal with the emotions and stress in their lives. Teachers can help to change that through the use of the simple activities and exercises that this book offers.

Diversity and Stress: Personality, Cultural Differences, and the Sexes

Genetics can influence an individual's susceptibility to stress. For example, genetics can influence the body's use of the neurotransmitters serotonin and dopamine, which are associated with pleasure and maintaining control (Karren, Smith, Hafen, & Frandsen 2010). However, even though genetics play a role in how well a person handles stress, learning positive coping skills is just as important. Students can learn positive coping skills through comprehensive stress management curriculums.

The Youth Risk Behavior Surveillance System offers information addressing racial and ethnic subgroups and health risks (Centers for Disease Control 2010b). While all students are facing increased risk, there are higher numbers reported in various subgroups. For example, nearly 7 percent of black students and 10 percent of Hispanic

students in the United States reported that they didn't attend high school because they felt unsafe either at school or while going to or from school; only 4 percent of white students reported feeling unsafe. Similarly, about 45 percent of black students and 40 percent of Hispanic students reported being in a physical fight one or more times in the past 12 months, whereas the number for white students was 32 percent. Table 1.1 offers more specifics about the crucial risk factors faced by our nation's minority students; further detail can be found on the CDC's website.

Some differences have been found between the sexes concerning stress. In *The Mindful Brain* (2007), Daniel Siegel, psychotherapist and clinical professor at the UCLA school of medicine, states that "female brain development appears to involve more integration, with a thicker corpus callosum" (p. 45). The corpus callosum connects the right and left hemisphere of the brain, and Siegel explains that male brains "are said to be more differentiated, or more specialized, allowing the separate regions to work intensively more on their own" (p. 45). Siegel differentiates between the functions of the two hemispheres of the brain as follows: The left side's special functions include "linguistics, linearity, logic and literal thinking" (p. 45), whereas the right side specializes in nonverbal communication, visual and spatial learning, memory, kinesthetic integration, attention, empathy, spontaneous emotions, and attentiveness. As Siegel points out, the right side is believed to mediate distress, whereas the left side is associated with positive affective states. The ability to connect and coordinate both areas of the brain is known as neural integration, which allows for balance and

Table 1.1   Selected Health Risk Behaviors by Race and Ethnicity

Health risk behavior	% African American students	% of Hispanic students	% of Caucasian students
Purposefully hit, slapped, or otherwise physically hurt by boyfriend or girlfriend (during last 12 months)	14.3	11.5	8.0
Seriously considered attempting suicide (during 12 months prior to survey)	13.0	15.4	13.1
Rode with a driver who had been drinking alcohol one or more times (during 30 days prior to survey)	30.0	34.2	26.2
Drank at least on drink of alcohol on school property on at least one day (during 30 days prior to survey)	5.4	6.9	3.3
Carried a weapon (at least 1 day in the last 30 days)	14.4	17.2	18.6

Reprinted from CDC. Available: www.cdc.gov/HealthyYouth/yrbs/pdf/yrbs07_us_disparity_race.pdf.

improved ability to manage and prevent stress. One way to bring about this balance is to practice mindfulness, which is discussed in chapter 4 as a positive coping skill.

In a study conducted in the United Kingdom by Jordan, McRorie, and Ewing (2010), male students were better able to make a successful transition into secondary school when they used emotional intelligence programs—including positive coping skills and anger management—in primary school.

Stress and Protective Factors

The field of mental health has traditionally focused on the study of maladaptive behaviors known as risk factors for mental disease. Slowly, however, the field is shifting toward what is known as the "positive psychology movement," which focuses on protective factors that help the individual to adapt (Karren et al. 2010; Rutter 1983).

One protective factor is resiliency, which is the ability to survive and thrive despite adverse circumstances. Students can build their resiliency by using the skills they develop in a comprehensive stress management program (see chapter 4 for an extensive discussion of resiliency).

Other protective factors include academic achievement, future-mindedness, critical thinking skills, and social and emotional intelligence. A statistical review (Collaborative for Academic, Social, and Emotional Learning 2008) of more than 700 social and emotional intervention studies found significant benefits for students. Their behavior improved, as did their standardized test scores. They also felt better about themselves and experienced decreases in anxiety and depression. Many school districts now include social and emotional learning in their curriculums (Viadero 2007). The State of Illinois has adopted standards for social and emotional learning (SEL) that address criteria including self- and social awareness, self-management, decision making and responsible behavior, interpersonal communication, and maintenance of positive relationships (Illinois State Board of Education 2010). Social protective factors include physical and psychological safety, connectedness to school, support from home, positive social norms, structured activities, and positive adult–student interactions (Find Youth Info 2010).

In a study of 613 children from age 8 to age 12, including 51 percent Hispanic and 49 percent non-Hispanic whites, Taxis et al. (2004) found that social connectedness and use of positive coping strategies significantly mediated the perception of stress. Similarly, a school program using a strengths-based approach with low-income African American parents found that connectedness, interpersonal communication including empathy, and rule setting decreased total behavior problems and parent–child relational stress (Sheely & Bratton 2010).

Horowitz and Garber (2006) used a meta-analytic statistical method to compare 30 studies addressing prevention of depression symptoms in children. They found multiple interacting causes of depression, which means that effective intervention must involve multiple components, including recognition of negative thinking, improvement in interpersonal relationships, and a reduction in maladaptive reactions to stress. This analysis is supported by multiple studies of the efficacy of school-based depression prevention programs by researchers at the Penn Resiliency Program (Gillham, Brunwasser, & Freres 2007), which emphasizes cognition and problem-solving skills.

Teachers need to develop strategies tailored to the age group of the students with whom they will be working. Each group—early childhood, elementary, middle school, and high school—has a unique set of stress risks and protective factors, including resiliency characteristics.

Early Childhood Students

Preschool children's response to stress can be affected by several developmental factors, including cognitive function, control issues, awareness of self and others, and attachment relationships (Barton & Zeanah 1990). A preschooler typically responds to stress by regressing into immature and disorganized behavior (e.g., having a meltdown or temper tantrum). Preschoolers' second most common reaction is attention seeking. They may also withdraw from social interaction and show changes in play patterns—for example, using play either to retreat from a difficult situation or as a reaction to it (Barton & Zeanah).

Common stressors for this age group include lack of quality child care arrangements, birth of a sibling, and parent employment obligations and limited time available to spend with the child. Stressors that go beyond the everyday include divorce, hospitalization, abuse or neglect, witnessing of violence, and the loss of a parent (Barton & Zeanah 1990).

Toxic stress can impair a child's development of certain circuits in the brain during early childhood (Middlebrooks & Audage 2008). In addition, high levels of cortisol can lead to suppression of the immune system and affect learning ability and memory function in later years.

Preschool children can benefit from various protective factors, including resiliency. It is critical to provide these young people with structure, stability, and a high quality parent–child relationship. Teachers can also serve as strong protective factors by being available as positive models for attachment. At the preschool level, learning relies heavily on the various senses; as a result, stress management activities for this age group should actively engage children in seeing, listening, touching, tasting, smelling, and moving.

Resilient preschoolers are self-confident, independent, involved in play, and able to use advanced skills in communication, locomotion, and self-help. They tolerate anxiety and frustration and are ready to take realistic risks and seek out help. They also relate well to their peers and teachers and are socially mature (Kimchi & Schaffner 1990).

Elementary Students

Stressors affecting elementary students include school demands, separation from parents and being away from home all day, acceptance of new authority figures, socializing with a larger group of peers, pressure for academic achievement, and various fears—for example, fear of success, of wetting oneself, of going unchosen for a group or team, and of failure (including test anxiety) (Middlebrooks & Audage 2008; Sears & Milburn 1990). In addition, students in the upper elementary grades vary widely in their physical and emotional maturation patterns (Humphrey 1993), and this variation can cause considerable stress, as when a student is the tallest or the shortest in class.

Protective factors for this age group include support from family, clear expectations, and an external support systems such as teachers and extended family members and other care takers. Teachers can encourage and reinforce coping efforts and positive strengths, and provide the teaching of appropriate coping skills. At about the age of 6 or 7 years, students begin the important developmental steps of learning to reason and establishing the foundation for communication skills such as listening actively, speaking mindfully, and attending to nonverbal communication (e.g., body language, eye contact).

Resilient elementary-age children are good students, enjoy their classmates and teachers, and pursue hobbies. They exhibit a wide range of constructive and creative coping skills, and they enjoy humor and get along well with others while developing meaningful friendships (Kimchi & Schaffner 1990).

Middle School and High School Students

Adolescence is a period of unique stress, and a wide variety of stressors compound this life stage—for example, pubertal growth, hormonal changes, changes in relationships with parents and peers, and cultural and societal expectations. All of these stressors involve movement toward independence as the adolescent moves away from the structured environments of home and school and into a broader social environment (Hendren 1990) that may include substantial exposure to crime and violence. This shift may be occurring earlier these days due in part to children's access to digital resources (e.g., social networking sites) and the potential for cyberbullying.

© Image Source

Resilient elementary-age children cope better with stress—thanks in part to meaningful relationships with peers.

The adolescent's move toward autonomy can result in parents feeling conflicting emotions about the adolescent's development as well as more conflicts between parents and adolescents during this stage. If the parent is also experiencing stress (e.g., divorce, employment troubles, or the responsibility of caring for aging parents), this too will affect the stress of the adolescent. For example, the parent may model ineffective coping strategies such as excessive outbursts of anger or drinking too much alcohol, or disclose too much information on topics that adolescents are not able to deal with, such as marital problems. According to neurologist Frances Jensen, the prevailing adolescent tendency toward moodiness, self-centeredness, and constantly changing plans—which can be quite frustrating for parents and teachers—may be linked to differences in brain anatomy and physiology (Knox 2010).

Students at this age often make poor choices and then face the resulting consequences. This pattern may be due to the fact that the frontal lobe of the brain, where reasoning and critical thinking occur, is not fully developed in an adolescent. These connections within the brain are formed by myelin sheaths or fatty coatings of insulation that allow information to move quickly around the brain. Because the myelin sheath is not fully formed in adolescents, the information moves more slowly; this processing is also slowed by alcohol consumption and by stress.

The adolescent brain is also very excitable and able to learn quickly, but this excitability needs to be harnessed constructively. The negative potential of excitability involves the fact that not just desirable behaviors but also undesirable ones—such as addiction—can be learned faster. We can help students learn optimally and live healthy and happy lives by providing them with opportunities to practice their ability to focus and relax.

Specific adolescent stressors include peer pressure, stress due to pressure from parents, changes at school, divorce, relocation, legal stress, gender role expectations, physical illness, worry about one's changing body, and sexual mistreatment (Hendren 1990). Adolescents may also experience a great deal of stress due to the Western cultural uncertainty about when a person becomes an adult. This uncertainty is registered in the varying (and often confusing) legal ages for driving, purchasing alcohol or cigarettes, signing a contract, dropping out of school, being tried as an adult in court, consenting to sex, obtaining access to birth control or abortion, and enlisting in the armed services. Whatever its source, adolescents may display stress in the form of depression, substance abuse, disordered eating, or even suicide.

The most significant protective factor for adolescents is the development of effective coping skills, which are referred to in this book as positive skills. These skills include cognitive behavioral strategies, maintenance of friendships, problem solving, concentration, focus, social intelligence, self-efficacy, and internal locus of control. In addition, connectedness is an important protective factor. Connectedness is the positive interaction between students and their school when they feel cared for and an important member of the learning community (Barnes, Bauza, & Treiber 2003; Gillham, Reivich, & Shatté 2002).

Resilient adolescents are high functioning, active, future minded, achievement focused, responsible, and caring. They enjoy positive self-concept and self-efficacy and an internal locus of control. They have well-defined internalized values and are empathetic, socially intuitive, and mature (Kimchi & Schaffner 1990).

The Wellness Model

In the face of this grim reality of student stress, Stephen Covey (1989) provides a wonderful model for shaping and empowering students (see figure 1.1). Those who work with school-age children may find it hard not to be overwhelmed by concern about the ways in which stress affects our students' quality of life. Covey terms this the "circle of concern" and advocates that we focus on what we can do, which he calls the "circle of influence." This approach enables us to work proactively to help students build their positive skills, and thus the book you are now reading focuses on the circle of influence by presenting positive skills that we can help our students cultivate. We can use this approach both to foster positive environments for learning communities and to advocate for effective stress management.

We can address our circle of influence by providing students with activities and opportunities that help them grow in areas such as the following:

- Physical and environmental needs—Time for rest and sleep; movement; nourishing food; feeling safe; ability to relax
- Social and spiritual needs—Meaningful relationships with and support from family, peers, trusted adults, community; the ability

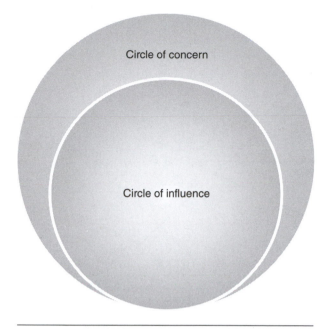

Figure 1.1 The circle of concern encompasses all of the stressors in a student's life. Focus your attention on the circle of influence which students are able to change and you can help students learn to take a more proactive and positive role in their stress management.

Adapted from Covey 1989.

to be empathetic; effective communication; enjoyment of nature

- Emotional and intellectual needs—Positive self-concept; sense of control; gratitude; ability to focus and concentrate; mindfulness; honest self-evaluation; leadership

Many other possibilities supported by research are presented in later chapters of this book.

Stress Management for Our Students

Stress evokes an image of physical symptoms, such as headaches, which are often treated without looking at root causes. A holistic approach to stress management allows for a different perspective. A holistic or wellness approach integrates all aspects of health into a unified "whole student" approach. Health involves not just treating symptoms but healing—bringing to wholeness and balance. The wellness interconnectivity model (see figure 1.2 on page 14) includes all the dimensions of human health: physical, emotional, intellectual, social, spiritual, and global or environmental. Each of

these dimensions influences the others, and an interconnection between the dimensions is crucial to overall health. Stress influences each of the dimensions of health, as when we feel physically exhausted, emotionally out of control, unable to work intellectually through a problem, socially disconnected from others or from ourselves, apathetic about war or urban decay, or lacking in inner peace or meaningful purpose.

The spiritual dimension may be misconstrued as a religious or theological one. Within the wellness context, the spiritual dimension involves the student's self-image and self-worth, meaningful connections with others, and a sense of something that gives his or her life meaning. The source of this meaningfulness depends on how the *student* defines and determines it—be it called God or a higher power or a connection to nature, art, or community. The biggest gift we can give our students is to teach them to maintain a healthy balance and integrate all of these important dimensions of their lives.

The medical community is slowly beginning to understand the integration between the various dimensions of health. Stress is a significant reason for visits to the doctor, and there is a slowly emerging paradigm shift away from a mechanistic medical model. The mechanistic model focuses on disease by means of a specialist who treats symptoms, but it neglects to look at the reason behind the symptoms or to see the individual as a diverse and complex whole. Treatment in this model emphasizes fixing risk or disease through medicine or surgery. An integrative model supports the importance of the connection between the mind and body. The mind has a profound effect on health, illness, and disease as well as healing and optimal well-being. This shift currently taking place involves a move toward a holistic protective factor or integrative strengths-based model that encourages positive behaviors. A strengths-based model empowers individuals to exert control and to plan the most beneficial choices and actions for their own health and healing.

In a meta-analysis of 19 studies of school-based stress management programs, Kraag, Zeegers, Kok, Hosman, and Abu-Saad (2006) found significant positive effects in the form of decreased stress symptoms and increased coping skills and positive behaviors. Although it is difficult to identify exactly which stress management components produced the desirable results, the overall evidence supports an integrative strengths-based model.

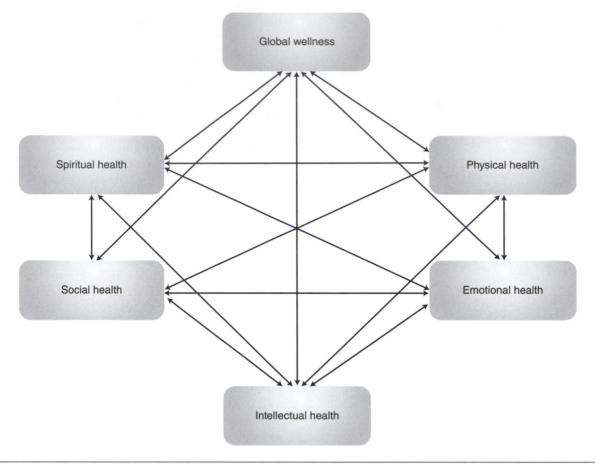

Figure 1.2   Wellness interconnectivity model.

Adapted from National Wellness Organization. Available: http://www.nationalwellness.org/index.php?id_tier=2&id_c=25

Helping Our Students Comprehend Stress Concepts

Eric Jensen's book *Teaching With the Brain in Mind* (2005) discusses the promising field of educational neuroscience. Jensen draws out important implications for parents, educators, and other caring individuals concerned with the growth and development of our students. Jensen and other educational neuroscientists believe that it is crucial for us to help students learn healthy strategies for communicating about and managing their emotions so that they can maintain their focus on learning and interpersonal relationships.

Learning is truly complex, and emotions can rule our ability to learn. We often think instinctually or reflexively in the moment, which makes sense in cases of immediate danger, but it is difficult to engage in higher ordered thinking when

we are feeling distressed, fearful, threatened, or disappointed. When students can realize the connection between getting upset and performing in a subpar manner as a learner, teammate, friend, or family member, they can learn to engage appropriate positive behaviors (Jensen 2005).

Summary

Considerable evidence indicates the far-reaching effects of stress in our students' lives. Stress management offers us a chance to develop skill in dealing with stress and establishing a positive climate for learning. In an optimal learning environment characterized by effective stress management, students are motivated to ask questions and become curious learners, apply information in meaningful ways, provide social support to others, engage in physical activity, use critical thinking, celebrate their learning, and commit to becoming lifelong learners and productive citizens.

Scientific Foundation of Stress and Stress Management

I am an old man and have known a great many troubles, but most of them never happened.

Mark Twain

This chapter provides a basic picture of the stress response and thus enables a better understanding of how stress affects health. Understanding the stress response allows us to see how stress management activities counterbalance stress or help bring the body back to wholeness or homeostasis—the optimal functioning and balance of the hormonal, immune, and nervous systems. This description simplifies the stress response, which in actuality involves more than 1,400 physiochemical reactions (Karren, Smith, Hafen, & Frandsen 2010).

Physiological Responses to Stress

When confronted with a stressor, the body follows a predictable chain of responses. If the stressor is *perceived* to be a threat, then both adults and school-age children tend to resort to the same habits or instinctive reactions that kept primitive humans alive when they confronted threats to their existence (e.g., vigilance against predators or enemies that might take their food, their offspring, or their lives). The stress reaction provides the body with the strength, energy, and focus to deal with the threat by either fighting or running away. This is all well and good if there is an imminent physical danger; the problem lies in the fact that the body doesn't know whether a stressor is physical or a perceived threat to one's intellectual, emotional, spiritual or social well-being—it simply launches into its prehistoric defense system against any perceived threat. For example, during a nightmare, a person can wake up sweating and with a racing heart because his or her body has kicked into fight-or-flight mode as if there were a physical threat.

In the United States, most people do not frequently face threats or stressors that are acutely physical in nature. It is true that students sometimes face such threats—for example, terrorism alerts, hurricane watches, and physical threats from bullies. Most threats, however, are emotional in nature. They intimidate or impinge upon one's ego, sense of identity, or ability to thrive (Woolfolk, Lehrer, & Allen 2007). Regardless of the type of stressor, however, the same survival mechanism is invoked, and it involves various systems or glands that kick into gear in reaction or response to stress.

Homeostasis

Remember that the body is wired for survival and cannot distinguish between a physical threat and an emotional one. If we recognize a mistaken perception ("It was just a branch in the road, not a snake!") to be laughed off in the hope that no one saw, then we feel a sense of relief but also a degree of fatigue because the body was put through an enormous amount of activity that requires a lot of energy. At this point, the parasympathetic nervous system comes into play; known as the rest-and-digest system, it brings the body back to normal levels of functioning. The parasympathetic system attempts to restore all of the physiological aspects that were propelled into fight-or-flight mode (e.g., bringing down blood pressure and breathing rate)—that is, to return to homeostasis.

However, even when the stress is removed and the body tries to get back to homeostasis, cortisol and other hormones are not immediately removed by the system. Their continued presence can trigger the body to crave more fat and glucose to restock the depleted muscles and liver stores. Further, the unused fat and glucose dumped into the bloodstream to fuel the body's energy needs for the physical requirements of fight or flight are then converted to and stored as body fat that tends to accumulate around the middle of the body—close to the heart. This abdominal (or android) fat is considered a heart disease risk factor. Cortisol also sends the liver into overdrive in order to manage the elevated cholesterol levels that were dumped into the bloodstream during the fight-or-flight response. Elevated cortisol levels also damage white blood cells which are necessary to fight off infection and keep the immune system strong (Seaward 2006).

General Adaptation Syndrome

Hans Selye, one of the earliest investigators of stress, used rats as subjects in his research into the effects of severe environmental conditions (1970). Whether the rats were subjected to extremes of heat or cold, they showed a consistent pattern of response in the adrenal glands, as well as the thymus, spleen, and lymph nodes. Selye referred to this pattern as general adaptation syndrome (GAS) and found that it came in three distinct stages: alarm, resistance, and exhaustion (Selye 1970, 1974).

Alarm

In this stage, the fight-or-flight response kicks in as the autonomic nervous system and the endocrine system mobilize to meet the challenge of the stressor. First, the brain reacts to the stressor by sending information via nerve impulses throughout the body. The brain directs many voluntary processes involving muscle movement and involuntary or automatic activity, such as heart rate and the release of hormones.

Information obtained through the sensory organs (e.g., seeing a snake or hearing a verbal threat) is relayed to the hypothalamus (a part of the brain) for an immediate response by the sympathetic branch of the autonomic nervous system. The sympathetic branch then energizes the musculature system for action (e.g., to fight or run).

If the threat remains (e.g., if the snake gets closer or the verbal abuse continues), the hormonal system comes into play as well. This system takes longer to kick into full gear as the hormones travel through the circulatory system. In this process, the hypothalamus and the pituitary glands (both in the brain) release hormones (chemical messengers) that cause a multitude of reactions. The hypothalamus releases powerful painkillers called endorphins in anticipation of possible injury. The hormones epinephrine and norepinephrine are also released in order to boost breathing rate, heart rate, blood pressure, and the release of glucose and thus increase the amount of oxygenated and energy-stoked blood being delivered to the working muscles.

If the stress continues, the hypothalamus stays in charge and releases another hormone called, conveniently, corticotrophin releasing factor (CRF), a key hormone in the domino effect of the stress response. CRF signals the pituitary gland to release another hormone called adrenocorticotropic hormone (ACTH), which in turn signals the adrenal glands to release cortisol, aldosterone, and more epinephrine. What do these chemicals do for the stress response? In the case of any damage brought on by fighting or fleeing, they protect the body by decreasing inflammation and thickening the blood so that the body doesn't bleed to death; they also provide nutrients (including fat) to meet the demand for energy to fuel a continuing fight or flight.

When the body goes into fight-or-flight mode, its immediate needs take priority, and blood is diverted to the muscles and away from the digestive and reproductive systems. The needs of these systems, as well as those of the immune system, are put on the back burner. If the stress continues over a prolonged period of time (i.e., chronic stress), these systems become compromised; for example, digestion suffers, fertility problems may arise, and production of white cells and other immune cells decreases.

The thyroid gland also releases hormones to accelerate metabolism so that blood sugar is released into the circulatory system. This in turn causes insulin (a hormone) to be released in order to regulate blood sugar levels. If the body experiences prolonged stress, the strain of regulating glucose and insulin levels can cause problems such as diabetes or metabolic syndrome. The stress response also involves the release of cholesterol, which may be necessary in order to provide

Educators should not dismiss taunting and bullying as merely "kids will be kids" behavior. Such stressful incidents can increase the levels of cortisol in children's bodies, which in turn can lead to long-lasting physical damage.

energy if a person is facing a true fight-or-flight situation, but, again, the body responds with the same pattern regardless of whether the person is being chased by a pit bull or simply feeling anxious about taking yet another standardized test. Unfortunately, if the released cholesterol is not used for energy, then it needs to be stored, and it often ends up being deposited in the blood vessels, where it can contribute to heart disease. Similarly, the thickening of blood as part of the stress response accelerates clotting in case of injury, but it can also result in heart complications such as stroke or embolism (blood clot). Excessive levels of the emergency hormones in the body can cause immune deficiency, insulin resistance, increased blood pressure, and damage to nerves and brain cells (McGrady 2007).

Resistance

In the second stage of Selye's general adaptation model, the body works to adapt and become more resistant to chronic or long-term stressors. The body is now working overtime and remaining vigilant in order to be responsive to any further threats to the immune system. The body is thus stressed to a point where it is unable to return to homeostasis. In response, it overcompensates and reacts in a way that can cause excessive immune response, which may lead to allergic responses or susceptibility to autoimmune diseases.

Exhaustion

When the body experiences continued or chronic stress, it eventually becomes unable to provide resistance, let alone maintain homeostasis. The body becomes depleted and unable to rest and restore itself. This is what Selye referred to as exhaustion. Bruce McEwen uses the term allostatic load to refer to this cumulative effect of chronic stress—the wear and tear that finally results in exhaustion and leaves the body vulnerable to illness and disease (McEwen & Seeman 2009).

The Pathophysiology of Stress

When a person encounters a stressor, the brain is the first line of defense. It reacts by signaling the release of brain chemicals and hormones into the bloodstream. These chemicals are necessary for the brain to be sharp and immediately responsive to the threat, but this process can bring serious consequences. Chronically elevated levels of stress hormones can cause nerve damage, memory loss, impaired thinking, and, due to damage in the cells of the hippocampus, impaired learning (McGrady 2007).

Another modern phenomenon—one that would have been a decidedly unwise choice for our distant ancestors—involves not fighting or fleeing but ruminating, or staying focused on the problem and not a solution, which is also referred to as chewing and stewing. This response may lead to feelings of hopelessness, helplessness, and defeat. Remaining stuck in the stress response, the body continues to release cortisol and epinephrine. Later chapters of this book discuss research showing that the use of stress management tools such as meditation that can help a person get unstuck from ruminating or fixating on the stressor and shift into utilizing positive coping skills such as problem solving.

Elevated levels of epinephrine, norepinephrine, and cortisol (the endocrine system's primary hormones) are linked to health complications that include heart problems, diabetes, and stroke. Under prolonged stress, the body also becomes vulnerable to any and all microbes in the environment. Here's why: The immune system includes a network of organs, tissues, white blood cells, and other specialized cells whose role is to defend us against disease. Much of this system is regulated by the endocrine system, which uses specialized chemicals to communicate within the systems. When a person experiences prolonged stress, the elevated cortisol level hinders his or her body's ability to produce and maintain the lymphocytes—the white blood cells and natural killer cells that fight off threats to the immune system.

In addition, stress-related increases in blood pressure and heart rate strain the blood vessels and weaken their lining, which results in inflammation. The body works to repair this damage by depositing fat in the lining, which further narrows an artery that is already lined with plaque and thus slows down circulation. Remember too that stress also causes the blood to thicken and that this thickened blood is more prone to clotting. The body now faces a dangerous combination: Slowed circulation increases the risk of spasm, pain, heart complications, and stroke—and the possibility of clots traveling and occluding other blood vessels.

One risk factor for cardiovascular disease is physical inactivity, which can also exacerbate problems associated with the instinctive fight-or-flight mechanism. Specifically, when the stress response mobilizes various processes in the body, the physical activity of fighting or fleeing uses up the byproducts of the process—that is, the emergency hormones. However, because most modern stressors are not physical in nature, the body is not forced to move, and the hormones thus remain in the body and wreak havoc. In fact, the United States is one of the most sedentary nations in the world; many of us are out of shape and thus unhealthy. This fact is reflected clearly in the increasing health problems associated with obesity: increased rates of diabetes and hyperlipidemia (elevated blood cholesterol).

Physical activity also relates to stress in another important way. During physical activity, the body releases the hormones serotonin and dopamine, which positively affect our thoughts and emotions. For example, people who exercise regularly experience lower levels of mild and moderate depression.

During the stress response, blood is shunted away from the body's core to its peripheral areas—the arm and leg muscles that are used to run or fight. But a great deal of energy is needed to properly digest and metabolize food and make the resulting energy readily available to the whole body. When the digestive and assimilation processes are interrupted by stress, the gastrointestinal tract can suffer complications such as irritable bowel syndrome (IBS). Among children, the most often cited health complaint is stomachache, which can be the start of a lifetime of gastrointestinal problems.

Stress can also bring on other problems. For example, prolonged elevated cortisol levels can cause an inflammation response and have been linked to cardiovascular disease, aggravated pain responses, Alzheimer's disease, immune system complications, and reduced bone formation, which may lead to osteoporosis (Benson & Proctor 2010). In addition, stress can cause overstimulation of muscles that leads to activity such as nervous tics or uncontrollable movement (e.g., shaking hands). It can also render the muscles unable to execute coordinated movement, which increases the likelihood of mistakes such as overreaction or overcompensation in a stressful situation (e.g., oversteering a car or missing an easy basketball shot). Research also shows that long-term stress can deplete endorphin levels and thus aggravate back pain and headaches.

Finally, the skin, which is the largest sensory organ in the body, is most vulnerable to the effects of stress. Research has linked anger to the skin disorders of hives, rash, acne, and eczema (Arck, et al. 2006). Even more striking, when someone is experiencing stress, his or her wounds do not heal quickly; in fact, patients going into surgery are encouraged to practice stress management activities (e.g., imagery) to help their incisions heal. This point brings us to the important association between mind and body.

The Mind–Body Connection

The link between stress and disease is becoming stronger and stronger in the scientific literature (Benson & Proctor 2010). This link can be seen dramatically in lifestyle diseases, such as heart disease and cancer, that are influenced by behaviors such as smoking and being inactive, but many more lifestyle behaviors are also linked intricately to stress. For example, someone experiencing stress at work may respond by smoking or drinking. Students who are exhausted by stress may choose to watch nonstop television or act out in class. Lifestyle diseases manifest not only in adulthood but also in children, among whom we are seeing more and more type 2 (i.e., adult-onset) diabetes.

The emerging field of psychoneuroimmunology (PNI) examines the relationship between thoughts and feelings (psychology), the nervous system (the relaying of messages back and forth between the brain and the body via hormones and neurotransmitters), and the influence on our health (illness) and healing (immunology). The nervous system innervates the thymus, spleen, lymph system, and bone marrow—all of which are part of the immune system. If the brain sends a message saying "This is a threat," the nervous system kicks out fight-or-flight messengers (emergency hormones). At this point, the body is focused only on preserving itself against the threat in the moment; it is not concerned with the long term. The immune system is put aside, because diseases and illness are just not important when you are about to become someone else's lunch. The body has to prioritize. The downside is that these emergency chemicals send the immune system into a tailspin, which is especially damaging when the stress is chronic because the body remains on constant alert and never gets to recuperate. This process drains the immune system and leaves the body vulnerable to any bacteria or virus that comes along. A healthy immune system can immobilize most foreign

Prolonged stress may cause students to adopt unhealthy lifestyle behaviors, such as constant snacking and television watching.

invaders, but students and staff alike can be hit with illnesses such as the flu or an upper respiratory infection immediately after experiencing a period of prolonged stress such as the holidays or a round of school testing.

Another important area of mind–body connection involves the placebo effect, which says that the expectancy of improvement influences the health-related outcomes (Oken 2008). In conducting research, the powerful effect of the patient's belief in the efficacy of a therapy, medicine, or surgery accounts for 30% of the effectiveness (Abascal, Brucato, & Brucato 2001). The placebo effect is so important in pharmaceutical research that it must be factored in when making claims about the efficacy of a drug (Oken 2008). The power of the mind–body connection is paramount in stress-management tools such as prayer, relaxation, and meditation because it is the belief in these tools' ability to positively affect stress management and the resulting improved health outcomes that helps them to succeed. It is only recently that medical centers and hospitals have included behavioral medicine among their practices, and many outstanding pioneers in the field deserve mention and further investigation. Andrew Weil has written about his work with patients using a holistic approach that he calls integrative medicine, which includes both allopathic medicine (the Western model of surgery and drugs) and other practices such as massage therapy, nutrition, stress management, and acu-

puncture. Similarly, Dean Ornish and Deepak Chopra have each researched and written extensively on their pragmatic work with patients. Dr. Ornish and researchers' groundbreaking study (1998) found through a lifestyle invention approach including stress management training, there was a reversal of coronary artery disease. Another pioneer, Jon Kabat-Zinn, has worked extensively with mindfulness-based stress reduction and pain management. These forward thinkers are providing models for the integration of protective factors into health care, and their work can also provide evidence to support a lifestyle approach to lifelong health and happiness. According to Ornish's nonprofit Preventive Medicine Research Institute, lifestyle approaches need to be started early (e.g., in early childhood education) and maintained throughout the stages of life (Ornish n.d).

Summary

The first step to teaching our students about stress is to help them understand the science behind stress and then bridge this information to an understanding of how stress management tools work to decrease or lower stress reactions. This can help them learn to deal proactively with stress. The next chapter provides the evidence and framework for bringing stress management into our learning communities.

CHAPTER 3

© Monkey Business/fotolia.com

Advocating for Stress Management in Schools

Every human being is the author
of his own health or disease.

The Buddha

iven that students spend a good part of their day at school, it has been suggested that schools should be viewed as stress reduction agencies (Humphrey 1993). If students are given information and enabled to develop the skills for effective stress prevention and management, then many of the behavioral problems experienced at schools would be diminished, and school would be a safer and more respectful environment for both staff and students. This chapter provides evidence-based best practices for integrating stress management into the academic curriculum, establishing stress management programs (e.g., after school), and implementing stress management projects.

Advocacy means promoting and encouraging positive health practices and taking the steps to make a real difference on a health issue. Members of the entire learning community need to become strong advocates for students on the crucial health issues of stress and stress management. As advocates, we should educate all members of the learning community about the importance of stress and stress management. One obstacle to such work appears in the form of unwarranted bias against certain stress management tools that may be assumed to derive from religious practices. In reality, stress management tools are universal: self-awareness, focus, compassion, empathy, self-care, responsibility, relaxation, sound decision making, interpersonal communication, kindness, impulse control, patience, social support, and cooperation are not owned by anyone but are secular human abilities that we all need to cultivate. Our task as educators is to step back and ask what is really important in the health and happiness of our students—and how we can help them to live healthy and happy lives. The ideas provided in this book invite you to experiment with your students and make creative adjustments to meet the unique needs of your learning community.

It is well known that merely teaching a topic is not as effective as providing students with opportunities to engage with the topic in ways that are relevant and meaningful to their lives. This type of integration is vital to stress management. For our students to learn the content and develop the skills of stress management, this topic should be incorporated into a comprehensive school health program (CSHP) model (Centers for Disease Control and Prevention 2008). This model includes eight interactive components (see figure 3.1).

Table 3.1 provides examples of how each area of the coordinated school health program could play a role in advocating for stress management. The examples are not exhaustive, and chapters 4, 5, and 6 provide more coverage of stress management advocacy.

What Do Healthy Schools Practice?

The Partnership for 21st Century Skills fosters collaboration between the U.S. Department of Education and major corporations and individuals who advocate for student readiness in the 21st century. Specifically, schools must prepare students to be responsible citizens, and this process includes providing health and wellness education; students should be enabled to achieve health literacy, which refers to the ability to obtain accurate and

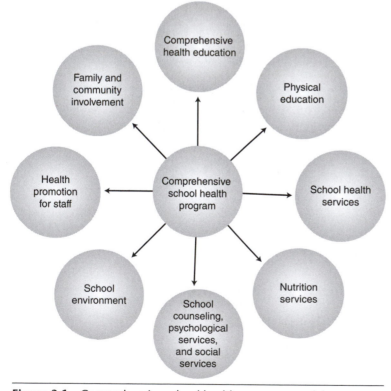

Figure 3.1 Comprehensive school health program model.

Adapted from CDC. Available: http://www.cdc.gov/healthyyouth/CSHP/

Table 3.1   Infusion of Stress Management Tools Into the Coordinated School Health Program Model

School health program	Stress management tools
Health education	Stress management is a required content area and includes experiential learning activities to provide practice across early childhood to grade 12 curriculums. Learning objectives are aligned with the National Health Education Standards.
	Design projects to increase students' skills in advocating for stress management for their peers and school (e.g., public service announcements, posters, skits, peace tables, stress management toolkits for each classroom, guest speakers, visiting master teachers).
	Stress management is infused into other subjects (e.g., English, social studies) by means of activities such as storytelling, journal writing, and studying contemplative practices or integrative medicine (see the National Institutes of Health website for information about complementary and alternative medicine, including meditation and yoga).
Physical education	Display posters that encourage the use of stress management tools.
	Model stress management tools (e.g., progressive muscle relaxation) at the end of physical education activities.
	Model methods of conflict resolution "on the court" (e.g., when students disagree about rules).
	Emphasize the importance of daily physical activity and recess for all students since the health benefits of physical activity carry over to stress management and ultimately to learning as well!
Health services	Refer students with signs and symptoms of stress to health service personnel (e.g., school nurse, psychologist).
	Educate staff members about signs and symptoms of stress.
	Provide a safe space for students to confidentially seek out help for all health issues—including mental health.
Nutrition services	Provide nutritious, healthy meals and a café environment that contributes to healthy eating.
	Display posters that encourage the use of stress management tools.
	Provide healthy snack choices for vending, concessions, and school sales.
	Serve breakfast.
Counseling, psychological, and social services	Identify at-risk students who would benefit from stress management programs.
	Serve as liaisons, consultants, and guest speakers on mental health issues.
Healthy school environment	The basic tenets of a holistic model of stress management (e.g., safety, respect, responsibility, caring) are implemented throughout the school environment.
	The entire learning community advocates for healthy and balanced living (e.g., intervening in cases of bullying, training staff and students in peer mediation, implementing cross-generational mentoring programs).
	Display posters and art pieces that encourage the use of stress management tools (e.g., peer mediation, respectful communication, peaceful resolution of problems).
	Both students and adults (parents, staff, and administrators) resolve disagreements in a positive manner.
	Parent–teacher organizations (PTOs) can raise funds to purchase materials (CDs, blankets, yoga mats) and furniture (small tables, bookcases, or storage units and comfortable chairs) for a peace corner—that is, a stress management space—for each classroom in the building.
	Supplies for stress management activities are viewed as necessary budget items (e.g., music equipment, stress balls, art supplies, yoga mats).

(continued)

Table 3.1   *(continued)*

School health program	Stress management tools
Health promotion for staff	Provide training to identify students who would benefit from a stress management program, such as an after-school program or help with using specific tools (e.g., time management techniques, peer mediation, study habits, strategies to reduce test anxiety).
	Provide stress management activities for staff members before school and after school, including yoga and relaxation, meditation, smoking cessation, and healthy eating habits.
	Provide incentives (e.g., gift certificates) for staff members to participate in stress management activities.
	Provide support for infusing stress management into the curriculum or for leading special projects, activities, or after-school programs. Recognize that professional development is vital and encourage teachers to seek out continuing education credits in understanding stress and stress management.
Family and community involvement	Provide parents with information about stress and stress management activities for their children (e.g., newsletters, web pages, blogs).
	Assign a stress management topic or activity (e.g., meditation, yoga) for students to study or do at home with family.
	Invite parents to participate in training to help their children practice stress management tools. Make learning visible!
	Invite parents to participate in stress management activities. Hold stress management health fairs for parents and community members. Encourage parents to participate with their children.
	Invite a variety of community members to serve on your wellness advisory council, including members of the media, religious organizations, community organizations who serve youth, health care centers, and local businesses.
	Engage community members as volunteers. For example, ask senior citizens to serve as mentors for students.
	Make sure students are actively involved and take ownership by designing stress management activities, projects, and programs. Service learning is an excellent way to engage students in advocacy for stress management.
	Encourage the learning community to apply for grants that encourage stress management for students.

relevant health information and apply it in health-enhancing ways (Partnership for 21st Century Skills 2009). These skills involved with increasing health literacy closely align with the skill set recommended by the Partnership for 21st Century Skills which includes critical thinking, problem solving, communication, cooperation, creativity, and collaboration (Partnership for 21st Century Skills 2009). In addition, the National Health Education Standards (NHES) provide an excellent framework for integrating these 21st-century skills and health literacy skills (see the standards sidebar on page 4), since the skills advocated align with each other. The National Health Education Standards are addressed in detail in chapter 4.

The Youth Risk Behavior Surveillance System (YRBSS) surveys 9th and 12th graders in the United States about risky and protective health-related behaviors. A state-by-state survey is also available that can provide critical information about the needs of your students.

The YRBSS statistics highlight the critical need for comprehensive stress management programs throughout out the students' time at school from early childhood education through 12th grade. The complete survey is available online (Centers for Disease Control and Prevention 2010c), and the following list provides a brief look at statistics indicating a need for comprehensive stress management:

National Health Risk Survey of 9th and 12th Graders: A Case for the Importance of Stress Management Curricula

- 18 percent of students had carried a weapon (e.g., gun, knife, club) on at least 1 day during the 30 days before the survey.

- 8 percent of students had been threatened or injured with a weapon (e.g., gun, knife, club) on school property one or more times during the 12 months before the survey.

- 32 percent of students had been in a physical fight one or more times during the 12 months before the survey.

- 6 percent of students carried a weapon on school property at least one day during the 30 days before the survey.

- 14 percent of students had seriously considered attempting suicide, and 6 percent of students had attempted suicide one or more times, during the 12 months before the survey.

- 20 percent of students had been bullied on school property during the 12 months before the survey.

- 73 percent of students had had at least one drink of alcohol on at least 1 day during their life, and 42 percent of students had had at least one drink of alcohol on at least 1 day during the 30 days before the survey.

- Only 18 percent of the students met recommended levels of physical activity by doing any kind of physical activity that increased their heart rate and made them breathe hard some of the time for a total of at least 60 minutes per day on each of the 7 days during the 7 days before the survey.

- 33 percent of students watched television 3 or more hours per day on an average school day.

Compiled from http://www.cdc.gov/HealthyYouth/yrbs/pdf/us_overview_yrbs.pdf

Equally important are the protective factors, which allow members of the learning community to focus not only on reducing risk but also on what they can do to help students improve their health. A report on violence prevention from the Centers for Disease Control and Prevention cites the following protective factors:

Individual and Family Violence: Protective Factors

- Intolerant attitude toward unhealthy behaviors
- High IQ
- High grade point average
- Positive social interaction
- Religiosity
- Connectedness to family or adults outside the family
- Ability to discuss problems with parents
- High perceived parental expectations about school performances
- Frequent shared activities with parents
- Consistent presence of parent during at least one of the following times: upon awakening, when arriving home from school, at evening mealtime, and going to bed
- Involvement in social activities

Reprinted from CDC. Available: www.cdc.gov/ViolencePrevention/youthviolence/riskprotectivefactors.html

Peer or Social Violence: Protective Factors

- Commitment to school
- Involvement in social activities

Reprinted from CDC. Available: www.cdc.gov/ViolencePrevention/youthviolence/riskprotectivefactors.html

Bullying Policy

Bullying can be a major stressor for many of our students. It involves acting intentionally in an attempt to hurt someone by hitting, pushing, kicking, teasing, insulting, harassing, threatening, humiliating, or hurting another's feelings. In a national survey of students grades 6-10, it was reported that at least once in the previous two months, 21 percent had experienced physical bullying or had physically bullied someone. Additionally, 54 percent had experienced verbally bullying or had verbally bullied someone, while 52 percent experienced social bullying or had socially bullied someone, and 14 percent had experienced electronic bullying or had electronically bullied someone (Wang, Iannotti, & Nansel 2009).

In many schools, bullying is a systemic issue, meaning that the entire school system is involved. Therefore, in order to address bullying effectively, the entire learning community—including parents—must subscribe to and own any policies or programs adopted. It is beyond the scope of this text to provide a specific bullying prevention curriculum. However, many of the activities presented in the book can be used to lay a foundation for building a schoolwide climate of social and emotional intelligence, safety, respect, responsibility, and caring. In order to be effective, the school needs a system that encourages students to serve as advocates and speak out to an adult when they know of a bullying situation. The school also needs to establish a system of consequences that will be applied when the bullying policy is violated.

Ideas for Bullying Prevention Policies

- No student will bully another student.
- All students will help other students who are being bullied.
- All students will make attempts to include students who are being left out.
- All students will commit to informing an adult when someone is being bullied.

Reprinted from National Youth Violence Prevention Resource Center. Available: http://www.cdc.gov/violenceprevention/pdf/YV-FactSheet-a.pdf

School Connectedness

Academic success goes hand in hand with the overall health and the well-being of our students. Leading national education organizations support the importance of embedding stress management skill development for all students (Association for Supervision and Curriculum Development Position paper 2004a). This development should include school connectedness—the sense of belonging or connection that students feel toward their school, teachers, and peers. Connectedness involves building emotional and social skills in a positive learning environment for all: students, teachers, staff members, administrators, family members, and the community (Centers for Disease Control and Prevention 2009).

Connectedness is associated with students with decreases in substance use, violence, anger, and stress (Rice, Kang, Weaver, & Howell 2008). Strategies for strengthening school connectedness include consistent classroom management procedures and expectations, as well as recognition and rewarding of students who meet these expectations. When students are more actively engaged in classroom activities that include cooperative learning and interaction among students, they are more likely to bond with each other and with their teachers (Catalano, Haggerty, Oesterle, Fleming, & Hawkins 2004). One of the performance indicators for the national health education skill of accessing information and services involves seeking a trusted adult who can help promote the student's health (Joint Committee 2007). Students will be more likely to seek out adult help if they feel positively connected.

Make Your Day is a schoolwide classroom management program (Burns 1990) based on the philosophy that everyone is responsible for doing his or her best. If someone

© Photodisc

Students who feel connected to each other, to their teachers, and to their school environment feel supported and happy.

interferes with this expectation, students and teachers are empowered to communicate their feelings and perceptions of the problem and work to resolve it. Students know the clearly and positively defined expected behaviors—and the consequences of not practicing the expected behaviors. Positive behaviors are recognized and reinforced regularly by administrators, faculty, and staff.

Asset-Building Approach

Edwards, Mumford, Shillingford, and Serra-Roldan (2007) provide substantial support for a positive approach to helping students learn about stress and improve their stress management skills. Their approach is based on what they refer to as an asset-building or strengths-based approach. Asset building addresses both internal assets (e.g., ability to make positive choices, confidence, and sense of purpose) and external assets (e.g., positive experiences with people, such as teachers, and institutions, such as schools). Edwards and colleagues looked at peer-reviewed studies of asset building and concluded that successful programs include opportunities for mentoring, community service, training programs for parents and teachers, infusion of asset development in lesson plans, and schoolwide group activities. Gillham, Reivich, and Shatté (2002) also provide support for the effectiveness of a positive youth development approach based on asset building. These authors have extensively researched positive youth development approaches focused on building students' strengths in order to reduce the risk of substance abuse, violence, pregnancy, and poor academic performance (Gillham, Reivich, & Shatté; Gillham & Reivich 2004).

Creating a Well-Learning Community

Parents who demonstrate affection, consistent discipline, and supervision are crucial to building students' assets and reducing risky behavior (Fulkerson et al. 2006). In addition, Fulkerson et al.'s review of literature found an asset in the habit of eating meals together as a family. At family meals, parents can model communication and social support, which in turn helps students demonstrate positive social behaviors. Dr. Amy Saltzman, who works with underserved students in the San Francisco Bay Area, encour-ages parents and students to work together to learn about and practice stress management tools to practice at home and incorporate into their daily lives as families (Saltzman & Goldin 2008).

Role Models for Stress Management: Wellness for Faculty and Staff

In order for students to understand stress and practice stress management, it is critical for all members of the learning community to serve as role models, and many of the suggestions presented in this book can be modified for adults to practice. Priority must be placed on establishing a community that practices stress management because students easily pick up on the many mixed health messages circulated by adults and society at large. For example, tobacco and alcohol are intended for adult consumption only but are purposely marketed at our youth. The need for educators to be cognizant of how stress permeates learning communities is heightened when those communities face an economic climate characterized by downsizing, budget cuts, and resulting economic hardship in many families.

Teachers, parents, staff members, and administrators need to take to heart the airline safety instruction to "put on your own oxygen mask first" so that you will be able to help others. We need to take a moment to take a few deep breaths, set our intentions, and become mindful of our own stress in order to model stress management as a lifelong skill. When we practice stress management, we can be more effective in our work. Instructors who practice stress management are less reactive to students yet more attentive and attuned to them.

Classroom Programs

Stress management curricula need to be taught by faculty and staff who not only practice the skills in their own lives but also are dedicated to teaching these skills to students. It is crucial to provide these educators with support and training (Nation et al. 2003).

See the sidebar on page 28 about classroom stress management for examples of best practices supported by research. These are exemplary, evidence-based practices for stress management in the classroom.

Classroom Stress Management Programs Hall of Fame

- Broderick and Metz (2009) examined a pilot study of 120 high school female seniors participating in a mindfulness curriculum named Learning to BREATHE. The curriculum included the themes of body awareness; understanding and working with thoughts and feelings; reducing destructive self-judgments; and integrating mindfulness into daily life. When compared with a control group, curriculum participants reported decreases in stress, tiredness, and pain and increases in calmness, relaxation, and self-acceptance.

- King, Vidourek, Davis, and McClellan (2002) studied the Healthy Kids Mentoring Program, which included activities for relationship building, improvement of self-esteem, goal setting, and academic tutoring. Mentors included community members ranging from high school students to senior citizens. Significant improvement was shown in self-esteem; academic achievement; and positive connectedness with school, peers, and family. Lessons learned from this research emphasize the importance of support from parents, administrators, and the community.

- The Penn Resiliency Program (PRP) is an outstanding evidence- and school-based intervention that leads to increases in optimism and decreases in depression and stress symptoms. This program includes cognitive behavioral tools as well as goal setting, assertiveness, and mediation training. For more information, see the University of Pennsylvania Positive Psychology Resilience Research in Children website at www.ppc.sas.upenn.edu/prpsum.htm.

- MasterMind: Empower Yourself With Mental Health is a flexible, low-cost, 6-week program that is classroom based (Tacker & Dobie 2008). It includes activities and instructional tools for creating a safe atmosphere in order to increase knowledge and encourage discussion of mental health topics. Students practice stress management tools individually, in groups, and in peer-teaching-peer activities. The researchers report that the peer-teaching-peer activities—which provide a means to ask questions anonymously—and the activities in which students recognized other students using stress management tools were the most effective components of the program over the long term in reinforcing health concepts and behaviors.

- Barnes, Bauza, and Treiber (2003) demonstrated the beneficial impact of a school-based meditation program. Inner-city African American adolescents who participated in daily group meditation sessions both at school and (on weekends) at home for 16 weeks were compared with members of a control group who participated only in general health education sessions. This program positively affected school discipline actions among students who meditated, including tardiness, absenteeism, behavior problems, and fighting. The findings also indicated a positive effect on female students' ability to effectively express their anger.

- Benson et al. (2000) examined middle school students' academic progress and participation in a relaxation curriculum. Classroom teachers were trained in relaxation exercises, and academic success outcomes were measured by grade point average, work habits, cooperation, and attendance. Students who participated for two or more semesters in the relaxation curriculum scored significantly better than their counterparts in academic success outcomes over a 2-year period.

- McCraty, Atkinson, Tomasino, Goelitz, and Mayrovitz (1999) investigated the effect of an emotional self-management intervention curriculum among middle school students. These students achieved significant improvement in stress and anger management, risky behavior, maintenance of focus, and relationships with family, peers, and teachers.

(continued)

(continued from previous page)

Students were able to sustain these behaviors at a 6-month follow-up.

- Bothe & Olness (2006) found that 10 minutes of stress management practiced every day in an elementary classroom significantly decreased stress and increased students' ability to relax. The intervention included deep breathing, stretching, and guided creative imagination activities. Classroom teachers led the activities for 4 months with third graders and reported that the students settled down and were ready to engage in work after the stress management sessions.

- Second Step, a violence prevention curriculum, incorporates lessons for developing skills in empathy, problem solving, and anger management. Research into this curriculum across pre-K through middle school populations has shown that improvement in social and emotional skills leads to decreases in physically aggressive behavior, bullying, and substance abuse and to improvements in impulse control, anger management, and interpersonal problem solving (Committee for Children 2010).

© Stockdisc Royalty Free Photos

It is important to keep the family involved in stress reduction programs so that students are supported in the home environment as well as at school.

After-School Programs

Pierce and Shields (1998) investigated approximately 700 students who participated in an after-school group program called "Be a Star" that addressed decision making, cultural aware-

ness, personal competency, and education about tobacco, alcohol, and other drugs. Students were assigned to either the "Be a Star" program or to a traditional after-school program, and each group met once a week for 90 minutes. The results showed that students who participated in the "Be a Star" program scored significantly higher than did those in a control group that addressed decision-making and interpersonal skills, cultural awareness, and negative perceptions about alcohol and drug abuse.

Another program, Kids in Cooperation with Kids, used physical, cognitive, and experiential approaches to increase students' ability to recognize and manage stress. This 10-week program sponsored by the Boys and Girls Clubs of America involved mostly at-risk African American students in an urban setting (Rollin, Arnold, Solomon, Rubin, & Holland 2003). The results indicate the importance of using multiple approaches to provide a comprehensive program.

Summary

This chapter offers a brief glimpse at the mounting research that marks the need for effective stress management programs in our schools. The best model involves a comprehensive approach in which all areas of the school are involved, including students, parents, staff, administrators, and community members. Chapter 4 discusses more of the protective factors in stress management, as well as ways to incorporate the development of these factors in schools.

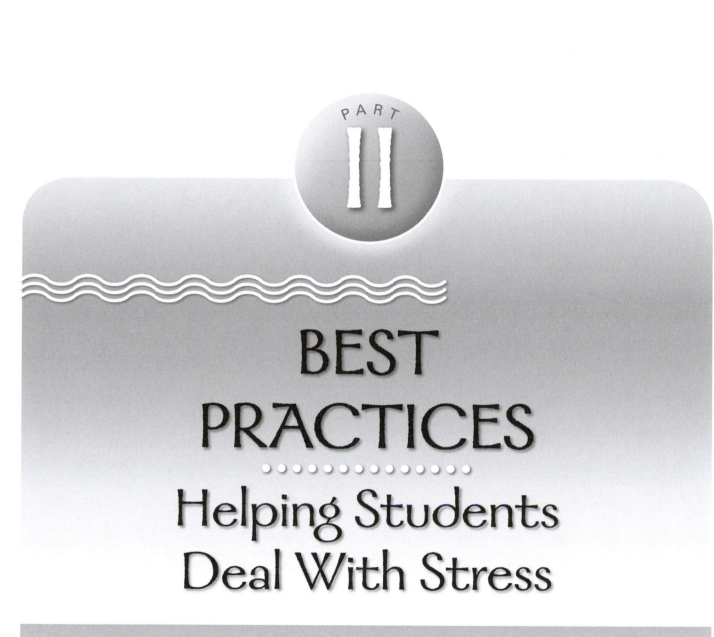

PART

II

BEST PRACTICES

· · · · · · · · · · · · · · · ·

Helping Students Deal With Stress

Fostering Positive Skills to Cope With Stress

"Flexing"—
A deliberate choice to do something else
other than the usual stress response.

Fox and Kirschner (2005)

This chapter highlights key coping strategies, as well as activities to help students develop their ability to use those strategies. Learning coping strategies helps our students be in the best frame of mind and body to make wise choices and thus ultimately to be successful. Positive beliefs and effective proactive behaviors lead to success, which in turn breeds more positive beliefs and behaviors, thus perpetuating a positive cycle.

Positive psychology is a new movement that researches and encourages programs focusing on students' strengths (i.e., taking a wellness approach) rather than on their weaknesses (i.e., a disease approach). We know from working with students that they are more likely to be motivated to learn and change behaviors when they feel supported and when they find themselves in an environment that focuses on their strengths. The strengths-based approach addresses positive emotions such as happiness and optimism; positive personal traits such as self-efficacy, confidence, mindfulness; and the positive quality of one's relationships with self, peers, family, and community (Seligman, Reivich, Jaycox, & Gillham 2007).

This chapter discusses components of a strengths-based approach and presents activities that foster those strengths. The activity descriptions include suggested grade levels, but you will need to consider the developmental level of each of your students in order to determine individual appropriateness. You can also address specific needs of your students by modifying the prompts and instructions as you deem necessary.

Many of the activities begin with the prompts "mindful sitting" and "peaceful inside." When the instructor asks students to come into mindful sitting, this is a cue for them to sit still, focus, and become ready to listen to instructions. The prompt "peaceful inside" is a cue that students are taught in order to calm themselves and achieve mental quiet and stillness.

The activities in this book can be adapted to any group you may be working with. For example, students in wheelchairs can do the various activities in their chairs. Students can use props such as pillows or bolsters to facilitate sitting upright for mindful sitting.

Mindfulness-Based Stress Reduction

Mindfulness-based stress reduction (MBSR) has played an important role in our understanding of stress management. Dr. Jon Kabat-Zinn of the University of Massachusetts Medical School has been using MBSR with various population groups, including adults and children, for more than 30 years (Center for Mindfulness, Medicine, Health Care and Society n.d.). Mindfulness has been described as paying full attention to the present moment without judgment or attachment. Mindfulness means resisting the tendency to allow our energy to be carried away by nonproductive and habitual thoughts such as "I stink at school" or "No one likes me." These thoughts can detract from the quality of life right now. Deborah Schoeberlein (2009) discusses five competencies in emotional and social learning: "self-awareness, self-management, social awareness, relationship skills and responsible decision making" (p. 37). These are the same competencies indicated by the National Health Education Standards. Mindfulness utilizes these competencies by asking us to be more curious and caring about our inner world and therefore more curious and caring about the outer world too.

Schoeberlein (2009) points out the importance not only of teaching mindfulness but also of having both the instructor and the learning community model mindfulness. Modeling mindful behavior is important for learning. Instructors can set the tone for mindfulness and optimal learning through the quality of their attention—for example, in the transition times before and after class, or between activities within a single class period (Schoeberlein 2009).

Examples of transitions are included in various sections in this book; here are a few:

- Singing bowl—A bowl made of brass or other metals that, when struck with a wood mallet, vibrates to make a chiming or singing sound
- Poem or daily reading by the instructor or students
- Clapped-out rhythm by the instructor that is repeated by students without talking as they take their designated seats
- Presentation of an interesting object for students to observe without speaking
- Practice of entering the room in silence
- Practice of sitting down, finding "your mindful body," and noticing the energy in your body and mental activity

Students will respond well to rituals that involve being mindful. These activities can easily be incorporated into the classroom. Students often look forward to participating in and assisting in leading these activities.

Mindful Sitting

This activity helps students sit tall, straight, and still and be ready to pay attention.

Start

Seated

Prompt

Sit tall and strong with your feet on the floor, your hands relaxed, and your eyes looking at me. Let your body become very still. Show me you are ready to start our next activity by showing mindful sitting.

Finish

Check to see that all students are practicing mindful sitting. Review with students the qualities of mindful sitting.

Peaceful Inside

"Peaceful inside" is the students' cue to become still and arrive at a place that they create inside where they feel calm and relaxed. This activity will be used consistently throughout the book.

Start

Mindful sitting or lying down

Prompt

You will create a special place for yourself called peaceful inside. When I ask you to come into peaceful inside, this is your reminder to become still. Come to a place you make inside yourself where you feel calm and relaxed. We can practice going to this place together. You can also go into your peaceful inside when you are stressed or upset.

Finish

Observe that students are practicing peaceful inside and make further suggestions (e.g., "be so quiet that the person next to you cannot hear you," or "slow down your breathing so it is soft and easy") to help them settle down.

Shift Meditation

This activity allows students to mindfully shift their focus by using the image of a laser beam.

Start

Seated or lying down

Prompt

Get comfortable and enter a relaxed breathing pattern. Now, use an imaginary laser beam to begin scanning your body. Bring your laser beam of focus and awareness to the top of your head and work your way down, noticing any areas of comfort (relaxation, warmth, softness, ease) or of discomfort (aches, tiredness, tension, stiffness). Scan your body slowly, paying attention as you shift the beam of focus from one area to the next.

Use your laser beam of focus to bring your awareness to any sounds you can hear. Listen carefully for loud sounds; listen attentively to soft sounds, including your breath.

Bring your focus to rest on your breath. Pay close attention to the breath as it enters your nose, your head, your throat, your heart, your belly. Continue to rest quietly with relaxed breathing for a few more moments. Then, open your eyes and quietly return your attention to the room, without talking. If you are lying down, slowly sit up.

Finish

Ask students to share their experiences with shift meditation and how it is helpful to use the laser point as a focus tool to be mindful of the body, sounds, and breath.

Singing Bowl

This is a wonderful way to start an activity and bring the group into focus. Attending to the chiming allows students to practice focusing and paying attention to only one thing; it can also serve as a calming ritual. A singing bowl makes a chiming sound when struck with a wooden mallet.

Materials

Singing bowl and mallet (see figure 4.1)

Start

Mindful sitting. Strike the singing bowl, then lead the class according to the prompt. Next, ask a student leader to strike the bowl and go through the prompt three times with the class.

Photo courtesy of Educational Innovations, Inc.

Figure 4.1 A singing bowl can be used to help bring students to attention in a calm way.

Prompt

1. Do 3 big belly breaths: 1 . . . 2 . . . 3.
2. Listen to the singing bowl; when the sound stops, raise your hand.
3. After the fourth and final chime (the third by the student leader), continue to sit quietly for a few moments, then slowly open your eyes.

Finish

Ask the students to share in one word how they feel right now.

Mindfulness

Elementary through young adult

STANDARD 7—practicing health-enhancing behaviors

Mindful Path Walking

In this mindful activity, students use walking as their focus and pay attention to the mechanics of their walking and breathing.

Start

The mindful path will be for each student a specified area of approximately 10 to 15 feet (preferably outdoors). The activity can be done in bare feet on grass for a nice change. You can set a timer for this activity and let students know that when they hear the timer or the singing bowl, to quietly come back to the instructor. Using a timer allows you to slowly increase the amount of time students practice walking mindfully.

Prompt

1. Today we will practice a mindfulness activity called "mindful path walking." In mindful path walking, we bring awareness to how we walk by slowing down each step enough to focus and be mindful of just walking.
2. Watch carefully, here are the mechanics of the walk: lift your heel, pick up your foot, roll onto your heel, transfer your weight from your leg onto your foot, push down, and then shift to your other foot. (Instructor demonstrates.)
3. Set up your mindful walking path—count out 10 to 15 long steps. (The amount of steps you tell them will vary on the amount of space available.)
4. Begin to walk slowly on your mindful walking path, attend to your breath, and be careful not to touch anyone else while walking. When you come to the end of the mindful walking path, slowly turn and return to the start of your path. Slowly start your walking mindful walking path again. Continue mindful walking on your mindful walking path.
5. Your breath should come in and out through your nose with your mouth sealed; if the walking becomes too vigorous, slow your pace enough to breathe through your nose with your mouth closed.
6. If you become distracted, stop walking, take a breath, and slowly start again—taking one step at a time.
7. When you hear the chiming bowl (or soft whistle or timer ringing), finish your mindful walking and return quietly to me.

Finish

Ask students to share their experience and reactions to using walking as a mindful activity.

Take a Walk!

For younger children, Take a Walk! is a mindful walking activity given more of a game-like emphasis by having students focus on various kinds of walking.

Start

In a specified area (preferably outdoors), instruct students to walk in various patterns or styles of walking. This activity can be done in bare feet on grass for a nice change.

Prompt

We will pay attention to walking slowly and to our breath. Be careful not to touch anyone else in our mindful walking area. Walk in the following ways:

* As if you don't want to go to school
* As if you are a secret spy
* As if you have stubbed your toe
* As if you are carrying heavy books
* As if you are really excited that you just finished a major accomplishment

When you hear the chiming bowl, stop walking, slowly come back to our circle, and become ready for your next directions.

Finish

Ask students to share their favorite way of walking. Ask students to share how it feels to pay attention to their walking.

Mystery Box: A Touchy-Feely Activity

In this activity, students practice their ability to be mindful of the sensation of touch.

Materials

Collect items such as feathers, leaves, plush toys, flower petals, rocks, and pinecones. For sensory integration, provide a word bank that students can use to identify feeling words (e.g., bumpy, smooth, soft, cool) with the object.

Start

Before doing this activity, help students come into a relaxed state—for example, by means of a relaxation pose or by using belly breaths (see chapter 5). The activity itself can be done in several ways, depending on the age of your students. Younger students can lie down on their tummy as the instructor gently brushes the student with the object on his or her arm or back; alternatively, the objects can be placed in students' hands with their eyes closed or covered by a blindfold. Older students can reach into the mystery box through cutouts that allow manual access but keep the objects hidden.

Prompt

We can use our hands to pay attention and be mindful when we touch things. Describe what you are touching and feeling before you guess what it is. Use feeling words, such as rough, smooth, and prickly. What was it like to touch something without knowing what it was?

Finish

Invite students to consider how the touchy-feely activity allows them to focus their attention on their sense of touch. Help them make the connection that they can use this same type of mindfulness to pay close attention to what they are doing. Ask them to talk about activities that they could do mindfully (e.g., drawing a picture or doing homework).

Mindfulness

Pumping Up:
The Remember Muscle Workout

Early childhood education through middle school

STANDARD **7**—practicing health-enhancing behaviors

The objective of this activity is for students to practice mindful focusing by recalling specific objects and, if appropriate for their age, the order of the objects.

Materials

On a tray, place several objects—for example, an apple, a Beanie Baby, and a ruler (use fewer than three objects in early childhood education and more in working with older students). The objects could be linked to curriculum themes such as colors, geometric shapes, or holidays. You'll also need something (e.g., bandana, towel) to use as a cover for the tray.

Start

Mindful sitting. Cover the tray when presenting it to the students, then remove the cover.

Prompt

1. Take a picture in your brain of what you see on the tray. Freeze the picture in your mind. (Pause and watch students to make sure to provide enough time to allow the students to look at each object on the tray.) Remember what is on the tray. (Now cover the tray.)
2. What do you remember about the objects—for example, color, shape, texture?

Finish

Invite students to relax their breathing and remember their favorite object shown to them today. Ask them what was special about their favorite. Discuss examples of other places or situations when we can use our memory muscles (e.g., remembering the proper spelling of words).

Mindfulness in Nature

In this activity, students take time to observe and be mindful of the outdoors.

Start

Pick a favorite tree or outdoor scene that students can pay attention to on a weekly basis. This activity can be done either from an observation point such as a classroom window or by having the students go outdoors to observe. For younger ages, the instructor can record the log entries with input from the students.

Prompt

For this activity, you will keep a log (written or electronic). You will use your log to attend to and reflect on details of the nature scene as it changes throughout the various seasons.

Finish

Invite students to share their experiences of being mindful of nature. Discuss some examples of situations when we need to mindful of nature (e.g., when storms are coming in or taking care of the environment).

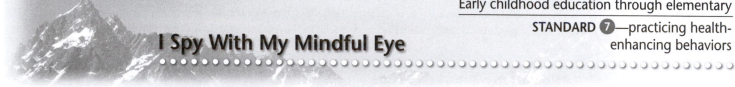

I Spy With My Mindful Eye

This is the quintessential game that many of us have played on long car trips. It is also an exercise in mindfulness. Doing this activity outdoors can bring into play a rich variety of colors, shapes, and textures. You may be surprised at how many of us (including our students) miss the obvious visual objects that are right in front of us!

Start

Select (or ask a student leader to select) an object in the immediate environment.

Prompt

I spy with my mindful eye something that is . . . (indicate a color, shape, or texture). Now we will take turns suggesting what the object might be. (Have students take turns asking questions until someone guesses the object correctly.)

Finish

Ask students what they saw today that they had never noticed before. Invite them to identify and share about the object that was most interesting—and why. Ask students to reflect on a time they may not have paid attention to something important (e.g., tripped over their toys left in the middle of the room).

Space Out Concentration

This mindfulness activity is a variation on "I spy." The focus can be trained on sounds, sights, or body positions. Students can use the popcorn method, in which they "pop out" responses, albeit in a respectful manner. The activity can also be done silently.

Start

Mindful sitting

Prompt

1. This activity is about paying attention. Take a look around the activity space and, without shouting, state something that you see when I call your name. (Continue to field responses and consider pointing out items that have not been named.)
2. Okay. Let's try the same thing again, but this time name things you hear. (Continue to field responses and consider pointing out things that were not named.)
3. Now let's try it with five things you notice about how you are sitting. (Continue to field responses and consider pointing out things that were not identified.)

Finish

Invite students to reflect on areas of their daily living in which they might work to pay more attention (e.g., by listening mindfully).

Eating a Raisin

This activity allows students to develop mindfulness through their senses and build awareness of mindful eating—that is, taking time to intentionally taste, chew, and pay attention to the food they ingest.

Materials

Raisins (about three) for each student. If a student has an aversion or allergy to raisins, substitute another food, such as crackers.

Start

Mindful sitting

Prompt

Today we will pay attention to and be mindful of all the senses involved in eating a raisin!

1. Pick up the raisin and look at it. Notice its color, shape, texture, and weight. (Pause to allow time for this step. If students rush through it, repeat the instructions.)
2. Spend some time smelling the raisin. (Pause.) Place it between your lips but do not yet bite it. Feel the texture with your lips.

(continued)

Eating a Raisin   *(continued)*

3. Allow the raisin to fall onto your tongue and—without biting—taste the raisin. (Pause.) Move it around onto the different parts of your tongue. Now, bite down and chew the raisin for as long as possible before you swallow it. Count how many chews you can complete before you swallow the raisin.

4. Notice how your mouth feels once the raisin is swallowed. Notice the aftertaste of the raisin. (Pause.)

5. (Students can repeat these steps with the other two raisins. They can also use them if they skipped a step and need to start over with a new raisin.)

Finish

Invite students to discuss what it was like to eat more slowly than usual and to pay close attention to their eating. Ask them to talk about how eating mindfully might be a healthy habit as compared with eating too fast or eating too much, as we may do when we don't pay attention to our eating.

Mindfulness

Elementary through young adult

STANDARD 7—practicing health-enhancing behaviors

Tune In

We spend a lot of our time "tuned out." This mindfulness activity asks students to tune in and pay attention—to themselves!

Start

Mindful sitting

Prompt

Listen to your breath. Stretch your hands. Do some spider pushups. Bring the palms of your hands together with fingers matched up. Keep finger tips together and move palms out and in, pressing back and forth five times. Now, make fists with both your hands and start to move them in circles from the wrists. Make five circles one way. Stop and circle the other way five times. Flex your toes toward your shins, and then point your toes toward the floor. Keep flexing and pointing 5 times each direction. Stop and slowly do ankle circles, five times in each direction.

Finish

You can also use any of these tune-in activities:

* Listen to a clip of relaxing music.
* Read a poem.
* Focus on a candle flame (electric candles are super and pose no fire danger!).
* Focus on an art print in the room.
* Listen to all of the sounds in the room and outside of the room.

To wrap up the activity, ask students to share some of their favorite "tune-in" activities. Ask to students to share when they could use a tune-in activity in their everyday life (e.g., taking a break from studying or working on a homework problem to take a break and refocus).

Remember When?

This activity allows students to practice focusing on remembering information.

Materials

Reading book

Start

Mindful sitting. Read aloud a story of appropriate length for the age group.

Prompt

1. We are now going to do a movement activity. (Lead the class in doing yoga or a movement game for 5 to 10 minutes, depending on the age of your class.)
2. Now it is time for you to come back to mindful sitting. (Pause for students to get situated.) Take a few relaxing breaths.
3. (Now reread the story, pausing at the end of each page and prompting students to recall the story.) Raise your hand if you remember what happens next in the story. (Turn the page and continue reading.)
4. Practice being peaceful inside.

Finish

Ask students if there are times when it is hard to remember important information and discuss what things we can do to help us remember better.

Pigs Fly

This mindful movement activity promotes focus.

Start

Standing

Prompt

I am going to name an animal or object. When I name it, you will imitate the motion that the animal or object makes when it flies. If I name something that doesn't fly, remain still with your arms at your sides. (You can also use other animal movements, such as hopping, swimming, and slithering.)

Finish

Ask students to share what happened when they didn't listen carefully to all of the instructions in this activity. Ask students to share why it is important to listen and pay attention before doing an activity, such as taking a test or crossing the street on their bike.

How Do I Feel?

This activity works well as a beginning or closing activity for a session with students. It allows students to take time to attend to, reflect on, and articulate how they are feeling. It is important to give students practice in recognizing and describing their feelings in order for them to be comfortable with expressing all kinds of emotions.

Start

In a circle, either seated or standing

Prompt

We are going to take turns sharing how each of us is feeling. When it is your turn, start by saying "I feel . . ." and then say how you are feeling right now (e.g., tired, relaxed, confused). (Lead students in taking turns to share how they are feeling.)

Finish

Ask students what it was like to take time and pay attention to their feelings (e.g., we may be sad about a situation and can tell our friends how we are feeling and that we want to be alone today).

Talking Stick

This activity cultivates mindful listening and turn taking. The student holding the stick talks until he or she feels understood. The student is not to be interrupted. The talking stick can be replaced by any prop that the student holds to represent "holding the space." Be creative! You can use this activity to help students share their feelings after doing a stress management activity or session. You can also use it as a starting activity for the day, in which case it might include the following elements: something good that happened today or something positive about the group or an individual student.

Materials

Talking stick (wood dowel of 10-12 inches or like object such as a plastic wand)

Start

In a circle, either seated or standing

Prompt

We are going to take turns expressing how we feel. When you are sharing, you will hold the talking stick to show that it is your turn and no one else should be talking. When someone else has the stick, you should respect that person by listening quietly. Each person in our group will have a chance to share. If you prefer not to share, you have the right to pass. (Lead the students in taking turns sharing how they feel. You might want to limit each turn to 15 seconds or to a single word [or three] as a challenge to be mindful in speech by being sincere yet succinct. This is recommended as a student could dominate the talking stick and ramble.)

Finish

Once the sharing circle is finished, you can ask students how it feels to be listened to. Discuss why it is important to take turns to listen and to talk mindfully (e.g., so that no one dominates a conversation and so that everyone can understand us).

Mindfulness

Early childhood education through middle school

STANDARD **4**—interpersonal communication

Telephone Game

This activity uses the traditional "telephone game," sometimes also known as "whisper down the lane," to help students see the value of using active listening skills.

Start

Mindful sitting in a circle

Prompt

1. We are going to play the "telephone game." I will whisper something to the student next to me, and that student will whisper to the next person, and we will keep going this way all the way around the circle. (Start the game by whispering to the first student. Once the last student says aloud what he or she heard, move to prompt 2.)

2. Here is what I actually said when I started the game. (Restate what you said to the first student. Rarely is the final student's statement even close to the original statement.)

3. We are going to play the game again in just a few minutes. But first, let's talk about how we can make sure that what I say to the first student makes it all the way around the circle without getting changed. (Lead students in brainstorming about active listening skills such as repeating, speaking clearly, listening quietly.)

4. (Play the game again using the active listening skills that students brainstormed.)

Finish

Ask students why active listening is important in school and life overall. Discuss why we should make sure that we are understood and also that we understand others by asking for clarification to make sure we clearly understand what someone is telling us. Students can make a classroom checklist to use in practicing and as a reminder to use active listening.

Building a Story

This activity requires students to listen to each other's storybuilding sentences.

Start

Mindful sitting in a circle

Prompt

We are going to build a story together by taking turns adding sentences to the story. I will start the story, and we will then go from student to student to build the story up. (Start the story with a catchy opener—for example, "It was a dark and stormy night. There was a crashing sound in the basement, and Joe was home alone." Then lead the students in taking turns to add one sentence each to the story.)

Finish

Ask the group to reflect on the importance of listening carefully and attentively when people are talking. Ask students to share a time they may not have listened carefully when someone was talking (e.g. directions for a test).

Mindful Log

Mindfulness is an integral tool for stress management, and one key to success is to find ways to include mindfulness in everyday routines. This activity asks students to select everyday activities and practice doing them with a mindful intention—or to reflect on a day when they caught themselves being mindful.

Start

Students use their personal journals for this activity.

Prompt

In this activity, you will use your journal to log moments when you find yourself being mindful during the day. Another way to practice mindfulness is to pick an activity that you do every day and do it mindfully by paying full attention to the activity. (e.g., brushing your teeth or cleaning up your room). At the end of each day, take five minutes to reflect on the experience of paying attention to mindful moments or your chosen mindful activity.

Finish

After a week, invite students to share about what they noticed and how it felt when they did activities more mindfully. Ask students to reflect how mindfulness could be used in other situations in their lives, such as writing a paper. Ask students to reflect how practicing mindfulness works as a stress-management tool.

Mindful Work Habits

In either a discussion or a written exercise, ask students to reflect on specific areas of learning in order to help them think of ways they can focus and concentrate on their work in those areas.

Start

Students use the Mindful Work Habits worksheet (page 199 of appendix A) for this activity.

Prompt

1. We will spend some time looking at our learning habits today. Fill out the Mindful Work Habits worksheet completely from your experience. (Allow enough time for students to complete the worksheet.)

2. Remember that to set a goal, you need to make it measurable and specific and include action steps and a deadline. Did you do that? Double check your papers.

3. Let's go around the room and summarize from your worksheets what you think are your best study habits. If you hear any new ideas from your classmates, feel free to add it to your own list to try out on your own.

4. Now that you've heard everyone's good ideas, set a goal for yourself to practice your best study habits for the next week. Keep track of your progress on the worksheet.

Finish

After the week is over, ask students to process how setting a goal toward practicing their best study habits was effective and to think of ways to make it more effective (e.g., setting a schedule to study at the same time every day).

Name _____

Date _____

Mindful Work Habits

Describe your work space at home or where you study.

1. Is it absolutely quiet? _____

2. Are you alone or are others there? _____

3. Are you sitting? On a chair or couch? On the floor? _____

4. What is the best time for you to work? After school, after you have done physical activity? Or later at night? _____

5. How do you break up your study time? Fifteen minutes and then a stretch, or longer periods of time? _____

6. When reading, how long can you focus on the materials in one sitting? _____

7. How do you decide what you will study? Do you use a to-do list or a day planner? _____

8. What are some ways in which you could make your study habits more mindful? _____

From N.E. Tummers, 2011, Teaching stress management: Activities for children and young adults (Champaign, IL: Human Kinetics).

RU Listening?

This activity uses role playing to help students recognize when they are not listening and when they are practicing active listening. You can use the RU Listening Script on page 200 of appendix A, create your own, or have them improvise.

Start

Mindful sitting

Prompt

We are going to do some role playing. Two students will do the role play, which will be a scene in which student 1 is trying to communicate but student 2 is not listening. During the role play, the rest of us will think about the times when student 2 does not listen and times when he or she does listen. (Prompt the two students to start the role play.)

Finish

Students will recall their observations of the role players' listening and not listening. Ask students to share their thoughts about situations in which they can practice mindful listening. They can share examples of times when they were not mindfully listening and any consequences that resulted. They can also share about times when active listening helped them succeed.

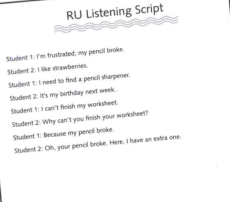

RU Listening Script

Student 1: I'm frustrated; my pencil broke.

Student 2: I like strawberries.

Student 1: I need to find a pencil sharpener.

Student 2: It's my birthday next week.

Student 1: I can't finish my worksheet.

Student 2: Why can't you finish your worksheet?

Student 1: Because my pencil broke.

Student 2: Oh, your pencil broke. Here, I have an extra one.

From N.E. Tummers, 2011, *Teaching stress management: Activities for children and young adults* (Champaign, IL: Human Kinetics).

© iStockphoto/Juan Monino

Mindful listening can help a person experiencing stress feel that someone is there who really cares and listens to his or her problems. It can also help students avoid stressful situations simply by paying attention and not leaving a friend to feel ignored.

STANDARD **7**—practicing health-enhancing behaviors

Quiet Time

Quiet time is a ritual that honors silence and respect for the silence of others. This activity needs practice and reinforcement and is worth the effort in order to create a stress-reducing environment in the classroom. It is recommended to use a timer set for a predetermined amount of time as it helps students to realize how much actual time they are silent.

Start

Designate (or have students generate with a guided discussion) the rules and procedures for quiet time. It is a good idea for quiet time to occur in a space away from where students normally study or learn, such as their desks. Instead, come into another space, for example, on the floor either seated or lying down. This allows for the students to associate quiet time as a means to take a break away from their desks where they need to be actively engaged in learning.

Prompt

We are going to practice having quiet time. I will signal the start of quiet time by giving you a cue (e.g., using the singing bowl or flicking or turning down the lights). During quiet time, all work and talk should be stopped. (If there is any chatter or noise, gently but firmly reinforce the importance of silence.) When you hear the timer's bell, you will know that quiet time is finished. At that time, return to your seats and, sitting as quietly as you can, come into peaceful inside.

Finish

Ask students to share their experiences with quiet time. For some students it will take considerable practice for them to be quiet. Students could share when they might need quiet time (e.g., after a test or after lunch).

Resiliency

Resiliency is the ability to survive and thrive. Resilient students are able not only to survive the various obstacles that arise in life but also to thrive. They deal with stressors by strengthening their internal resources or coping skills—that is, their resilience skills (Henderson, Bernard, & Sharp-Light 2007; Krovetz 2008). Resiliency also refers to a student's external protective factors, which include components of the student's learning community: school, home, neighborhood, and peers (Krovetz; Reivich, & Shatté 2002). The following list highlights the essential protective factors for building resiliency skills.

Internal Resiliency

- Social competence—the ability to foster positive relationships by means of empathy, communication, and cooperation
- Problem solving by means of flexibility, persistence, and help seeking
- Independence through confidence, self-efficacy, and self-awareness
- Cultivation of a sense of higher purpose, which includes aspirations, optimism, future mindedness, and goal setting

Adapted from Reivich and Shatte 2002; Seligman et al. 2007.

External Resiliency

- Caring adults
- Sense of belonging and connectedness
- Positive expectations for all students
- An environment that encourages meaningful participation and positive peer interaction

Adapted from Reivich and Shatte 2002; Seligman et al. 2007.

Resiliency can be fostered in numerous ways by embedding opportunities for students to practice these skills. They can then use those skills in real-life situations and thus manage their stress more effectively. Any aspect of resilience can be chosen as a theme for a day, a week, or an entire school unit. Examples include creativity, flexibility, commitment, friendship, humor, wisdom, optimism, and generosity. The chosen theme can be engaged by means of readings, plays, skits, posters, poems, slogans, cartoons, story writing, and quotations. Students can become resiliency detectives who look for resiliency themes both inside the school (e.g., in themselves, other students, and faculty members) and outside of the school (e.g., in the family or community and in news stories).

Resiliency

Elementary through young adult

STANDARD **2**—analyzing influences

What's in My Backpack?

This activity helps students recognize the qualities of resiliency that they use every day.

Start

As a lead-in for the activity, help students discuss and list the qualities of resiliency. Then have students form pairs for doing the activity.

Prompt

Show your partner one thing in your backpack or purse that shows your personal resiliency. Explain to your partner how the object is connected—for example, a photo of your best friend (social support), a book you read for pleasure (love of learning or escaping into fiction), or your calendar or day planner (self-motivation and goal setting).

Finish

Ask students what surprised them about the activity. Ask them to share what qualities of resiliency they use most often. Ask students to reflect on resilient people they know and what those people do to cultivate resiliency in their lives.

Resiliency

Elementary through young adult

STANDARD **6**—goal setting

Booster Shots

This activity uses group brainstorming to come up with ways to boost students' resiliency.

Start

Review with students the qualities of resiliency, then have them form small groups for doing the activity.

Prompt

We need to boost our resiliency skills. In your small group, brainstorm ways to boost your resiliency. Consider both your internal assets (e.g., humor, self-confidence for learning a new dance routine) and your external assets (e.g., completing a service project, taking time to talk with a trusted adult about planning for college).

Finish

Have each student write a measurable goal for using resiliency boosters during the next week and specify measureable actions they will commit to taking.

Resiliency

Changing the Perception of Me and My Friends

Middle school through young adult

STANDARD **2**—analyzing influences and **8**—advocacy

In this activity, students analyze how their lives are influenced by other people's perceptions of them. Students can take this further by planning and implementing a service project.

Start

Discuss the concept of social norms. Most people's behaviors are based on their perception of how other members of their social group behave. Emphasize that even though these perceptions are often incorrect, they carry normative power. For example, adults may believe that all students procrastinate or spend too much time sending text messages. This activity helps students work to change negative perceptions of young people by doing advocacy projects.

Prompt

1. (Students can work individually, in small groups, or as a class.) Brainstorm ways how you and your peers are perceived by adults in your life and by society at large (e.g., as losers, druggies, slackers, texters, overachievers, jocks, stylish dressers, and so on).

2. Brainstorm about how you would like the adults in your life and society at large to perceive you and your peers from a strengths-based approach (e.g., as empowered, generous, caring, creative, critically thoughtful).

3. Brainstorm ways in which you might bring about change in perceptions of you and your peers from a strengths-based approach. Your list might include creating public service announcements, designing and implementing service projects, becoming mentors, or starting a peer mediation program in your school.

Finish

If you had students work individually or in small groups, ask them to share their brainstorm lists with the whole group. To expand on this activity, students could select an area of health they feel is a critical need such as bullying or dating violence. Have students plan and implement a health advocacy service project to address those areas (e.g., a public service announcement about dating violence for a local cable television station).

Strengths Survey of Significant Family Member or Other Adult

This activity asks students to interview a significant family member or other adult in their life in order to learn about that person's strengths.

Start

The student selects a family member or other trusted adult to interview.

Prompt

1. Select a family member or trusted adult to interview about his or her strengths.

2. Here are some ways to conduct a good interview

   * Formulate your specific questions ahead of time to make sure you will help guide the person to talk about his or her strengths in detail.

   * An interview should be like a conversation, so don't just read your questions to the person, but know the questions and look at the person when you ask them. Take notes of the major points of the person's response, not every word they said. Make sure to listen carefully to their response.

   * Set up a convenient time of about 10 to 15 minutes to talk with your chosen adult. Take a few minutes at the end of the interview to review your notes and ask for clarification or explanation on any questions you might have. Take the time to thank the interviewee for his or her time and ask if your interview summary is accurate.

3. After you conduct your interview, write two or three paragraphs to share with the class about the person's strengths. Reflect on how the example of this adult's strengths can help you develop your own strengths.

Finish

Lead a group discussion in which students formulate a master list of the strengths they learned about in their interviews.

Hardiness

We can help our students become successful by giving them opportunities to practice the characteristics of hardiness. Kobasa (1979) studied people who seemed to weather stressful situations and found that they had the following persistent characteristics: a strong sense of commitment, an internal locus of control (i.e., the belief that one can control or at least influence one's efforts toward desired results), an adventurous and engaged attitude toward stepping up to challenges, the idea that things make sense in view of a positive future, and finally a sense of

humor. Students can ask themselves the following key questions when faced with a challenging situation:

* Control—How can you feel in control? A sense of internal control can be developed by learning how to reconstruct or reframe and respond with constructive action to solve the problem that created the stress.

* Commitment—How can you build and improve your commitment to reach your highest potential?

* Challenge—How can you view a problem as a challenge? Compensation is the ability

to focus on strengths rather than weaknesses and to take personal responsibility.

- Choice of lifestyle—How can you improve your lifestyle choices, such as sleep, relaxation, and eating healthily

- Connectedness—How can you improve your social support? How can you be a better support to others?

Based on Kobasa 1979.

Hardiness Discussion and Writing Exercises

Middle school through young adult

STANDARD **2**—analyzing influences and **7**—practicing health-enhancing behaviors

This activity asks students to reflect on the characteristics of hardiness as evidenced in their own lives.

Start

Review with students the characteristics of hardiness.

Prompt

Using the Hardiness Discussion and Writing Exercises worksheet (page 201 of appendix A), write about each of the qualities of hardiness, then consider connectedness in your own life. Finally, reflect on what you feel is your dharma—your life purpose—and how self-responsibility relates to dharma.

Finish

After students have spent time writing in response to each of the seven prompts, invite them to share their responses. Lead them in a discussion to further explore hardiness in their lives.

Name _____   Date _____

Hardiness Discussion and Writing Exercises

Write about each of the qualities of hardiness.

1. When have you shown these qualities in your own life? _____

2. When have you observed these qualities in others? What were the specific situations? _____

3. How could you cultivate these qualities more in your daily life? _____

4. Consider your connectedness. Who do you feel connected to? _____

5. Think about two ways you can improve your connectedness. _____

6. What do you feel is your dharma—or your life purpose—and what can you do now to help you move toward and realize this life purpose? _____

7. What does self-responsibility mean? How does self-responsibility relate to dharma? _____

From N.E. Tummers, 2011, *Teaching stress management: Activities for children and young adults* (Champaign, IL: Human Kinetics).

What Habits Do Successful Students Practice?

Middle school through young adult

STANDARD **2**—analyzing influences, **7**—practicing health-enhancing behaviors, and **8**—advocacy

The idea for this activity came from a schoolwide project that one of my students observed during student teaching. In the project, a middle school adopted *The Seven Habits of Highly Effective People* by Stephen Covey (1989) as the basis for a term-long, schoolwide effort. Many of the habits of highly effective people overlap with the characteristics of hardiness.

Each week, one of the seven habits was explored in detail through readings, experiential activities, and small group projects. In 2005, Covey added an eighth habit to move beyond effectiveness and to cultivate the motivation to make significant changes in one's life. His son Sean Covey (1998) has written a book about these habits for teenagers.

(continued)

What Habits Do Successful Students Practice *(continued)*

Start

Students can discuss the common aspects of the eight habits and the characteristics of hardiness. Students can then select a specific characteristic they would like to explore in detail. This activity can be done as an individual student assignment, a whole class assignment, or as a schoolwide project.

Prompt

Choose a characteristic of highly effective or hardy people that you wish to explore in detail. You can explore the characteristic in numerous ways—for example, by looking for it in book or movie characters, sports figures, celebrities, world leaders, or by visiting Stephen Covey's website (www.stephencovey.com/7habits/7habits.php).

Finish

Invite students to share their exploration results creatively—for example, in poster presentations or videos in order to advocate for their learning community to recognize the importance of cultivating these characteristics.

Social and Emotional Learning

Emotional intelligence and social intelligence involve the ability to recognize and deal proactively with one's own emotions and to recognize and empathize with the emotions of others (Lantieri 2008). Social and emotional intelligences include the following skills:

- Awareness—This skill involves tuning into one's feelings. This awareness of the student's internal world helps him or her to make healthy choices about the external environment.

- Management of emotions—Instead of merely reacting to strong feelings, students make better choices when they can respond with a calm and focused mind.

- Empathy—Students notice and tune in to the emotions of others; this is also known as social awareness. The typical human brain is hardwired for this connection to others (Siegel 2010).

- Relationship—Emotional and social intelligence work together when difficult emotions surface and cause friction and conflicts between people. By helping others, we deepen our own lives. Therefore, it is necessary to listen and tune in to the energy of the other person or of the group. Students can be assertive while at the same time finding harmony so that relationships persevere through hurt feelings or misunderstandings.

Social support—the sense of belonging, of acceptance, of being loved and needed—also constitutes a critical aspect of mental health and student wellness (Karren, Smith, Hafen, & Frandsen 2010). Students who possess a strong, positive social support system will seek out positive relationships when they are confronted with stressful situations. Social support can be informational, emotional, financial, or material. Another kind of social support—known as the voice of reason—comes from a trusted individual who provides honest yet caring assessment of situations. The quality of all these supportive relationships is more important than the sheer number of one's friends or acquaintances (e.g., having 500 online social network friends instead of three really close friends you spend quality face-to-face time with).

Research has found improvement in academic success, increased creativity, and decreased anxiety as a result of increased training in social and emotional intelligence skills. Students who have gone through social and emotional intelligence skill development are better able to concentrate, be empathetic, exercise self-control, and enjoy increased self-esteem (Lantieri 2008).

Social and Emotional Learning
Elementary through young adult
STANDARD **2**—analyzing influences and
7—practicing health-enhancing behaviors

Stress Detective

One of the keys to understanding stress and its effects in our lives lies in the skill of noticing when stress starts to creep into our lives. Often, we are too busy to notice!

Start

Mindful sitting

Prompt

In this activity, you will use the Stress Detective Log (page 202 of appendix A). Keeping a log of stressful events in your life will help you be on the lookout for little stressors before they become big ones. You may also identify patterns in your stressors, such as being unorganized in the morning and thus late for the bus. You can then come up with solutions to reduce these stressors in your life—for example, getting your backpack ready for school on the night before.

Finish

Helping students to recognize sources of stress in their daily lives is an important step in finding tools to help them manage their stress. Discuss as a class some of the solutions that students discovered from filling out their Stress Detective Logs. If necessary, share some of your own solutions you've observed in your own experiences and observations to help students grow beyond what they are already doing.

Name _____
Date _____

Stress Detective Log

Stressor	Situation and time	Proactive response or activity
(Example) Can't find homework.	3 minutes before the bus is picking up for school. Mom is yelling at me to be ready for school bus.	Take a few deep breaths. Take 5 minutes before going to bed to set up backpack each night—making it a habit.
(Example) Too tired, too much homework.	8 p.m. After dinner and basketball game.	Organize study area—shut off phone. Use study hall time to study and not socialize.

From N.E. Tummers, 2011, *Teaching stress management: Activities for children and young adults* (Champaign, IL: Human Kinetics).

Social and Emotional Learning
Middle school through young adult
STANDARD **6**—goal setting

Wellness Brainstorm

This activity allows to students to examine not only physical signs and symptoms but all aspects of their health.

Start

Use the wellness model in the Wellness Brainstorm worksheet (page 203 of appendix A) to encourage students to generate ways to increase protective factors and decrease their risk factors in each of the components of wellness.

Prompt

In this activity, you will use the handout to explore your personal strengths and challenges in each of the areas of the wellness model. Personal strengths include protective factors that are healthy behaviors or habits. An example of this in social health is talking to a mentor.

(continued)

Wellness Brainstorm   *(continued)*

Challenges are risk factors that are unhealthy behaviors or habits that keep us from being our best in that area of health. An example of this in intellectual health might be procrastinating on school projects so we do not show our best work.

Take time to reflect on your perception of your challenges as failures or setbacks either as motivators to learn and grow from or as stumbling blocks that lead you to quit or give up. You will also share recent examples and write strategies that you could use to change negative attitudes to more constructive ones that recast stumbling blocks as positive challenges. You will then discuss the importance of lifestyle and identify an area in your life that you would like to change.

Finish

Have students select an area of their daily lifestyle habits and write a goal for which they will monitor their progress in order to make a positive change. Accountability is an important aspect of adopting healthy behaviors. Therefore it is important for the students to have a system of monitoring their progress that is objective. An example of objective monitoring is breaking the goal down into measureable units such meditating for five minutes daily or setting up a time to speak assertively in person with someone they have a conflict with rather than avoiding them or gossiping about them with others.

Wellness Magazine

Middle school through young adult

STANDARD ❷—analyzing influences and ❼—practicing health-enhancing behaviors

In this activity, individual students create a mini magazine which reflects their personal definition of wellness. It can be either a hard copy project or an electronic version (e.g. PowerPoint or web page). You can show your students examples of popular print magazines to demonstrate the importance of the cover, the editor's letter, and the various sections of content—in this case, addressing the dimensions of wellness.

Materials

Heavy construction paper and coloring materials (colorful markers, paint and brushes) and old magazines for cutting out pictures, or computer access for each student

Start

Students will design their wellness magazine to be formatted like a print magazine including a cover, an editor's page, and a section for each of the dimensions of wellness.

Prompt

1. Create the cover for your magazine. Make sure that it entices readers to open your magazine and gives them an idea of what the magazine is about. It should be colorful, easy to read, and attractive.

2. Next comes the editor's letter. This page is all about you. It describes your definition of wellness and how wellness plays an important role in your life.

3. Now develop your wellness sections. Make a section for each dimension of wellness: physical, emotional, social, occupational, spiritual, intellectual, and environmental. You can use any method to show how important each dimension of wellness is in your life. For example, in the physical dimension, you might show a picture of yourself doing your favorite physical activity, discuss your favorite health foods, or identify a piece of music that helps you relax.

Finish

Have the students present their magazines to the entire class. If their work is in digital form, they can save these electronic portfolios about their wellness to modify and expand as they continue on their wellness journey.

Social and Emotional Learning

All levels

STANDARD **7**—practicing health-enhancing behaviors

Gratitude Journal

Cultivating gratitude is an important skill for students to practice. This allows students to be grateful for what they do have. Improving their attitudes about gratitude shifts their emotional and social learning to looking for strengths and positive aspects of their lives and radically changes their perspective and outlook.

Materials

Each student will need a journal.

Start

Provide each student with the Gratitude Journal worksheet (page 205 of appendix A)

Prompt

Use the prompts on the worksheet to maintain a daily gratitude journal. Gratitude takes us out of our egos and into our hearts.

Finish

Have students maintain the journal for a period of time from a week to a month and then use it to reflect on times when they have experienced gratitude. Encourage students to share this activity with their families and initiate a family gratitude journal. Ask students to share aspects of their gratitude journal with the rest of the class.

Name _____   Date _____

Gratitude Journal

I am grateful for _____

_____

_____

I am appreciative of _____

_____

_____

I am so fortunate to have _____

_____

_____

Thank you for _____

_____

_____

From N.E. Tummers, 2011, Teaching stress management: Activities for children and young adults (Champaign, IL: Human Kinetics).

Scaffold Meditations

Scaffolding involves building upon a base. In this creative writing activity, students develop their own meditations. The first sentence provides the base, and each following sentence includes the previous sentence, thus creating what are called "nested meditations" (Anderson 2010). This activity helps students think creatively and expressively about their strengths.

Start

Share with students examples of previous students' scaffolding meditations or ones you have created to provide an idea of the scaffolding process.

Prompt

1. Write a simple statement about one of your strengths—for example, "I am strong in mind and body."

2. Now write the first statement again and add to it: "I am strong in mind and body and I am happy."

3. Next, add onto the second sentence: "I am strong in mind and body and I am happy when I practice yoga."

4. Add a fourth sentence: "I am strong in mind and body and I am happy when I practice yoga and stretch out to life's possibilities."

Finish

Ask students to share by reading their pieces aloud to the class, taking time to breathe before reading each sentence. Use the scaffolding meditations as a meditation activity. Students can display their scaffolding meditations in the classroom to inspire their classmates to take time to reflect on their strengths during the day.

Loving Kindness

This activity provides a way to offer loving kindness to ourselves in order to be able to offer it to others. The intention is to take care of ourselves and extend loving kindness as we reach out to others. Cutting ourselves some slack and showing loving kindness is an important task. We may be unhappy with our behavior, but who we are as people is the most important thing.

Start

Peaceful inside

Prompt

1. Listen quietly as I speak aloud each of the following statements of loving kindness. Repeat each one silently after I finish reading it. (Read the following, pausing between each to allow time for student reflection between the statements.)

   * May I be happy just the way I am.

* May I be at peace with whatever happens.
* May I be safe.
* May I live in the wisdom of my heart.

2. Now, repeat these same statements with the intention of expressing loving kindness toward the people in your life—family, friends, community, and country.

3. Finally, repeat the statements with the intention of expressing loving kindness toward people who pose difficulty in your lives and to all beings—people you know, animals, and nature.

Finish

Have students share about the people they might include in their extensions of loving kindness; this group can include people we don't know who are experiencing hardship (e.g., those suffering due to a disaster in another country) as well as difficult people in our own lives (e.g., a mean crossing guard or a lunchroom attendant who doesn't smile). Students can also discuss possible reasons that people might behave in certain ways in order to develop empathy toward and understanding of those people.

Social and Emotional Learning

All levels

STANDARD **7**—practicing health-enhancing behaviors

A Beam of Kindness

This loving kindness activity allows students to come up with their own wishes for someone they care about and form their own message to send. Here are two examples of beams of kindness: "I wish that you feel better." "I wish that you recover quickly from your operation."

Start

Peaceful inside

Prompt

Imagine in your mind's eye the person to whom you wish to send the beam of kindness. Imagine a beam of emerald green light shining out from your heart and reaching the other person's heart. Create a short statement that is your wish for this person. Repeat your wish silently three times.

Finish

Ask students how it feels when they send people they care about a beam of loving kindness. Discuss with students how it feels to imagine that others could be sending beams of loving kindness to them.

Practicing Random Acts of Kindness

In this activity, students generate ways to practice random acts of kindness—thoughtful and caring acts for which they are not acknowledged or rewarded.

Start

Have students brainstorm as a class ways to be kind or nice without being told or prompted to do so. Examples include saying thank you and please, asking if they can help out, and spontaneously sharing with others. Students can then set a goal for practicing random acts of kindness or keep a log of such acts that they perform during the day. Alternatively, the entire class or group can set a goal to do random acts of kindness as a project—for example, planning a special day for another group (e.g., participants at a senior center or the secretaries at the school). More information about how students and groups have practiced random acts of kindness can be found at a website (www.payitforwardmovement.org/) created by Catherine Ryan Hyde, author of the book *Pay It Forward*.

Prompt

1. Let's take some time to list as many ways as possible that we could be kind or nice to others without being told to do this.

2. Has anyone noticed someone else in the class being kind or nice? Could we add what they did to our list?

3. We are going to do an experiment called random acts of kindness. Random means not doing something because you are supposed to, but rather like a surprise. Random acts of kindness are sincere, thoughtful, and caring acts that you do for others without being asked. Set a goal to practice a random act of kindness.

Finish

Invite students to reflect on their own reactions and others' reactions to their random acts of kindness. Ask students how being kind changed how they felt about themselves and others in the class.

Helping others can help students feel good about themselves and ease the stress that the other person is experiencing.

Wise Owl Speaks

This activity uses a checklist for students to monitor how they speak to each other according to the Wise Owl Checklist (page 206 of appendix A) giving criteria for positive interpersonal communication. The owl can symbolize an animal that shows wisdom by taking its time to speak and making sure it is the right time to speak, using keen observation skills, knowing how to hoot (communicate) or stay silent, and being careful about the words it uses.

Start

Have students discuss the characteristics of good interpersonal communication. Review each of the wise owl speaks criteria and ask students for examples for each area.

Prompt

Take a moment to think about a time you tried to communicate with someone and they did not listen or would not do what you asked them. For example, maybe you asked a friend to share their favorite toy they were playing with, but they did not want to share. Use the Wise Owl Checklist to think about ways you used and did not use the wise owl checklist. Make sure to review the checklist, to help you remember to communicate in good ways in the future.

Finish

Students can share experiences they have had when they did or did not use the wise owl checklist. You can reinforce lessons learned in this activity by talking or reading about literary examples in which the characters do or do not follow the practices of wise owl speaks and the importance of good interpersonal communication skills.

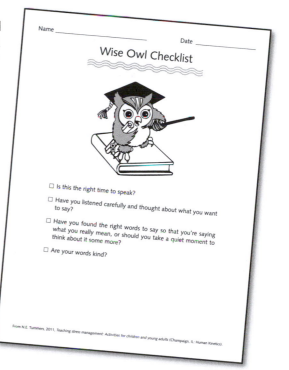

Name _____ Date _____

Wise Owl Checklist

☐ Is this the right time to speak?

☐ Have you listened carefully and thought about what you want to say?

☐ Have you found the right words to say so that you're saying what you really mean, or should you take a quiet moment to think about it some more?

☐ Are your words kind?

From N.E. Tummers, 2011, *Teaching stress management: Activities for children and young adults* (Champaign, IL: Human Kinetics).

This activity helps students build their awareness of what pushes their buttons or ignites their anger reaction.

Start

Pass out the What Pushes Your Angry Buttons? worksheet (page 207 of appendix A).

Prompt

Today we will be spending time looking at the emotion of anger. Use the handout to learn about your angry buttons. The anger reaction is usually quick and messy, and then it settles down. If you can catch yourself, you can give yourself a time-out until you settle down and become centered and grounded. This way, you can choose to respond with self-responsibility rather than just reacting.

Finish

After students have finished checking off and listing what pushes their angry buttons, have them select one or two of the ways in which they most typically react. Then ask them to develop a step-by-step plan to make the decision to respond with self-responsibility in the midst of a stressful situation.

Name _____   Date _____

What Pushes Your Angry Buttons?

Review the following list of frustrating situations and make a check mark by any that you have experienced. You can also write in any additional ways you react when angry.

☐ Being late   ☐ Losing stuff
☐ No money   ☐ Disorganized people
☐ Friends gossiping   ☐ Long lines
☐ Parents' expectations   ☐ People changing plans at the last minute
☐ Parents fighting   ☐ Friends who won't stop texting you
☐ Slow computers   ☐ Rules
☐ Boring classes   ☐ Losing an important game
☐ Forgetting something important   ☐ Group work
☐ People who interrupt   ☐ Being ignored
☐ People who are rude   ☐ Being treated unfairly
☐ Your boss   ☐ Being disrespected
☐ Waiting for downloads   ☐ Being lied to

Other button pushers (list):

_____
_____
_____
_____

From N.E. Tummers, 2011, *Teaching stress management: Activities for children and young adults* (Champaign, IL: Human Kinetics).

Dealing With Difficult Situations

This activity allows students to analyze the external influences (e.g., people who gossip) in situations that ignite their stress response. Students then decide to use various methods to deal proactively with these difficult influences.

Start

Have the entire class identify and analyze external factors to which they tend to react with anger. Examples might include media, family, peers, society, technology, ethics, culture, and laws. Then divide the class into small groups of three or four students to use the Dealing With Difficult Situations worksheet (page 208 of appendix A).

Prompt

Often, what stresses us is outside of our control. These are called external influences. Can anyone give me an example of an external influence? (Students can provide ideas such as parents; school work; friends.) Brainstorm as many difficult situations caused by external influences your group can come up with.

Using the Dealing With Difficult Situations worksheet, consider what proactive choices your team could use to deal with difficult situations.

Finish

Ask students to share the situations in which they could deal proactively with their stress from external influences.

Name _____   Date _____

Dealing With Difficult Situations

Work on your own and check off the methods that you use to deal with difficult situations.

☐ Walk away

☐ Just be nice

☐ Be direct

☐ Take turns

☐ Hang out with someone else

☐ If I can't say something nice, just be quiet

☐ Come up with a solution

☐ Use an I-message

☐ Set a boundary

☐ Be clear and stick to my word

☐ Ignore them

☐ Step into their shoes

☐ Ask them questions

☐ Ask a friend or trusted adult for an objective point of view

☐ See the situation from a different point of view

☐ Take calming breaths and ask for what I need

☐ Make a choice not to be influenced by this situation—try to keep your emotions separate from the situation so that you can look at it objectively

☐ Tell the person I don't know and will get back to them

☐ Agree to disagree

☐ Affirm that I can only change my point of view, not theirs

Other ways to deal with difficult people (list):

_____

_____

_____

_____

From N.E. Tummers, 2011, *Teaching stress management: Activities for children and young adults* (Champaign, IL: Human Kinetics).

Social and Emotional Learning

All levels

STANDARD 7—practicing health-enhancing behaviors

Count to 10

Use the following saying from Thomas Jefferson as a class motto: "When angry, count ten before you speak; if very angry, a hundred."

Start

Mindful sitting

Prompt

Think of a situation in which you feel frustrated or angry. Now count down from 10—slowly. Take a moment to look again at the situation with a calm and centered intention.

Finish

Invite students to break down the stressful situation and reflect on how and when using the "count to 10" tool could be used in their lives.

Talking About Feelings

Students of all ages need to practice the skills of emotional intelligence. This includes an awareness of and the healthy expression of the full range of emotions. Without this practice, students might learn that feelings are bad or something to be ignored.

Start

Mindful sitting

Prompt

Today we will be talking about feelings. Let's start by naming some small feelings we experience in our daily lives. (Ask students for responses and write them on the board. Next, discuss a time when you experienced a relatively mild feeling. For example: "I was happy when I found a parking spot this morning right away so that I could be on time and ready for school." Demonstrate by acting out the happiness you felt.) Now, I'd like to hear about a situation in which you had a small feeling. When it is your turn, describe the situation and what you felt, and then demonstrate that feeling.

Finish

Encourage students to identify and name feelings. During the discussion, emphasize the importance of not labeling feelings as bad or good and that there is a continuum of all kinds of feelings.

Facing Fierce Feelings

The skill of dealing with difficult or strong emotions—that is, facing fierce feelings—can be developed through the following activities. Each activity can be practiced several times and then built upon by doing the subsequent activities. These activities allow students to recognize strong feelings and practice the skill of self-regulation. In addition, students learn to recognize and acknowledge strong feelings in others.

Understanding Strong Feelings

Students will discuss dealing with strong emotions by exploring various scenarios.

Start

Model for your students a strong or fierce feeling—for example, "I was very scared when my car broke down and I did not know where I was. It was cold and dark out." Then act out how you felt in that situation.

Prompt

Act out what you might feel and what your reaction might look like in the following situations. (Here are some examples or you can make up your own scenarios to reflect the age and circumstances of your group. Alternatively, you can invite students to share their own stories of strong or fierce feelings and demonstrate the feelings by acting out them out.)

* How frustrated would you feel if you couldn't find your mittens to go out and play?
* How happy would you feel if you did well on a math assignment?
* How frightened would you feel if the lights went out in the middle of a storm?
* How sad would you feel if your best friend moved to another state?

Finish

After the activity, invite students to reflect on what it was like to think about facing strong feelings.

Stop, Drop, and Be Calm Tool

Early childhood education through middle school

STANDARD 7—practicing health-enhancing behaviors

This activity introduces a quick-and-easy tool to help students self-regulate and become calm.

Start

Standing in a circle (with the graphic of the Stop, Drop, and Be Calm traffic light [page 209 of appendix A] as a visual aid to help students remember to stop, drop, and be calm)

Prompt

1. How can we calm down and face our strong feelings? We can use this tool called Stop, Drop, and Be Calm. This tool has 3 simple steps: let's look at the traffic light.

   a. When we feel a strong feeling, we see the red light. Say stop to yourself when your thoughts start to race and you feel panicky. (Model putting a hand out to indicate the action of stopping.)

   b. Next, we see the yellow light. It reminds us to get mellow. Drop your hands to your belly and take three to five deep relaxing breaths. (Model belly breathing.)

   c. Next comes the green light. It reminds us to be cool green, serene, calm. Say to yourself: "Be calm."

2. Now, let's practice using the Stop, Drop, and Be Calm tool. (Walk students through the steps.)

3. (Model the process for students by describing a situation you faced. Here is an example.) When I got lost in my car and it was dark and cold, I found myself feeling scared and upset. I used the Stop, Drop, and Be Calm tool to help me calm down so I could think and pay attention to what I could do in the situation. Now, let's practice together.

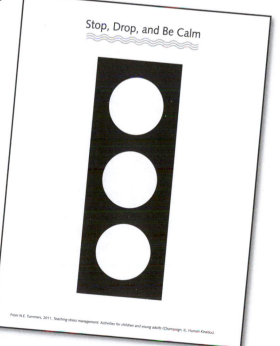

Stop, Drop, and Be Calm

From N.E. Tummers, 2011, *Teaching stress management: Activities for children and young adults* (Champaign, IL: Human Kinetics).

(continued)

Stop, Drop, and Be Calm Tool   *(continued)*

4. I will now describe a situation. After I am done, I want everyone to demonstrate all three steps to using the Step, Drop, and Be Calm tool. Are you ready? Here are the situations:

   * Your shoelace breaks and you are late for the school bus.
   * Your little brother breaks your favorite toy.
   * You are not invited to your friend's birthday party.
   * You are in the school play and can't remember your lines.

Finish

Review the Stop, Drop, and Be Calm tool. Have students look again at the traffic light signals and discuss what each light signals. It is important to reinforce the three steps by practicing them frequently. If a student, or even the entire class, ever needs to self-regulate, ask them to look at the graphic as a reminder and walk them through the three steps.

Facing Fierce Feelings

Early childhood education through elementary

Stop, Breathe, and Act Smart Tool

STANDARD **7**—practicing health-enhancing behaviors

This activity is a modification of the Stop, Drop, and Be Calm tool. The students act out the three parts of the traffic light to help them calm down. Students also recognize when they are at the almost moment discussed in chapter 1 (Saltzman 2010). The almost moment is that space between recognizing a feeling and acting upon it. It is represented graphically in this activity by the flashing yellow light. When we see a flashing yellow light, we stop and look both ways before proceeding.

Start

Mindful sitting in a circle

Prompt

1. We will use a traffic light to help us remember what to do when we get frustrated or upset.

2. (Show the traffic light on page 210 of appendix A, point to the red circle, and hold one hand out in front of you to indicate stop.) The red circle means to stop our fierce thoughts and take deep breaths. (Demonstrate bringing both hands to your lower belly and moving your hands as your breath slows down.) We can take as many breaths as we need in order to calm down.

3. (Show the traffic light and point to the yellow signal.) This step gives us time to think about the problem so that we can act smart instead of acting frustrated or upset.

4. (Point to the green circle, then point to the middle of your forehead.) The green light

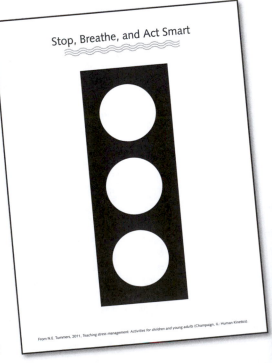

Stop, Breathe, and Act Smart

From N.E. Tummers, 2011, *Teaching stress management: Activities for children and young adults* (Champaign, IL: Human Kinetics).

reminds us to bring our attention to the best way to think about the situation and resolve the problem in a positive way.

Now, it is everyone's turn to model and act out the three parts of this tool: stop, breathe, and act smart.

Finish

Ask students to think about things that might signal to them that they are in a yellow light situation—that is, things that signal an almost moment (e.g., when the student might almost hit his or her brother or scream at a classmate). Ask students to identify situations in which they might use this tool.

Facing Fierce Feelings

Facing Feelings Step-by-Step Tool

Middle school through young adult

STANDARD **2**—analyzing influences and **5**—decision making

This activity helps older students be aware of and acknowledge difficult feelings.

Start

Mindful sitting in a circle

Prompt

In this activity about facing feelings, we will practice being aware when difficult feelings and thoughts pull us away from feeling centered and grounded and learn to deal with them in a healthy and responsible manner. When we are facing a difficult situation, our habit may be to react without remaining calm, centered, or grounded. This is different than when we respond well to a situation. In the almost moment, we take the time to feel calm, centered, and grounded to make the best decision on the best response for us (Saltzman 2010). We nearly reacted, but did not because we chose to respond by remaining calm, grounded, and centered. Being grounded means to be steady and confident. Being centered means to be focused and present in the here and now.

Let's work together to examine this situation by using the Facing Feelings Step-by-Step Tool.

1. Take a moment to recall a difficult situation. Picture this situation as if you're watching it on a big movie screen. Press the pause button and take deep belly breaths. Take as many breaths as necessary to feel calm. (Pause to allow deep breaths.)

2. Acknowledge the feelings experienced in this difficult situation. Observe the feelings as they are, without trying to change them. Just sit with these feelings. Bring your awareness to the almost moment, the moment before you act on these feelings. Think about what your immediate reactions to the feelings in this difficult situation are.

3. Take a few breaths to become calm, grounded, and centered. Now think about what might be a better response rather than an immediate reaction to the feelings you are experiencing in this difficult situation.

4. Choose the best response for you right now. Note that the best response may involve doing nothing.

Finish

Have students share in a discussion or by journaling what it was like to think about using the Facing Feelings Step-by-Step Tool in a difficult situation.

STANDARD **5**—decision making and **7**—practicing health-enhancing behaviors

Logging Strong Feelings

By logging or writing about facing fierce feelings, students can consider how best to handle strong emotions.

Start

Students should each have a Strong Feelings Log (page 211 of appendix A) or blank piece of paper and a space in which to write.

Prompt

Use the worksheet (or blank piece of paper) to write or draw about a situation in which you had a fierce feeling—and how you reacted to it. Next, write about a situation in which you had a fierce feeling and used calming tools to respond in a proactive and healthy way.

Finish

Have students share how they deal in responding proactively to strong feelings. Allow students to compare and contrast a response to strong feelings done in a reactive and unhealthy way versus a responsive healthy way and why the healthy way is the best choice for them.

Name _____ Date _____

Strong Feelings Log

Strong feeling situation	Physical reaction	Emotions	Thoughts

From N.E. Tummers, 2011, *Teaching stress management: Activities for children and young adults* (Champaign, IL: Human Kinetics).

STANDARD **5**—decision making

Problem Diary

This activity allows students to work through a problem step by step and use the skill of decision making. Taking the time to sort out a problem is a valuable tool in developing impulse control. This activity allows students to practice stopping and considering consequences before deciding on an action—and to do so in a confidential and safe environment. Each student will be given copies of the Problem Diary worksheet (page 212 of appendix A) that can be put into a folder for each student to decorate as their own problem diary for their private use.

Materials

Folders and supplies for decorating the folders

Start

Students should keep a problem diary in a designated and secure space such as your locked desk or cabinet. This activity can be done by the whole

Name _____ Date _____

Problem Diary

1. How are you feeling? _____

2. What is the problem? _____

3. What are some actions you can take to solve this problem? _____

4. What might be some of the consequences of these actions? _____

5. What is the best solution, and what is your plan? _____

6. Reflect on your plan. What worked? What would you change? _____

From N.E. Tummers, 2011, *Teaching stress management: Activities for children and young adults* (Champaign, IL: Human Kinetics).

class or if a student feels they need to take a time out, the individual student could do their writing at the classroom's peace table or a desk or area designated by the instructor.

Prompt

Today you will creating your problem diaries. You can use these diaries using the Problem Diary worksheet to work through any problems you may be experiencing. Diaries can help us to think through our problems step by step. All of the Problem Diary worksheets will be kept secure so that only you and I will be able to read them. When you create your diary, the Problem Diary worksheets will go in a folder that you can decorate so it is your very own special place to think about your choices when facing a problem.

Finish

You can provide feedback directly to individual students or you can address and discuss general problems with the whole class. If you see any indication of neglect or abuse in a student's life, it is important to take appropriate action by bringing the facts to an administrator or school counselor.

Facing Fierce Feelings

Early childhood education through middle school

Noticing Feelings in Others

STANDARD **2**—analyzing influences and
7—practicing health-enhancing behaviors

This activity gives students practice in recognizing how others are feeling, which is an important part of the social and emotional skill of empathy—the ability to share others' feelings and emotions.

Materials

Photos or pictures cut from magazines of people of all ages showing strong emotions

Start

Mindful sitting in a circle

Prompt

1. Today we are going to talk about noticing how other people are feeling. I am going to start by showing you some pictures. (Share pictures of children showing strong feelings, such as anger, frustration, and sadness. As you show each picture, ask students about what feeling they see.) What are some ways that you can tell what the child in the picture is feeling? A worried look, a clenched fist, a red face? What are some ways that you notice when you yourself are experiencing a strong feeling?

2. Feeling angry or upset isn't wrong. The problem comes if we react without thinking through the feeling and do something that hurts someone or damages something. (Provide examples, such as yelling at someone or saying something mean.)

3. When we use calming tools, such as talking to ourselves and working through the problem—or leaving the situation and going to the peace table—we can calm down and then respond to feelings in a healthy way.

Finish

Have students share about the ability to recognize their own feelings and the feelings in others. Ask students for examples of reacting to feelings without thinking and conversely examples of responding to feelings in a healthy way. Reinforce the importance of self-management—the choice to respond to feelings in health-enhancing ways.

Acting Out Feelings

In this activity, students learn about nonverbal ways to communicate feelings. In fact, nonverbal cues contribute a considerable amount to interpersonal communication.

Materials

Index cards on which are written various feelings (e.g., angry, sad, snobby, sad, afraid, rejected, ignored, hot, helpless, eager)

Start

Mindful sitting in a circle

Prompt

I am going to pass out some index cards. Each card has a feeling written on it, and you (or your team) will act out the feeling on your card without speaking. The rest of the class will try to guess the feeling you are acting out.

Finish

Discuss the activity. How important is nonverbal communication? How important is it not only to hear words but also to pay attention to nonverbal cues and their connection to the words? Why is this essential?

Finding the Calm in the Middle of the Brainstorm

In this activity, students brainstorm suggestion for tools that they can use to help them calm down. They can then set a goal of using these tools.

Materials

Drawing paper and coloring markers

Start

Mindful sitting

Prompt

Make your own drawing or develop a mind map to display for yourself as a reminder to use your calming tools. A mind map is a visual representation of a central idea or problem (the middle circle). Mind maps are used for decision making, problem solving, or organizing information. The middle circle is then connected to outer circles which rep-

Finding the Calm

Name _____ Date _____

I feel calm when I...

play outdoors · dance · read · do a puzzle or word game · play with my little sister or dog · use a stress ball · do a breathing or relaxation tool · make something · do something for someone else · listen to soothing music · talk to a friend · take a break

1. Brainstorm a list of tools that you can use to help yourself calm down.

(continued)

From N.E. Tummers, 2011, *Teaching stress management: Activities for children and young adults* (Champaign, IL: Human Kinetics).

70

resent major solutions or areas necessary to map out related to the central theme. Finally, if necessary, create another layer of circles to depict ideas or steps necessary to complete each of the outer circles. For this activity, your mind map will become a diagram showing all of your ideas for calming down and how to implement each of them. For an example of a mind map, see the figure in the Finding the Calm worksheet (page 213 of appendix A).

Finish

Display the drawings in the classroom as visual reminders of the varied calming tools we can all use. The tools can also be shared with students' parents, and students can discuss ways to stay calm at home. Students can set a goal to utilize their calming tools.

Temperature Rising and Chilling Out

Elementary through young adult

STANDARD ❷—analyzing influences and ❼—practicing health-enhancing behaviors

In our digital age, the old-fashioned mercury thermometer display might be a thing of the past, but this activity allows students to describe situations that push their buttons, recognize how their body and mind react in these situations, and identify ways to calm down or cool off.

Start

Mindful sitting

Prompt

1. Using the Temperature Rising and Chilling Out worksheet (page 215 of appendix A) with the blank thermometers, start at the bottom of the thermometers (with the words "no problem") and write in words on the vertical axis to describe yourself as you get more upset (e.g., frustrated, cranky, annoyed). The top of the thermometer represents "boiling mad."

2. Next to the feelings you have written, note situations that push your anger buttons and describe how your body feels as the temperature climbs (e.g., red in the face, out of breath).

3. On the bottom of the worksheet, next to the ice cubes, write words, sentences, or draw symbols to repeat silently to yourself that it's time to cool off.

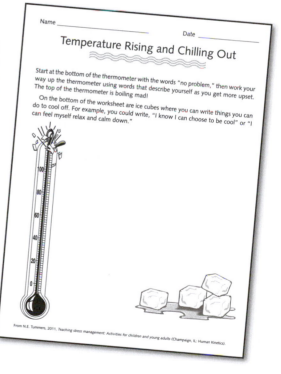

Finish

Display the thermometers and ice cubes in the classroom as visual reminders to attend to our feelings and use our tools to become calm and cool.

Worry Meetup

This activity allows an anxious or overwhelmed student to set aside worries when it is inappropriate to allow them to be a distraction (e.g., during class time) but also arrange for time later to focus on the worries. The student can use his or her creative imagination to set aside the worry by visualizing putting it into a box, a computer file, or any other storage option for later consideration. These become their "saved worries."

Start

At the designated time, the student and a trusted adult or peer mentor can discuss the saved worries and ways to address them so the student can feel a sense of control. This scheduled time is important to do on a consistent basis, perhaps weekly, so that continuing issues can be addressed. You can set aside time for yourself or another trusted adult or peer mentor to meet with each student in a private quiet spot.

Prompt

(This prompt is an example for how the trusted adult or peer mentor might guide a discussion with a student.)

1. Our meetings together will be a special time to talk about your saved worries in a safe environment where you can feel calm, centered, and grounded. Let's take a few calming and relaxed breaths together before we start our talk today.
2. Is there a saved worry you'd like to talk about today?
3. What are some ways you could address this saved worry in a health-enhancing way?
4. By the time of our next meeting, what is an action step you would like to take toward dealing with this saved worry?

Finish

Students can journal about their saved worries and their ability to deal with them proactively to enhance their health. The student can share their journals with you or their other trusted adult or peer mentor during the meeting and can use the journal to document the action steps they have been working on. This can help give the students a sense of control and self-efficacy because, not only are saved worries talked about, but the student is taking actions toward a solution. By discussing the actions taken, the trusted adult or peer mentor can aid the student in processing when the actions were effective and troubleshoot what might be different actions to take.

Act Out Emotions

In this activity, students use role playing as a way to express their feelings.

Start

First, warm up the class with the following activity for acting out emotions: Standing in a circle, one student (or the instructor) names an emotion and, without speaking, acts out the emotion. The next person acts out the same emotion—that is, how he or she would experience it. Each member of the circle acts out the emotion, one at a time, and the group can do several rounds (i.e., several emotions). Then divide the students into teams for the main activity.

Prompt

I am giving each team a list of emotions and a scene. (Alternatively, each team of students can write their own scenarios involving the specified emotions.) The members of your team should plan and act out your scene in such a way that all of the listed emotions are demonstrated. (The list might include five emotions, and the scene might take place in a setting such as a video arcade or a homecoming basketball game.) At the end of your scene, the other teams will list all of the emotions that your team demonstrated.

Finish

Discuss with students the importance of paying attention to our own as well as others' feelings.

If My _____ Could Talk, It Would Say . . .

This is an esteem booster and a sharing activity.

Start

Mindful sitting

Prompt

Imagine an object that you use every day. If it could talk, what might it say about you? For example: "If my (computer, gameboard, skateboard, backpack, sneakers, dog) could talk, it would say . . ." When it is your turn, start your sentence this way and fill in the blank with positive statements about yourself.

Finish

Have students discuss how it feels to make positive statements about themselves. Discuss with students why it is important to do this.

Active Listening

So much of the stress we experience in life involves our relationships with others. With this in mind, we can see the importance of empathy as part of healthy communication. It allows us to listen to another person's story. When we cultivate empathy, the focus is no longer on us.

Start

First take time to discuss what active listening involves—listening for constructive feedback rather than focusing on defending oneself. An active listener lets go of always having to be right. Here are several keys to active listening:

1. Make your utmost goal to understand the speaker by putting yourself in his or her shoes and seeing his or her perspective. Notice the person's body language, tone, and choice of words.

2. Keep your own thoughts to yourself and turn down the mental volume of your commentary and response to what the other person is saying. Just commit to listening. Use body language that shows you are paying attention (e.g., eye contact, nods, appropriately serious facial expression).

3. Ask relevant questions to determine whether you understand clearly or need more details.

4. Repeat in your own words in order to summarize what you feel you have understood.

Prompt

Break into pairs and practice active listening using the suggested topics on the Active Listening Topics worksheet (page 216 of appendix A). (Have one student talk for a set period of time while the other student listens actively without interruption; then have the students switch roles. Allow each partner to take several turns.) What did your partner do to show active listening?

Name _____   Date _____

Active Listening Topics

1. Tell me about the funniest situation you have ever experienced.

2. Tell me about a person you admire and why you admire him or her.

3. Tell me about the proudest moment in your life.

4. Tell me about your dream career.

5. Tell me about your favorite memory.

6. Tell me the hardest thing about romance.

From N.E. Tummers, 2011, Teaching stress management: Activities for children and young adults (Champaign, IL: Human Kinetics).

Finish

Have students process the steps to active listening and discuss what it feels like to be listened to.

Using Feeling Sentences

Straight-talk messages, also known as I-messages, offer a constructive way to communicate honestly—to manage emotions by stepping away from the drama rather than getting caught up in the story or in one's personal attachment to a situation. The purpose of straight talk is to focus on the facts and stay neutral. Using I-messages is an important lifelong skill that allows us to communicate how we feel while taking responsibility for effective communication.

Start

Mindful sitting

Prompt

I-messages tell someone how you feel, how you see a situation, or what you think. These messages use the word *I* instead of the word *you*. This approach lets the other person know how you feel and allows him or her to respond to your feeling. Here are some examples: "I feel happy because I am going to visit to my grandmother." "I feel sad when no one wants to share their toys with me." Now, let's share about situations in which we have experienced hurt or frustrated feelings and talk about how to reword statements as I-messages.

Finish

Have students write I-messages on large pieces of paper to display in the room as reminders to model good use of feeling sentences.

© Photodisc

Knowing how to communicate effectively helps students develop a strong social support system that can help them in good times and bad throughout their lives.

Rewrites!

In this activity, students rewrite a dialogue using the Straight-Talk Building Blocks worksheet (page 217 of appendix A).

Start

Students first write from their own experience about a situation in which their feelings were hurt; the write-up should include dialogue.

Prompt

Rewrite your dialogue situation using the straight-talk building blocks (see the worksheet).

Finish

Have students share their first and second straight-talk dialogues. Allow students to share situations where using straight talk would have been a healthy choice.

Name _____ Date _____

The Straight-Talk Building Blocks

Rewrite your dialogue situation using the straight-talk building block procedure shown below. Examples of dialogue to rewrite:

- Your mom keeps yelling at you over little things.
- You text and leave messages for your friend, but he or she never texts or calls you.
- Your big brother keeps telling you what to do and annoyingly play-punching you.
- Your boyfriend is ignoring you and pays more attention to his friends than to you.
- A kid you don't even know keeps calling you names in the hall.

1. State what is happening objectively. _____

2. Explain how it makes you feel—not putting down the other person by telling them how they should feel, but stating how you feel. _____

3. State specifically what you want in the form of a request. _____

4. Invite the person to respond to your request and ask for agreement. Example: "I feel (what you are feeling) when you (what the person did). I want (what you want the person to do)." Then ask for agreement. _____

From N.E. Tummers, 2011, *Teaching stress management: Activities for children and young adults* (Champaign, IL: Human Kinetics).

Compliment Central

This activity helps students practice making sincere and meaningful compliments.

Start

Mindful sitting in a circle

Prompt

Compliments are nice things we say to someone else. A compliment needs to be sincere and honest. We can offer a compliment when we like something about a person and want to let him or her know how we feel. In this activity, you will take turns complimenting each other by using one of the categories of compliments shown on the Compliment Categories handout (page 218 of appendix A). (Lead the activity. Point out to students that the categories build up from a foundation of casual or merely polite compliments to the peak of more meaningful compliments.)

Finish

Have students share how it feels to receive and give compliments. Help students understand the importance of being gracious in receiving compliments and authentic and sincere in offering them.

Compliment Categories

The way the person behaves: "I appreciate it when you take turns."

The way the person is: "I like that you smile all the time."

What the person does: "That is awesome you can roller skate."

What the person has: "Those are cool shoes."

How the person looks: "I like your smile."

From N.E. Tummers, 2011, *Teaching stress management: Activities for children and young adults* (Champaign, IL: Human Kinetics).

Facing Fierce Feelings
Elementary through middle school
STANDARD **7**—practicing health-
enhancing behaviors

Pats on the Back

This activity allows each member of the class to recognize positive aspects of other students.

Materials

One large piece of heavy construction paper (12" x 18") and markers for each student

Start

Each student has a piece of heavy paper taped to his or her back. Each student has a marker to write carefully on each students' attached paper.

Prompt

With your marker, carefully write one positive thing about each of the other students in your class. (When all are done, make a classwide list on the board.) Now, let's discuss the positive comments people made about each other. (Point out the difference between superficial comments, such as "you have nice jeans," and more substantial ones, such as "you are a team player and easy to approach.")

Finish

This activity can be repeated again in a few weeks. This allows students to become more aware and "catch" other students doing positive things so that future comments are more meaningful.

Assertive Bill of Rights

In this activity, students design an advocacy campaign for their classroom or entire school to promote effective interpersonal communication and respect for other students.

Start

Review the skill set for the national health education standard 8, advocacy (Joint Committee 2007). This standard includes the following skill cues:

* Taking a clear health-enhancing stand
* Being well aware of one's target group
* Encouraging and motivating others
* Showing passion and conviction

Prompt

In this activity, you will work together to create your own Assertive Bill of Rights (see the sidebar on page 78 for an example), then design a campaign using posters, public service announcements, and skits to convey your message. Be sure that you use all of the skill cues we discussed that should be used for advocacy.

(continued)

Assertive Bill of Rights

- Say no and mean it when someone makes a request you do not want to do.
- You don't have to have the answer on the spot: "I'll get back to you."
- You have the right to change your mind.
- You can learn from your mistakes.
- Admit when you are wrong.
- Ask for help.

- You have a right to your opinions but you can't force them on someone else.
- Be open—be flexible to changing your opinion.
- Keep to the topic and to the point. Avoid giving too much information!
- Avoid slang and prejudicial words.

Finish

Students can display their advocacy posters around the school. They can also serve as peer educators who go into classrooms to conduct short lessons that advocate about being assertive.

Facing Fierce Feelings

Elementary through middle school

STANDARD ❶—core concepts

Recognizing the Players in Conflict Resolution

In this activity, students learn to recognize the various players involved in a conflict situation.

Start

Read aloud a description of a conflict situation. The situation could be pulled from the news, from a book the students are reading, or from a situation the instructor has observed among the students.

Prompt

Now, as we discuss the conflict situation, you will identify the key players:

- Victim: Who is targeted in the situation?
- Bully: Who started the situation?
- Bystanders: Who allowed the situation to happen and didn't do anything to help resolve it?
- Mediator: Did anyone try to help the players resolve the situation?

Finish

Have students discuss how each of the players in the situation could have avoided or helped resolve the conflict. It is important that each member of the situation has the responsibility to resolve the conflict rather than one person being "right" or "the winner."

The Rules of Fighting Fair

In this activity, students establish rules for fighting fair (with some guidance from you).

Start

Many of our students have never been shown how to disagree with someone without "beating them up" through either words or physical actions. The media rarely portray fair fighting, focusing instead on the attitude of "let's kick some gluteus," so perhaps it is no wonder that our students often resort to fists and put-downs.

In this activity, the class brainstorms rules for fighting fair. Students must be allowed to generate the rules because if they do not own these rules, they will not use them. You can, however, guide students, and you can find sample rules for fighting fair in the sidebar.

Prompt

Fighting fair means resolving conflict with respect. In this activity, we will brainstorm rules for fighting fair with each other. This means that when you disagree with another person, you do not attack them—with words or actions. Remember that in brainstorming, there are no wrong ideas.

Finish

Once all ideas are presented, guide the group in coming to a consensus about which rules work the best. The rules should be clear and as brief as possible. See the Sample Rules for Fighting Fair sidebar for examples of actions to take and some to avoid. The emphasis should be on the yes list in the sidebar, and the rules should be displayed in the classroom.

Sample Rules for Fighting Fair

YES LIST

- Stick to the problem, not the person.
- Commit to finding solutions.
- Use active listening.
- Take responsibility.
- Be assertive.
- Be honest—tell the truth.
- Be empathetic.
- Take turns.
- Respect the rights of others.

NO LIST

- Threats
- Name calling or put-downs
- Rudeness
- Profanity
- Behind-the-back comments

Finding a Resolution: Role-Playing Negotiation

Elementary through young adult
STANDARD ④—interpersonal communication
and ⑥—goal setting

In this activity, students first understand the roles of various players in resolving a situation. They are then given situations to resolve. Finding a resolution involves working through and solving their own issues rather than going to the teacher to handle things for them.

Start

Give the students situations in which to resolve conflict. You can create scenarios or use situations that you have observed among your students.

Prompt

1. First, let's learn about three key roles in resolving a conflict situation:
   * Negotiators are the parties trying to solve a problem.
   * The mediator is a neutral party who facilitates communication and helps the negotiators use the rules for fighting fair and good interpersonal communication—especially I-messages and active listening. The mediator remains neutral and provides empathy without judging.
   * The arbitrator or ombudsperson is another neutral party who provides suggestions that steer the negotiators toward a consensus and resolution.

2. Now, break into your teams (of perhaps four members each) and work your way through your scenario. Each student in your group should take a turn serving in each of the three roles—negotiator, mediator, and arbitrator. The mediator reads aloud the situation and facilitates the following steps:

   Step 1. Each negotiator uses I-messages to tell his or her side of the situation without being interrupted.

   Step 2. The negotiators take turns suggesting ways to resolve the conflict. Both parties share the responsibility of solving it. The arbitrator can be asked to step in to provide ideas for achieving resolution.

   Step 3. Both negotiators come to a resolution and state the steps that they will take to implement it.

3. Observe each other as you try on each of the roles in finding a resolution. Give each other feedback about how well you fulfilled your role in resolving the conflict.

Finish

Help students to identify the responsibilities of each of the conflict resolution roles. It is important to provide practice for students to explore the responsibilities of each role. Beyond this activity, you can encourage students to use these steps in the classroom when conflicts arise. Resolutions can be recorded in a peacekeeping log where all the parties sign an agreement to their role in the resolution—for example, a negotiator's next steps that he or she has agreed to take. The mediator's commitment is to check in with the negotiators within 48 hours to see if all parties are taking their action steps. When conflicts arise, a designated area—the peace table—can be used as a space in which to work for resolution. This area can be decorated with images of peacekeepers (e.g., Gandhi) and the rules for fighting fair.

Case Studies

Case studies provide a way to apply content and skill to a specific situation. A case study brings into play a more objective and meaningful application of stress management tools. Case studies also allow students to practice empathy by putting themselves into the shoes of the person described in the case.

Start

Develop the character of the case study based on the needs of your students. For an example, see the Sample Case Study sidebar.

Prompt

1. What stressors is the character facing?

2. What signs and symptoms suggest that the character is experiencing stress?

3. Did the character's actions create, add to, or reduce his or her stress?

4. What do you think the character needs to know about stress and stress management?

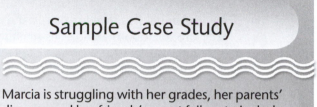

Sample Case Study

Marcia is struggling with her grades, her parents' divorce, and her friends' recent failure to include her in plans they make. She feels that she isn't smart enough and that she is not popular because she is overweight. She decides to go on a diet and exercise as much as she can, even late at night in her room. She begins to feel exhausted most of the time and considers using diet pills to help her move toward her perfect weight.

Finish

Have students discuss their answers to each of the prompts. Ask students to identify stress management tools that could be applied to the situations provided and share their own situations where they could use these stress management tools as well.

Time Management

Learning to plan for the best use of our time is a lifelong activity. For students, enormous stress can be produced when they feel overwhelmed by the combination of schoolwork, after-school activity or a part-time job, and social pressures. Students may respond to such stress ineffectively by procrastinating because they do not know how to break down projects, assignments, and study time into manageable pieces.

Time Management
Elementary through young adult
STANDARD **5**—decision making

Decision Making

National health education standard 5 states that "students will demonstrate the ability to use decision-making skills to enhance health" (Joint Committee 2007). Indeed, one of the biggest stressors a person can face is the need to make a good decision. This activity helps students work through the necessary steps for doing so.

Start

Give each student a copy of the Good Decision Checklist (page 219 of appendix A), then have them use the checklist to analyze stressful scenarios created either by you or by the students in order to make them relevant to the group.

Prompt

In the stressful situation I just described to you, look at your Good Decision Checklist and write down, in order, each of the steps for making a healthy decision about this situation.

Finish

Have students share their scenarios and their steps for making good decisions. Why is it important to do each of the steps and in order? What are steps we often skip over when making a decision? Why is it important to consider all the options and consequences associated with each of the options?

Name _____   Date _____

Good Decision Checklist

☐ Can this decision be made on my own, or do I need help? What kind of help is best for this situation?

☐ What are the healthy options in this situation? What is best for me and my family? Did I consider all of the options and possible consequences for each option?

☐ What are the potential outcomes in both the short term and the long term for each of the healthy options?

☐ How effective was my decision? What could I do different next time to make it healthier?

Scenarios
Pair up with a partner and generate solutions for the following situations:

1. Provide an example of a not-so-good decision you made in the past. Use the Good Decision Checklist to decide which step you skipped or did not fully execute. _____

2. Provide an example of a decision that you made impulsively without thinking through all the steps. _____

3. Provide an example of a time when a decision was needed but you procrastinated until it was too late to make a good or achievable decision. _____

4. Provide an example of a situation in which you did not give your opinion and others made the decision for you. _____

From N.E. Tummers, 2011, *Teaching stress management: Activities for children and young adults* (Champaign, IL: Human Kinetics).

File It

In this activity, students demonstrate the ability to organize their time and find a time management system to use consistently. Organizing oneself and managing one's energy constitutes a critical life skill. Because we all have our own ways of processing information and learning, no single time management method works for everyone; therefore, it is necessary to model various methods of time management for students. This activity provides just one example to help students examine how they use their time.

Start

Mindful sitting

Prompt

List all of the activities you did in the past 48 hours (besides such mundane actions as sleeping), then file each activity into one of the following four categories:

File 1: Important and immediate action is needed

File 2: Important but immediate action is not needed

File 3: Not important but immediate action is needed

File 4: Not important and immediate action is not needed

Next, examine how much of your day is spent in files 3 and 4. For example, an item might end up in file 3 simply because you forgot to do your chores and thus had to do them (urgently) when you should have been doing something important from file 1 or 2. You will probably find that you spend a lot of time on "time waster" items in files 3 and 4 (e.g., watching TV, hanging out).

Finish

Have students examine methods for keeping themselves organized by revisiting their goals and setting deadlines in their monthly and weekly calendars; listing their action steps in order; and setting up a system for accountability and reward (e.g., watching a favorite TV show or calling a friend, both of which are good stress management tools when used appropriately).

Goal Setting

As Napoleon Hill once said, "A goal is a dream with a deadline." For our students, learning to set goals with action steps is an important health-enhancing behavior that will serve them well for a lifetime. Students often have goals but lack the skill to write realistic action steps for achieving them. Equally important is the ability to reevaluate action steps in order to make changes and stay motivated to achieve one's goals. Without effective action steps and the ability to reevaluate, students often get stuck.

In this activity, students use goal setting to enhance their health; specifically, they write goals using the steps presented in the Formula for Goal Setting worksheet (page 220 of appendix A).

Start

Provide each student with the Formula for Goal Setting worksheet.

Prompt

Select a personal goal related to stress management (e.g., meeting the deadline for college application essays or planning for the science fair). Now write this goal using the formula for goal setting. Make sure to be specific and clear about what needs to be done to reach this goal.

Finish

Students can hold themselves accountable by tracking their progress toward meeting their goal. This process allows them to make adjustments in order to stay on track.

Name _____

Date _____

Formula for Goal Setting

1. Awareness: Think about what you want and brainstorm or research things that will help you to accomplish that. For example, you might think about a problem you are having and think about what, specifically, could help make the situation better. List those thoughts, ideas, and possible resources here.

2. Own it: Many times, goals are expectations created by parents, teachers, or coaches. In order to achieve goals, it is critical to exercise self-responsibility and make sure that it is a personal goal and under your control. When the goal is seen in a positive light—this is what I want—it is more likely to be achieved than when it is seen as a punishment and forced upon you. My goal is: _____

3. Action: What are the specific steps for action? Break the goal down into bite-size pieces known as action steps and set a deadline for each step. My action steps are: _____

4. Specific measures: Often, we don't really know what we want, and thus the goal is ambiguous or vague, which makes it difficult to know what we need to do. Action steps need to involve specific, measurable actions. The ways that I will objectively measure or evaluate progress towards my goal include: _____

From N.E. Tummers, 2011, *Teaching stress management: Activities for children and young adults* (Champaign, IL: Human Kinetics).

Learned Optimism and Locus of Control

In working with students, Seligman and colleagues (2007) observed what they came to call learned helplessness, in which a student shows a lack of motivation, distorts situations, and uses helplessness as a negative coping strategy in order to cause others to step up and do the work or excuse the student from the pressure of meeting expectations. For example, a student might continue to use excused absences and hand in late work supposedly due to an illness even after he or she has recovered.

Seligman's team (2007) went on to develop a construct called learned optimism. Thus they hold that both helplessness and optimism are not inherited but are learned behaviors, which means that optimism can be taught. One's level of optimism is rooted in what is called the locus of control. A student perceives his or her locus of control by means of his or her explanatory style (Seligman et al. 2007), which includes the following three aspects:

- How much responsibility the student takes for the situation
- How much responsibility the student assigns to others
- How much importance the student assigns to luck or chance

Here is an example of an explanatory style with an external locus of control: "All my teachers gang up on me and are so unfair." Such an explanatory style can bring on self-limiting beliefs, which may take the form of familiar self-fulfilling prophecies, such as "I am too stupid to do that" or "I am too slow."

When a student faces a difficult situation by focusing on his or her ability to take responsibility for it, he or she is exhibiting an internal locus of control. Here is an example: "My English teacher is hard, but I can ask her for help to make sure my paper is heading in the right direction." In contrast, a student with an external locus of control assigns responsibility for outcomes to someone or something else—for example, "the teacher is having a bad day," or "people just don't like me," or "it was fate (or chance)." Putting the blame on others leaves one with very little to power to make the situation better and thus can lead one to feel like a helpless victim. By taking responsibility, however, the student is able to choose how he or she will respond in the situation.

One critical skill in learned optimism is that of disputation (Seligman et al. 2007), which involves putting thoughts to the test in order to see whether they are true. We tend to be very critical in our thinking about ourselves for varied reasons, such as believing in the negativity brought on by parents, teachers, or peers. Such thoughts can easily be blown out of proportion and become distorted. Here are some types of distortions:

- Making an unnecessarily big deal out of a situation or catastrophizing

- Jumping to conclusions
- Thinking perfectionistically (characterized by "should" and "always")
- Having a sense of entitlement, as if things should or must happen according to one's own agenda
- Thinking in all-or-nothing terms, for example it has to be perfect or don't even bother doing it. Another example of all-or-nothing thinking would be thinking, "I am a stupid or bad student" instead of "I am challenged by math, but I'm a great speller" (Seligman et al. 2007).
- Thinking that everything is awful, for example, assuming that when one thing goes wrong, everything goes wrong, and it will always happen that way

The skill of disputation directly opposes distortion (Seligman et al. 2007). Disputing in this sense involves logically and rationally putting beliefs to the test by looking for evidence to back them up. Defeating or negative thoughts that do not hold up to disputation can then be disposed of in favor of what is true. This is self-responsibility.

Learned Optimism and Locus of Control

Middle school through young adult

STANDARD **7**—practicing health-enhancing behaviors

Put It Up for Debate

In this activity, students practice using disputation to handle stressful situations.

Start

Review with students the steps for disputation. Model an example to illustrate these steps. Provide students with scenarios to work with; alternatively, have students write their own situations.

Prompt

Examine the stressful situation and use the Steps for Disputation worksheet (page 221 of appendix A).

Finish

Have students share their situations and their steps for disputation. Ask students to share why it is important to use disputation to examine their thinking.

Steps for Disputation

Name _____ Date _____

1. Look at the evidence (the facts) to support stressful thoughts. Look for assumptions—conclusions made without sufficient information. When approaching challenging beliefs, beware of the tendency toward tunnel vision; it is better to widen the focus instead. _____

2. See if there is a positive explanation for the situation. _____

3. Put the situation in perspective. How important will this be tomorrow or next week? How can the situation be viewed in a more holistic and healthy way? Try to change your framing of the situation and use less dramatic or less emotionally packed language to describe it. _____

4. If you are not part of the solution, the problem will remain. What proactive actions could you take in this situation rather than dwelling on the problem—chewing and stewing—which perpetuates the stress cycle? Set an intention of not allowing the disturbing thought to override your best response to the situation. _____

From N.E. Tummers, 2011, *Teaching stress management: Activities for children and young adults* (Champaign, IL: Human Kinetics).

Learned Optimism and Locus of Control
Elementary through young adult
STANDARD **7**—practicing health-
enhancing behaviors

Debbie Downer or Polly Positive

In this activity, students first act out their reactions to the scenario from a pessimistic perspective, then do so from an optimistic perspective.

Debbie Downer or Polly Positive Scenarios

- Ashley gets a C on her English paper.
- José misses the bus for school.
- Phillip gets put on the JV baseball team rather than varsity.
- Keisha doesn't get invited to a popular girl's party.

From N.E. Tummers, 2011, *Teaching stress management: Activities for children and young adults* (Champaign, IL: Human Kinetics).

Start

Teams of two or three students work together on a given scenario. Give each team the Debbie Downer or Polly Positive Scenarios handout (page 222 of appendix A).

Prompt

Your team will act out responses to your scenarios from two different perspectives: pessimistic and optimistic. First, act out the given scenario by responding with pessimistic thoughts, feelings, and reactions to the problem. Then shift gears and act out the scenario with responses that take an optimistic perspective in thinking and feeling about the problem.

Finish

Have the student teams take turns acting out their responses to the same scenarios in order to see how different teams came up with different positive perspectives. Ask students how it feels to look at situations from a positive perspective.

Affirmations

Many people spend a significant amount of time engaged in negative thinking. Some of this negative self-talk may result from negative statements made by parents, peers, or society at large. We can become conditioned to speak to ourselves in a negative manner: "I can't," "I never," "I don't." We also hear such statements on the unconscious level and sometimes let them set the scene for failure, which fuels a cycle of failure and pessimism.

The tool of affirmation involves noticing when negative talk begins and shifting away from it to embrace a positive frame of mind. Writing affirmations can be tricky, since such statements can feel false or silly due to the constant dialogue of criticism and negativity that is often assumed to be normal. Often, however, the characteristics we desire are already there—we just need to get out of our own way and take effective action.

Affirmations are specific, succinct, personal statements written in the present tense. They address a feeling and, most important, are simple. It is said that energy follows intention, and asking students to be mindful of intention—their self-talk and the energy they bring to a task—can make all the difference. The practice of affirmation has many uses in both sport and business settings. Many successful people use affirmations to set themselves up for positive thinking. An Olympic athlete would not step onto the medal stand and think, "I really stink at this sport!" Nor should that be the way in which we speak to ourselves.

Writing an Affirmation

In this activity, students both write and practice using affirmations.

Materials

Index cards

Start

Mindful sitting

Prompt

Affirmations should be realistic and meaningful. It is hard to repeat sentences that are false or insincere. Affirmations should also be specific. For example, "I will get good grades" does not work as well as "I will practice my spelling words until I get them just right." Affirmation statements can begin with "I can," "I am," or "I will."

Write your personal affirmations on an index card. Hold the card in your lap and quietly say the affirmations aloud on your exhalations. With each subsequent exhalation, allow the affirmation to be said a little more quietly, until the phrase is repeated silently to yourself. Pay attention to each word and take your time. All words in the affirmation matter. Take the time to say them with purpose and intention.

Finish

Students can take their affirmation index card home and practice stating their affirmations before school and at night for 7 consecutive days. After a week of using their affirmations, have students reflect by writing about or discussing their use of affirmation cards as a stress management tool.

Making the Shift

This activity allows students to notice their typical internal dialogue and rewrite unconstructive thoughts into positive affirmations.

Start

Mindful sitting

Prompt

Write down typical statements that you make to yourself. Now shift your perspective and rewrite these statements into positive affirmations. For example, "School is so boring and useless" might be rewritten as "I love to learn and apply new things to my life." Similarly, "No one likes me" might be shifted to "I am grateful for my true friends."

Finish

Have students write down their newly created "shifted" statements on an index card. They can take their affirmation card home and practice stating their affirmations before school and at night for 7 consecutive days. After a week of affirmations, have students reflect in a writing activity or class discussion on using affirmation cards as a stress management tool.

Slow Down Turtle

In this activity, we will use the metaphor of the turtle to illustrate perseverance and tenacity in our commitment to our goals.

Start

Mindful sitting

Prompt

Turtles are slow, but they are also determined to get to their destination. Is there a time when you hurry too much and don't get to where you need to be? Reflect on a specific goal you have that takes time and determination. Write an affirmation statement of your desire to accomplish this goal: "I will . . ."

Take the time to talk to yourself. Ask yourself, "What actions will I take to accomplish my goal?"

Finish

Students can write their "I will" statements on an index card, then take the card home and practice stating their affirmations before school and at night for 7 consecutive days. After a week of affirmation, have the students reflect in a writing activity or class discussion about the actions they took to accomplish their goals using affirmation cards as a stress management tool.

Heart Smart Stress Management

Research conducted by the Institute of HeartMath (www.heartmath.org/) provides an excellent example of best practices for stress management in public schools. In the research, students used tools developed by Dr. Doc Childre (1999) at the Institute, which is a nonprofit organization that promotes heart-based research. Part of the research focuses on entrainment, in which a student shifts from a stressful perspective and aligns his or her brainwave rhythms with the calming, centered, and positive-emotion-focused rhythms of the heart. The body and mind can then work more efficiently with decreased stress and anxiety.

Hitting the Pause Button

This heart-based stress management activity is adapted from Dr. Doc Childre's book *The HeartMath Solution* (1999).

Start

Mindful sitting

Prompt

Listen to each of the following steps for this activity. (As you read the steps, leave time between them for students to process each step—15 to 30 seconds for younger children and up to a minute for older students.

1. Think about one specific personal problem you are having. Notice the feelings that go with this problem and what is going on in your body and mind when you are thinking about this problem. Imagine that you are viewing this problem on a high-definition screen in your mind's eye. Take a few more moments to bring all your attention to this problem on the big screen in your mind. (Pause for 5 to 10 seconds.) Now hit the pause button and freeze this problem. (Pause.)

2. Take three deep relaxed breaths. Make an effort to shift from the problem you identified in step 1 and bring your awareness to the area around your heart. Breathe in and out of your heart for five big breaths while imagining your heart getting bigger and more spacious with each breath. Connect with the heart as you feel the pumping of your heart slow down. Feel your body relax as you breathe in and out of your heart space. (Pause.)

3. Recall an experience where you had a strong positive emotion, such as gratitude, joy, happiness, or love. What did it feel like to experience this positive emotion? Take five deep breaths as you recall and enjoy this positive experience. Picture this positive experience in your mind's eye—on the big screen in your mind—and really enjoy all the feelings associated with it. (Pause.)

4. Ask your heart what might be a more positive and effective way to deal with the problem you put on pause in step 1. View this problem through the open heart and mind. (Pause.)

5. Listen to your heart and resolve to set an action step you will take to respond to this problem. Take time to reflect on this exercise.

Finish

Have students draw, write, or talk with someone they trust about the problem and about the possible action steps they reflected on from their perspective of open heart and open mind. The possible actions may include doing nothing.

Based on Childre and Martin 1999.

Happiness

In the United States, the pursuit of happiness is one of our inalienable rights, but we often do so little to pursue it. Dr. Sonja Lyubomirsky, professor at the University of California, Riverside, and author of *The How of Happiness: A Scientific Approach to Getting the Life You Want* (2007), believes that 40 percent of our capacity for happiness can be within our power to create through our thoughts and attitudes. Lyubomirsky suggests that circumstances such as life situations have very little to do with being happy even though we direct a lot of our energy, time, and money into trying to address such circumstances. For example, we may think that having a brand new shiny car will make us happier, but this is not necessarily the case.

Happiness

All levels

STANDARD **7**—practicing health-enhancing behaviors

This Is My Happy Place

This activity reminds students that to some extent they are the drivers of their own "happy bus." This fact means that no one else can make them happy and, conversely, that they cannot make someone else happy. By taking the time to reflect on their "happy place" when faced with difficult feelings, they can recall a happy experience in order to reframe their reactions or to self-regulate.

Materials

Drawing paper, markers, and other art supplies

Start

Mindful sitting. Students can use the heart-centered activity "Hitting the Pause Button" (described earlier) as a springboard for this activity to allow for a shift from a negative focus and intention to a positive one. This activity helps students to understand the concept of savoring or taking the time to appreciate a happy experience.

Learning to mindfully remember happy times and events can help students through stressful times by giving them something positive to focus on.

Prompt

Share a time when you wanted to stay longer in a happy experience—you did not want it to end (e.g., a birthday party or a trip to an amusement park). Describe the thoughts and feelings you had when you were in this happy experience. Take your special happy experience and draw a picture of it.

Finish

Have students share their pictures of their happy places and display them in the classroom. Students can discuss situations in which they would benefit from remembering their happy places.

A Healthy Lifestyle Approach to Stress Management

A lifestyle approach asks students to look at what they can add to their lives that is enjoyable and proactively healthy. It involves shifting away from punitive "must do" thinking to a focus on what one can do to become happier and healthier.

Healthy Lifestyle

Elementary through young adult

STANDARD **7**—practicing health-enhancing behaviors

It's Raining Healthy Habits!

This is a brainstorm activity, meaning that there are no wrong answers, only a free flow of healthy habits that students can incorporate into their daily lives (see the Mind Map on page 223 of appendix A). It is important that students approach this activity without judgment about one activity being better than another—the more activities students can incorporate as healthy habits, the better.

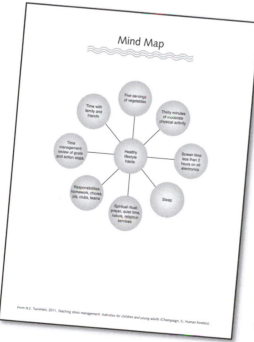

Start

Mindful sitting

Prompt

A healthy lifestyle involves habits and practices that promote wellness and happiness. Some you might do less often—maybe only weekly—such as attending a religious service; others you might engage in more often such as a physical activity. In this activity, you will use a mind map to come up with personal healthy lifestyle habits.

Take a look at each of the sample actions for a healthy lifestyle mind map. Create your own mind map with healthy lifestyle actions you might want to incorporate into your lifestyle either daily, weekly, or once in a while such as taking a vacation that involves a physical activity or volunteering every other month at your local food bank.

Finish

Have students discuss ways in which they can incorporate one of the healthy habits into their lives.

Better Sleep Habits Checklist

According to the nonprofit National Sleep Foundation (2010) children between the ages of 5 and 12 need 10 to 11 hours of sleep each night. Adolescents are especially at risk for not getting enough sleep due to long days in school, after-school activities such as jobs or sports, and time spent doing homework. According to the National Institutes of Health (2004), inadequate sleep is associated with poor school performance, increased substance use, depression, mood disturbance, poor self-esteem, and, not surprisingly, extreme sleepiness. The quality of students' sleep, in turn, is affected considerably by stress. In this activity, students learn about health-enhancing behavior and set a goal for establishing a better sleep routine.

Start

Have students discuss how many hours of sleep they personally need to be at their best. Each individual has his or her need for sleep, but you can provide general guidelines: 10 to 11 hours nightly for children between the ages of 5 and 11 and 8.5 to 9 hours for teenagers.

Prompt

Write a goal to establish a sleep routine by creating a checklist of things you will do before going to bed. This sleep routine might include making your room cooler and darker, turning off all electronics, doing a light stretching routine, practicing intentional relaxation (e.g., progressive muscle relaxation, relaxed breathing, or body scan), sipping herbal tea, taking a hot shower or bath, cleaning up and organizing your clothes, making a to-do list for the next day, listening to relaxing music, reading for pleasure or inspiration, establishing consistent sleeping and awakening times to maintain regular patterns for sleep (e.g., not just sleeping in on weekends), and monitoring caffeine use.

Finish

Have students maintain a record of their progress toward their goal for better sleep habits over a specified period of time and reflect on what worked for them in maintaining healthy sleep habits.

Recess

It is recommended that elementary students have at least 20 minutes of daily recess (National Association for Sport and Physical Education 2006). This position is supported by various organizations invested in the health of our students, including the U.S. Department of Health and Human Services, the U.S. Department of Education, and the Centers for Disease Control and Prevention. Recess provides students with time to practice many of the skills necessary for lifelong stress management, including movement, cooperation, interpersonal communication, focus, and conflict resolution. It is important for recess to be physically active which means that all students must have access to equipment and activity space that allows them to be physically active such as open space, balls, and jump ropes.

In addition, in *Spark: The Revolutionary New Science of Exercise and the Brain* (2008), Dr. John Ratey notes that unstructured active play without adult intervention is critical for enhancing brain function and providing a chance to repair the "corrosive effects" (p. 75) of stress. This position is also supported by professor of developmental cognitive neuroscience at the University of British Columbia, Dr. Adele Diamond (Spiegel 2008).

Diamond believes play to be an essential life skill that substantially influences our students' stress management ability. The play that Diamond speaks of is not adult mediated and therefore leaves students free to exercise and build "executive function," which is the ability to self-regulate and thus forms an integral part of stress management. Self-regulation includes controlling one's emotions, being centered and grounded, and exercising self-control.

Physical Activity

For a frazzled and depleted nervous or immune system, there is probably no more effective stress management tool than physical activity. It is well established that mild to moderate physical activity helps decrease depression and anxiety and improves mood. Research also shows that participating in physical activity improves brain function; for example, grade school students who participate in physical education classes improve their scores on standardized tests (Ratey 2008).

Everyone can enjoy physical activity, and the operative word here is *enjoy*. When an activity is enjoyable, we are more likely to do it consistently, and consistency is the key to making physical activity part of a lifelong healthy lifestyle. Thus we can help students get on the path to lifelong physical activity by helping them seek out and try a wide variety of physical activities (not necessarily sports) so that they find activities they enjoy.

Several organizations are dedicated to promoting and researching the benefits of movement on brain function. Brain Gym, for example, focuses on educational kinesiology by using specific exercises to enhance the connection between the body and the brain and thus help students focus and relax. To learn more, visit the group's website (www.braingym.org/).

Physical Activity
All levels

STANDARD 6—goal setting

Physical Activity Challenge

It is important to acknowledge even small increments of physical activity. Research indicates the health benefits of cumulative time spent in physical activity—it does not have to be done all at once. In this activity, we focus on finding time to get out and be active.

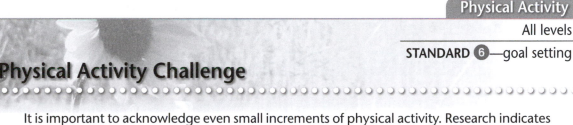

Start

Give each student a Physical Activity Challenge Calendar (page 224 of appendix A).

Prompt

Using the Physical Activity Challenge Calendar, circle the icon for physical activity (a puppy running) for every 10 minutes of continuous moderate activity in which you participate during a certain week. If you do the activity with your family, you should also circle the icon for family (a star). The physical activity could be an active household chore, such as walking the dog or vacuuming the house. Remember to record your activity each day for the next week.

Finish

At the end of the week, have students add up how many minutes the entire class spent engaging in physical activity. The challenge can be continued during the following week to see if the students can incorporate more physical activity.

Repeat to Delete Stress

The soothing repetitive nature of physical activity is thought to be one of the reasons that it can serve as an effective stress management tool. This lifestyle activity allows students to find such a physical activity and set a goal of doing it for a week.

Start

Display photographs in the classroom showing examples of soothing activities for the students to examine.

Prompt

Doing repetitive activity can be a way to soothe and relax yourself. Think of activities you enjoy that can be done over and over and are relaxing. Set a goal to incorporate one of these activities into your life each day for the next week. Here are some ideas: playing with a yo-yo, jacks, or a hula hoop; shooting basketball free throws; counting dance steps; doing music scales on an instrument while moving around; reciting a poem or rhyme while walking.

Finish

Have students share about their favorite soothing activity. They could also teach the class how to do their chosen activity.

Healthy Eating

Healthy eating is a skill that enables one to have a lifelong positive relationship with nutrition. It is critical not to label any food as bad but rather to instill the importance of making better choices. For many of our students, the unhealthy foods they eat affect their ability to learn and lead a healthy life. The problems include too much saturated fat, not enough fiber, not enough vegetables and fruits, and too many calories from added sugar, especially in soft drinks. Making a change, such as eating a healthy breakfast, can improve a student's learning and behavior.

Action for Healthy Kids is a nonprofit group whose website (www.actionforhealthykids.org/) provides an outstanding resource for promoting more physical activity and better eating habits among our young people. The group is the country's largest nonprofit and volunteer resource working with schools to help students learn to eat right and be active every day.

Eat for the Health of It

In this activity, students select their own healthy eating topic to research and teach to the rest of the class, school, or learning community through posters, videos, public service announcements, and oral presentations. One important aspect of health literacy is self-directed learning; when students can research their own interests in healthy eating, the results for advocating to other students can be powerful.

Start

Select various healthy eating topics as suggestions for students to explore.

Prompt

Select a tentative topic for your advocacy project—tentative because in some cases you may have a great idea but find only limited valid and reliable information on the topic. Thus, after you do a preliminary search for information, consult with me to refine your topic if necessary. Once you have a viable topic, design an advocacy project—such as a bulletin board, a cooking demonstration, a public service announcement, a video, an activity, or a health fair—in order to share about your topic and advocate healthy eating among your peers.

Finish

Have students discuss their experiences in advocating for healthy eating. It is important for students to understand that healthy eating is a personal choice. Students can help other students by advocating for making better choices but not by policing other's choices.

Student advocacy projects—in which students teach others about the benefits of healthy eating—help them become more aware of their own eating habits.

Sizing Up the Ads

This activity incorporates the health literacy skill of critical thinking and helps students analyze influences on their health habits—especially the pervasive influence of advertising. Manufacturers often use product packaging to make misleading claims about their foods. Being able to accurately read a food label is an important skill in accessing valid health information.

Materials

Various food print ads and product packaging and labels

Start

In this activity, students will study food print ads and product packaging and labels and learn to analyze influences and access information. Ask students to bring in ads, packages, and labels for foods they frequently eat to supplement ones you might find.

Prompt

In this activity, you will bring in food print ads, product packaging and labels, photos of food ads you see in your community, and video clips of food commercials to share with the class. Then, as a class, we will critically evaluate the nutritional claims made in the ads, decide whether the products offer healthy choices, and state the criteria that form the basis for our conclusions.

Finish

Have students display their various food products and analytic criteria in the classroom. Students can demonstrate to the class how they were able to critically evaluate the food products and suggest healthier choices.

Stress Reduction Tools

Breathing in, I calm my body.

Breathing out, I smile.

Breathing in, I enjoy the present moment.

Breathing out, I know this is a wonderful moment.

Adapted from Thich Nhat Hanh

This chapter briefly introduces the "how" of several kinds of tools that our students can use to reduce their stress, as well as creative ways to help students practice these skills.

Breathing Tools

Breathing exercises profoundly influence both the body and the mind, and relaxed deep breathing is the foundation of most stress management tools. For models of correct breathing, look at babies and animals. It appears that they use their whole bodies to breathe; they are engaged in diaphragmatic breathing, wherein the parasympathetic ("rest and digest") nervous system comes into play.

Many of our students have already lost the ability to breathe correctly and thus are using only one-third (or even as little as one-eighth) of their lung capacity. The reason is their tendency to slouch, which allows their postural and breathing muscles to become atrophied. When the body is thus caved in, it is difficult to take in a full breath of air and get that air to the lungs. This shallow breathing pattern, in which air fills only the upper chest, cues the sympathetic nervous system to engage in the fight-or-flight response, which sets off a chain reaction of elevated blood pressure and heart rate and subsequent fatigue and crankiness. The brain, now receiving insufficient oxygen and nutrients, becomes stressed, and learning is compromised. This happens because brain cells require oxygen more than any other tissue in the body—in fact, three times as much. In addition, when stressed, a person's first reaction may be to hyperventilate, meaning that his or her breath becomes choppy and shallow. Thus while the body is springing into action, only a small part of the brain is fully used. As a result, when students experience stress, they may be unable to access important information.

When breathing correctly, the body becomes energized during inhalations and gets rid of impurities, such as carbon dioxide, during exhalations. Mindful relaxed breathing can be used to improve one's blood pressure, heart rate, immune system, brainwaves, digestion, and even sleep patterns. As a result, when we help students retrain their breathing through better posture and deep relaxing breaths, we help them bring back equilibrium, stay energized, and focus on the task at hand.

A short anatomy lesson is necessary in order to understand why posture affects breathing and which muscles need to be retrained to help a person breathe correctly. During breathing, two areas of the body work together—the thoracic cavity and the abdominal cavity. The thoracic area contains the lungs and heart, and the abdominal area contains the digestive organs, including the stomach, kidneys, liver, pancreas, bladder, and small and large intestines. The key muscle used in breathing is the diaphragm, which is located horizontally across the trunk, at the bottom of the rib cage, separating the lungs from the abdominal area. The movement of the diaphragm is important to relaxed breathing. The diaphragm muscle works to make the lung cavity bigger, and as it moves downward the lungs can fill with more air. Conversely, as the air is expelled; the movement of the diaphragm upward helps make the lung cavity become smaller, thus pushing air out from the lungs. This relaxed breathing is also referred to as diaphragmatic breathing.

When we take full, deep breaths, other muscles come into play to allow the thoracic area to expand in more directions, thus permitting more air into the lungs. The intercostal muscles lie between the ribs and help the chest cavity expand outward to the sides. The muscles located at the collar bones, sternum, back, and neck help expand the cavity upward. Thus when all of these muscle groups work together, the thoracic area can expand in three directions.

Practicing relaxed breathing serves several goals:

- Slowing one's breathing
- Evening up the breathing cycles (matching the rates of inhalation and exhalation and smoothing the intake and exhalation of air)
- Lengthening exhalation, which is the most relaxing part of the breathing cycle
- Increasing the vital capacity or strength of the breath (how much air is taken in and expelled)
- Using breath to feel centered and calm

Belly Breaths

Belly breathing forms the basis for all relaxed breathing.

Start

Seated with hands resting on lower belly

Prompt

Take a deep belly breath with your hands on your belly. As you feel the breath come in, notice how your hands gently rise. On the out breath, feel your hands softly fall. Make sure that your breath is calm and relaxed. Continue to practice belly breaths.

Finish

Ask students to take a few moments to notice how their body feels after doing belly breathing. Ask them to share situations in which using belly breaths might help them feel calm, centered, and focused.

Breathing deeply from the belly—not shallowly from the chest—helps students relax.

Open-the-Throat Breath

This activity helps students understand that sometimes when they feel anxious their throat can become tight or constricted and that this effect can be exacerbated by poor posture.

Start

Seated or standing with the spine tall

Prompt

We're going to help you relax by bringing some gentle movement to your neck, throat, and head.

1. Do some shoulder shrugs and circles.
2. Slowly allow your chin to drop to your chest and trace half moons on your chest. Slowly bring your head back to neutral.
3. Slowly look over your right shoulder, inhale deeply and hold the breath while looking over your right shoulder. Gently dip your chin to your chest and exhale deeply.

(continued)

Open-the-Throat Breath   *(continued)*

Inhale deeply again and slowly look over your left shoulder. Hold the breath while continuing to look over your left shoulder. Gently dip your chin to your chest and exhale deeply. Inhale and exhale as many times as you need to completely relax your neck and shoulders.

4. Slowly bring your head back to neutral. Make slow circles with your nose as if writing big slow ovals on a chalkboard in front of your face.

5. Bring your shoulders up to your ears, then release your shoulders down again with the sound "ha." Do this two more times. On the next inhalation, yawn a big breath of air inward. Notice how it feels to have a relaxed and open throat area. On the exhalation, softly say the sound "ha."

6. Experiment with saying "ha" with your head back; with your neck long like a giraffe eating leaves from a tall tree; with your chin tucked in toward your chest; and finally with your head centered over your shoulders. Which position best enables you to have your throat relaxed and open?

7. Enjoy a few more relaxing exhalations, letting the "ha" resemble a deep sigh of contentment as it floats out of your throat—calm and relaxed.

Finish

Remind students that it is important to pay attention not only to their breathing but how the rest of their bodies affects their breathing. Sitting or standing up with a strong posture and using the diaphragm muscles will help their breathing become relaxed and calming.

Breathing Tools

Early childhood education through elementary

STANDARD **7**—practicing health-enhancing behaviors

"My Name Is . . ."

This is a breathing and group-building activity.

Start

Seated or standing with the spine tall

Prompt

Take deep belly breaths with your hands on your belly. Feel the breath come in and out of your belly—calm and relaxed. (For this next part, each student takes a turn.) As you breathe in, say, "My name is . . ." (Then the whole group says the student's name as they exhale, drawing out the full name.)

Finish

Ask students how they felt when hearing their name spoken by the whole group. Ask whose name is the longest, whose is the shortest. Emphasize a welcoming and respectful tone: "We love your name! It is important for each person in our group to feel welcome and to say his or her name with respect."

Wild Kingdom Breath

This activity allows for creativity, and young children love to imitate their favorite animals.

Start

Seated or standing with the spine tall

Prompt

When I name an animal, you imitate that animal. Make sure to use a big belly breath when you make the sounds!

* A lion—roar loud and low on your exhalation, stick out your tongue, and make your eyes really big!
* A bee—buzz deep down in your throat.
* A gorilla—tap your chest and open your throat to hear and feel the vibrations.

What are some other animal noises we can copy?

Finish

Show students photos of animals and point out how animals use their deep belly breaths to make noises and also to become restful.

Stretching Out the Breath

This activity helps students practice lengthening their exhalations. Emphasize the importance of not forcing the extra counts but slowly building up the length of the inhalation and exhalation.

Start

Seated or standing with the spine tall

Prompt

Count the number of seconds it takes you to inhale. Do this a few more times. Take the average and add one second. This is your exhalation number. After your next inhalation, see if you can lengthen your exhalation to your exhalation number. You can push all the air out of your lungs by bringing your belly button to your spine. Try this stretched-out breath a few more times, but remember not to force the exhalation. Just play with stretching it out.

Finish

Allow students to come back to a regular but relaxed breathing pattern. Remind students that the exhalation is the most restful aspect of breathing and to practice exhaling fully.

Mask Breath

This breathing activity helps students use the sound and feeling of their breath as a focal point.

Start

Mindful sitting

Prompt

Place your hands gently over your mouth and nose like a mask. Take deep breaths and hear and feel your breath as you continue to slowly breathe in and out.

Finish

Allow students to practice the mask breath and then come back to relaxed belly breaths. Explain that the sound of the breath can keep students focused on relaxed breathing which, in turn, helps them to become calm and focused.

Breathe In, Breathe Out

In this activity, students generate positive images that help them feel relaxed and happy. They also think of things they would like to "kick to the curb"—that is, get rid of.

Start

Mindful sitting

Prompt

In your mind's eye, think of an image that is positive and captures something that makes you feel relaxed and happy. Then think of something you want to get rid of. Here are some examples:

* Breathe in: rays of sunshine . . . Breathe out: cold rain.
* Breathe in: friendship . . . Breathe out: cliques.
* Breathe in: happiness . . . Breathe out: sadness.

Now, describe your images in words or draw them on an index card to serve as a cue for use during relaxed breathing.

Finish

Have students share their "breathe in, breathe out" statements, which can be enlarged and placed around the classroom as reminders for students to use this breathing tool in their daily lives.

ABC Breath

This activity allows students to practice their letter sounds and relaxed breathing.

Start

Seated or standing with the spine tall

Prompt

In a whisper, softly say each letter of your first name by drawing out the letter during an exhalation (one letter per exhalation). For example: If your name is Ann, exhale and say AAAAAA; exhale and say NNNNNN; and again exhale and say NNNNNN.

Finish

Encourage students to explore using other letters of the alphabet for this exercise. Ask them if they have favorite letters of the alphabet for relaxing. Can they describe why the sound of those letters is relaxing to them?

Whole-Body Breathing

This activity uses creative imagination and breathing.

Start

Mindful sitting

Prompt

In whole-body breathing, you will use your imagination to bring even more relaxation to your body and mind. Feel your feet planted firmly on the ground. Imagine your feet soaking up warm air as you breathe in. Feel this warm air swirling around your ankles, shins, and kneecaps. Rest here. Take a big inhalation and gently sigh out a big exhalation. (Pause.) As you inhale, feel the warm air swirling all the way up to your knees. Now pull the air up through your upper legs and hips. (Pause.) Feel the air continue to move up, through your abdominals and chest, into your back body and filling your entire core. Sigh out a deep exhalation. Take a deep relaxing inhalation, followed by an exhalation, and rest. (Pause.) On your inhalation, feel the warm air washing over your fingertips, up your arms, and surrounding your neck and shoulders with warm air. Feel the light, soothing, warm air saturate your skull and brain, and your face. (Pause.) Feel your whole body filled with this warm air. Take a deep breath and slowly return to this room. Slowly start to stretch and yawn to open your body. Rest in your peaceful and quiet spot.

Finish

Ask students to share what it is like to enjoy the relaxation they have created in their minds and bodies.

Quiet Down

This activity brings into play both breathing and the creativity of imagining the body engulfed in a smile.

Start

Mindful sitting

Prompt

Take a moment to notice anything that might be stressing you right now. Take three deep, calming breaths. Picture your whole body smiling. Make sure there is a smile on your face as well. Inhale through the bottom of your feet and pull the breath all the way up through your body to the top of your head. Now exhale all the way down, from the top of your head to your feet. Practice this breathing pattern on your own four more times.

Finish

Ask students to think of a word that captures how they felt before doing the activity and a word that captures how they felt after doing the exercise. (Or: On a scale of 1 to 10, with 1 meaning very relaxed and 10 meaning very stressed, what number captures how they feel after doing this exercise?) This allows them to qualify and quantify their stress management tools and tune into the effects of the activity.

Meditation

Students may hear the word meditation and start to act it out by crossing one leg over the other like a human pretzel and chanting weird sounds. For some, meditation can be confused with "thought stopping" or coming into a trance or "zombie state," but in fact a person is fully awake during meditation. We can help students understand what meditation is—and that it can be as simple as sitting quietly and focusing on a candle flame, repeating a word, saying a prayer, thinking about an intention or phrase, listening to music or a poem, taking time to reflect, or listening to one's own breathing.

Meditation is focused concentration. It is a lifelong skill that can enhance our students' ability to pay attention and get things done. A large amount of research into meditation has been endorsed by the National Institutes of Health (National Center, 2010b). Research on the benefits of meditation is revealing it to be a strong tool that anyone can use to become more focused, alert, mindful, creative, and relaxed.

Meditation not only decreases stress but also increases feelings of well-being and even happiness. In people who have practiced long-term meditation, changes have been found in the part of the brain—the prefrontal cortex—that is associated with happiness and wellness (Lazar et al., 2005). Practicing meditation has also been associated with decreasing headaches, lowering blood pressure, and reducing pain.

In our daily lives, we devote enormous time and energy to thoughts, even though not all thoughts deserve the attention and credit we give them. Thoughts are ubiquitous but transient, and we can consciously choose not to follow each and every one of them. Meditation asks us to become aware of thoughts—"Huh, I am thinking again"—and then use this awareness as a cue to gently come back to whatever focus tool we have selected, such as breathing. Awareness of thoughts is part of the meditation process, and thoughts should not be something that we fight or try to stop having; rather, we can lay them gently aside and choose to remain focused.

When teaching meditation, notice and tune in to your students' energy. It is hard for students to settle into quietude if they have "ants in their pants." Take time to do some yoga poses mixed in with creative movement. (See yoga poses and creative movement ideas starting on page 114). Consider doing "moving" meditation as well (see moving meditations starting on page 117).

Here are some suggestions to help you guide your students' practice of meditation:

- Emphasize a straight upright posture. It should not involve straining, but encourage students to become more and more comfortable with this focused and wide-awake posture.

- Possible cues include the following: "Listen to the sound of your breath as it slowly falls into a deep silence." "As your outer body softens, feel your inner body brighten." "Smile with your heart as you dissolve (melt, let go, toss aside) any lingering (leftover) tensions (tightness, aches)."

- Give your students permission to either close their eyes or soften their gaze and look down; these approaches can enhance focus.

- Remind students that this is a practice. In meditation, we practice over and over again, noticing if we become distracted by "stinking thinking." We then come back to our focus. This is in fact a necessary part of practicing—catching yourself when you wander away from the focus and gently remembering to come back.

- Try brief periods of practice; the rule of thumb is one minute per year of age (e.g., 5 minutes for a 5-year-old).

- Keep instructions as short and simple as possible; honor the quiet time and resist the need to fill up space with sound.

- Use a voice that is soft and gentle but strong enough that students do not fall asleep.

- Honor the experience. Students may be frustrated ("I can't do it!"). Like any skill, it takes consistent practice. You may find it helpful to remind your students that when they started to walk, it did not happen immediately—they fell on their diapered behinds many times but got back up and engaged in consistent practice. They do not need to feel that they are competing or "getting something."

- Help students process their efforts at meditation by debriefing after the activity. You might ask, "How does meditation help us? What helpful hints would you give someone who is just beginning to try meditation?"

Meditation

Elementary through young adult

STANDARD 7—practicing health-enhancing behaviors

Breathing In Cool Air, Breathing Out Warm Air

In this activity, the focus is on the nostrils and the feeling of the air coming in and going out.

Start

Mindful sitting. With younger students, you might show them a video clip or photo of the palace guards at the Queen's home in London. The guards cannot be distracted by tourists; they must stay focused on their task. The same is true in this activity as we attend watchfully to our nostrils and breath.

Prompt

In this breathing activity, you will attend to the feeling of air coming into your nostrils ("in cool") and the feeling of air flowing out ("out warm"). Thus the focus is on your nostrils. Inhale now and focus on the intake of air as cool. Try this focus on inhalation and the coolness in your nostrils for five more breaths. On your next exhalation, focus on the air coming out of your nostrils as warm. Try to keep this focus on exhalation and the warmth in your

(continued)

Breathing In Cool Air, Breathing Out Warm Air   *(continued)*

nostrils for five more breaths. When distractions pull you away, notice your distraction and return to the feeling of the air coming into and going out of your nose.

Finish

The more students can use their own imagination and creativity, the more effective the tools will be! For example, they can imagine inhaling and exhaling different colors (e.g., blue for calmness and red for frustrations). Ask students how using their imagination augments the effect of the breathing activity.

Meditation

Elementary through young adult

STANDARD **7**—practicing health-
enhancing behaviors

Sign of Peace

This activity focuses on a mudra—a symbolic pose or shape made by the fingers. This particular mudra, perhaps a familiar one, is formed by bringing the tip of the forefinger to the tip of the thumb in an O shape.

Start
Mindful sitting

Traditional symbolic gestures can serve as powerful cues for stress management.

Prompt

Bring the tip of your forefinger to the tip of your thumb in the shape of an O. This is called a mudra, a pose made by your fingers. Hold this "pose" lightly. Say silently, "I am peaceful." This mudra can be done any time you need to feel peaceful. You can hold this peace sign and sit quietly, saying the peaceful statement to yourself, for a peace break.

Finish

Discuss with the students the fact that they can use centuries-old symbolic gestures such as this one to remind themselves to calm down, relax, and become focused.

My Favorite Things

The score for the classic film *The Sound of Music* includes a popular song titled "My Favorite Things." This activity helps students focus on their favorite things when times get rough! It also provides a way for students to share about their favorite things and appreciate that we are varied in our preferences. In the activity, students make a collage of their favorite things by using cutouts, stencils, freehand drawings, and photographs. The collage can be laminated or put in a plastic sleeve for use as a focus tool during relaxed breathing meditation.

Materials

Craft supplies (e.g., magazines, stencils, construction paper, coloring tools such as markers or crayons, scissors, glue, stickers, photographs)

Start

Mindful sitting with " My Favorite Things" collage on lap or placed on table in front of student

Prompt

Take a few deep breaths. Focus your eyes softly on one of your favorite things in your collage. Take three deeper, relaxing breaths and think about how you feel when you are enjoying this favorite thing. If you get distracted, just bring your focus back to your favorite things. Now, gently shift your focus to another of your favorite things. Once more, focus on how you feel when you are enjoying this favorite thing. Now, put down your collage and take a few moments to come back to mindful sitting. Close your eyes and reflect on how you felt when you were enjoying your favorite thing.

Finish

Ask students to talk about situations they experience in which they could use this stress management tool. Students can also share their favorite things with the class and display their collages in the classroom as reminders of the power of this technique.

Taking a Test

Taking tests is a fact of life in most school districts, and for most students this process is accompanied by anxiety. You can help students handle this stress effectively by giving them chances to practice the skills described in this book throughout the school year. Please advocate for students to be allowed frequent breaks, recesses, and quiet time during the testing sessions at your school!

Start

Mindful sitting

Prompt

Imagine that you are sitting in the classroom on the day of our state testing (or SAT testing, or whatever test the students are taking). You have worked hard to get ready for the test and are looking forward to doing your best. Take a deep breath and notice how your body and mind feel when you are confident and focused yet also calm and relaxed. (Pause.) In your mind, picture the teacher putting the test on your desk. You listen carefully to the directions. You pick up the test and your pencil and begin your work by taking your time and carefully reading each question. If a question is confusing, you remind yourself to stay calm and relaxed by taking a few deep belly breaths. (Pause.) You go back to the question and do your best. It gets easier as you keep going through the test. When you get to the last question, you go back and recheck your answers. (Pause.) You are proud of yourself because you did your best since you were calm and focused. The test is over. You hand the test back to the teacher, put your pencil down, and take a big stretch, reaching your arms overhead with a big smile on your face. You are now getting ready to enjoy the rest of the day. (Pause.)

Finish

Ask students to share their experiences and feelings when taking tests. Have them discuss what they think of using this meditation in taking tests.

Blueprint

This meditation allows students to creatively plan out the steps for accomplishing a goal. To illustrate the nature of stepwise progress toward a goal, you might show a time-lapse video clip of a concert being set up or a building being constructed. At the end of the activity, have students take time to write their goal. Setting goals can be more effective when committed to writing as it enables students to take responsibility for what they have promised to themselves.

Materials

Index card for each student

Start

Mindful sitting

Prompt

Visualize in your mind's eye a goal that you would like to accomplish. Be very clear about how accomplishing this goal would look, sound, taste, feel, and smell. Focus on the positive emotions of motivation, pride, and accomplishment. As in time-lapse video footage, imagine each of the small steps necessary to accomplish your goal. Allow your creative imagination to go back and forth between the images of the steps required in order to make sure you have captured them all. Include all the details. (Pause for anywhere from 30 seconds to several minutes depending on the maturity of your group.) Now, slowly open your eyes and take three deep breaths. Take your index card and write down your goal.

Finish

Have students share their experiences and goals and what it would mean to them to accomplish the goal. Remind students of the fact that when they use their imagination to visualize a goal and then write it down, they set in motion powerful intentions to fulfill the goal.

Meditation

Elementary through middle school

STANDARD **7**—practicing health-enhancing behaviors

Shake It Up!

In this activity, you will call out different parts of the body, and students will gently shake and bring their awareness to that body part as a meditation focal point. When a body part is shaken, it is difficult to tense the muscle at the same time. Shaking out also aids circulation to that body part.

Start

Mindful sitting or standing

Prompt

Take a deep, relaxing breath. Gently start to shake your wrists and hands. Shake out any tension you might have in your wrists, palms, and fingers. Now, bring your awareness to your right pinkie finger. Focus on your right pinkie finger like a laser beam. (From here, use similar prompts to help students focus on other body parts, such as a thumb, the back of a hand, the palm, and so on.) As we finish this activity, take a few deep breaths, and with each deep breath allow your whole body to become still, quiet, and relaxed. Notice how you feel when your body is calm and relaxed.

Finish

Ask students to share how gently shaking different parts of the body helps them shake out any stuck energy or tension.

Spirit, Mind, and Body Scan

This activity focuses on different parts of the body. Make sure to provide enough time for students to scan and bring their full awareness to each body part.

Start

Relaxation pose (see figure 5.1)

Prompt

1. Imagine that you can look down on your body and see it relaxed and rested.

2. Lie on your back with your legs stretched out and slightly apart. Your feet should be turned out.

3. Position your arms about 5 to 7 inches (13 to 18 centimeters) away from the sides of your body at a 45 degree angle; your palms should be turned up and your fingers slightly curled.

4. You are going to scan or check your body. Starting at your toes, picture in your mind each part of your body as I name it. Notice how that part of your body feels. There is no right or wrong answer—just pay attention and notice. Let your breath be slow, easy, and smooth.

5. Gently shifting your attention, bring your awareness to your legs.

Figure 5.1 Relaxation pose.

6. (Continue through each of the body parts, pausing after each instruction and observing to see what students are doing: pelvis, lower abdominals and lower back, chest and heart space, neck and shoulders, scalp, face and throat, and arms and hands.)

7. You are now going to check in and scan your mind. Notice your thoughts and feelings. Without judging, take the time to pay attention. Are you feeling mostly positive? Are you feeling happy, centered, smiling? Or are your thoughts mostly negative—scattered, mad, sad, or bored? Whatever you are feeling is valid and okay. Just allow yourself to take an honest look.

8. The last area you are going to scan and pay attention to is your spirit—how you are feeling about your connection to yourself and to your family, friends, school, community, nature, or higher power.

9. Slowly start to come back from your scanning time to this room. Slowly and quietly, without letting the person next to you hear, wiggle your fingers and toes.

10. Now come into super hero stretch. Reach your fingers up and over your head to the wall behind you and point your toes in the opposite direction, reaching for the wall in front of you or the center of the circle. (Pause.) See if there is any other stretch that your body needs to do in order to feel balanced and ready for our next activity.

11. Slowly curl up onto your side in fetal pose and rest there with deep full breaths. (Pause.)

12. Slowly roll up and come into seated pose. Let's take a few minutes before we end class to just enjoy breathing.

Finish

In order to actively relax, we need to pay close attention to the tension we hold in our muscles. Often, we may not realize the stress we hold in our bodies and become used to the tension we hold in the muscles. The body scan helps us to pay attention to signals our bodies are sending us—let go of the stress! Ask students to share their experiences with this meditation focused on the body, mind, and spirit as a stress management tool.

Meditation

All levels

STANDARD **7**—practicing health-enhancing behaviors

Sound Meditation

This activity uses music as the focus for meditation. During the activity, play a musical recording with various sounds embedded, such as birds, ocean waves, a flowing creek, or a waterfall. You can also ask students to imagine specific sounds, such as a kitten's purr, raindrops on the roof, someone singing a lullaby, birds at a feeder, the drip of a faucet, or wind rustling leaves.

Materials

Music player and relaxing music with nature sounds

Start

Relaxation pose or mindful sitting

Prompt

1. Become as relaxed as you can in relaxation pose or mindful sitting. Then relax even more.

2. Connect with your breath. Slow it down, making it soft and smooth.

3. Listen carefully to the music. Pay attention to all the sounds you hear.

Finish

Have students share with each other by identifying their favorite sounds and instruments in the music track or by sharing their own favorite music for relaxation. They can also create playlists to use for this activity. Students should set aside time on a daily basis to listen to their relaxing playlists outside of class or the class can have scheduled relaxing music breaks.

Walking Meditation

This activity focuses on movements associated with walking. You can use various modes of walking to provide different focuses (e.g., walking quietly or as if on ice).

Start

Designate an activity space for students to move around in during this activity.

Prompt

Take 10 slow, deliberate steps, as if you are moving in a slow-motion movie. Walk as slowly as you can and exaggerate the picking up of one foot and the placing of it back on the floor (or ground) in front of you. Pay attention to all aspects of your walking. (Pause to allow students to walk in this manner.) What are your arms doing when you walk? Put your laser beam of focus on the movement of your arms. (Pause.) Now, walk as if you are on hot sand. (Pause.) Walk as if you are on an icy and slippery sidewalk. (Pause.) Walk as if you have to be quiet so that no one will hear you move. (Pause.) Walk as if you are a giant. (Pause.) Walk as if you are in your favorite place. (Pause.) As we finish walking meditation, slowly return to the circle and come to a stop. Close your eyes and take three deep, relaxing breaths. (Pause.)

Finish

Ask students to share about their experience in walking meditation. Remind students how a very simple activity done with a deliberate focus can help them to relax and become focused.

Outdoor Walking Meditation

Students use the outdoors as their focus in this activity, which is done in silence.

Prompt

How many smells can you notice? How many colors? How many sounds? How many sights?

Finish

Have students share the observations they made during their walking meditation while being silent and outdoors. Remind students that spending time in nature as well as becoming silent can be very soothing stress management tools.

Stretching Tools

Opportunities to move and stretch allow students to use pent-up energy and dissipate accumulated stress. Stretching is a natural tension reliever. When a muscle is tense it shortens and by stretching and lengthening the muscles, they relax. Here are some tips for teaching students how to stretch:

- In order for a muscle to stretch to its fullest, sustain the stretch without bouncing or excessive movement. Encourage students to hold the stretch for 5 deep, relaxing breaths. With each breath, the student can explore going deeper into the stretch—always being mindful, though, not to force or overextend.

- Ask students to come to their stretching point. At this point, the muscle is lengthened as much as possible without strain or pain; the stretching point can be sustained with full deep breaths. If the breath becomes strained or ragged, it probably means that the stretch is too intense.

- Our mind and body are integrated, and when we experience stress it is often expressed in our bodies, especially in vulnerable areas such as the shoulders, neck, and face.

Please see the resource section for information about a Human Kinetics publication by this author titled *Teaching Yoga for Life: Preparing Children and Teens for Healthy, Balanced Living* (2009).

Stretching

Elementary through young adult

STANDARD ❼—practicing health-enhancing behaviors

Neck Stretch

The area around the neck is often called the stress triangle. It includes the neck, shoulders, and upper back. This area is vulnerable to tension, and the neck muscles are subject to additional stress as it works to keep the head balanced on top of the spine, especially when the head is held jutted forward. This is comparable to holding a bowling bowl out at our sides for a long time—it gets heavy! No wonder the neck and shoulder muscles (trapezius) never get the chance to rest. It is hard for sensory nerve information to get to the brain when the neck is constantly contracted. It is also hard to pay attention to the rest of the body if tension gets stuck in the neck region.

It is important to help students feel the correct alignment for their head and neck. In figure 5.2, notice that the ears are aligned directly over the shoulders. The chin is parallel with the floor and pulled back rather than jutting out. The shoulders blades are pulled back and down, and the collarbones are pulled outward.

Start

Mindful sitting or standing

Prompt

1. Sitting or standing as tall as you can, bring your shoulders down and broaden your back. Create a lot of space in your neck area. Align your ears over your shoulders and over your hips in one vertical line.

2. Slowly bring your right ear toward the top of your right shoulder. Hold it there, making sure to breathe deeply. Send your breath to the left side of your neck.

3. Place your right hand on the right side of your head, as if your hand is a pillow on which the right side of your head is resting. Use your right hand

Figure 5.2 Correct neck alignment.

(continued)

Neck Stretch   (continued)

to slowly and gently guide your head back to an upright position. This movement allows your neck area to relax even more because it doesn't have to haul the very heavy head back! (Pause.)

4. Try it now on your left side. Slowly bring your left ear down toward the top of your left shoulder. Hold it there, making sure to breathe deeply. Send your breath to the right side of your neck.

5. Place your left hand on the left side of your head, as if your hand is a pillow on which the left side of your head is resting. Use your left hand to slowly and gently guide your head back to an upright position. (Pause.)

6. Now that you are done, does one side feel different from the other? Notice any tension in the stress triangle. Gently let the tension dissolve or melt like a snowflake on a warm sidewalk. Notice how letting go of the tension in your muscle can be like letting go of tensions in your mind. Imagine your thoughts just melting and floating away.

Finish

Ask students how their neck area feels when it is relaxed. When they remember to recognize and relax tension, their bodies can relax.

Yoga Tools

Yoga can serve as an effective stress management tool for children, particularly those with learning or behavioral challenges. For example, breathing exercises can serve as a natural relaxation method for students with attention deficit disorder (Zipkin, 1985). The benefits of participation in yoga have been observed at West Hollywood Opportunity School, an alternative public school for at-risk students in grades 7 through 12 (Stukin, 2001). Yoga is seen as an important outlet for students who have behavioral problems, have spent time in the juvenile justice system, or have failed in traditional school settings (Stukin). In addition, yoga has been shown to be an effective

teaching tool when working with students with Down syndrome, cerebral palsy, autism, sensory integration, and learning difficulties. Yoga can improve the ability of students with special needs to focus, attend, and follow directions in doing fine and gross motor activities (Klimas, 2003; Sumar, 1998).

It is best to use yoga mats for the activities described in this section so that students do not slip. These mats are also called sticky mats because they do just that—which means no slipping! The chapter covers several helpful yoga activities and poses for helping students reduce stress. Additional poses for use with students can be found in appendix B.

Yoga Movement

Early childhood education through elementary

STANDARD **7**—practicing health-enhancing behaviors

Save That Pose!

The objective of this activity is to have students delay assuming a yoga pose until after the music stops, thus developing impulse control.

Materials

Upbeat music and music player

Start

Standing. Demonstrate or show a picture of a yoga pose, making sure that all students see it. Then remove the photo or stop demonstrating the pose. Next, start the music and signal students to engage in a movement activity (e.g., running in place, dancing, or doing jumping jacks). Instruct the students to continue the movement as long as the music plays. When the music stops, students should demonstrate the yoga pose they saw.

Prompt

(Demonstrate or show a picture of the yoga pose.) Take a picture of this pose in your mind's eye and save it! Remember the yoga pose. When the music stops, you will show me the yoga pose you saved in your mind's eye. (Play the music for a short period, then stop it and watch for students to do the pose. Repeat this sequence of demonstrating a pose, playing music, and students demonstrating the pose when music stops for several different poses.) Which was your favorite yoga pose? Which was the first one I showed you? Can you remember it and do the pose again?

Finish

This activity helps students learn to delay their responses. Ask students for examples of situations in which they need to delay their responses or wait to do something (e.g., refraining from interrupting others when speaking).

Yoga Movement
Early childhood education through middle school
STANDARD **7**—practicing health-enhancing behaviors

Freeze It!

This is similar to the "Save That Pose!" activity in that it encourages gross motor activity, impulse control, and practice in remembering the predetermined shape, yoga pose, or position.

Start

Students standing in a circle. In the activity space, students are engaged in a movement activity, such as dancing, doing jumping jacks, or skipping. When students get an agreed-upon signal (e.g., clap three times or raise your hand), they *freeze it* and stop in a pre-determined shape, pose, or position and hold it without moving. There can be one pose or a sequence of poses. For a variation, have the students find an empty carpet square and come into a frozen version of the yoga pose on the square.

Prompt

I am going to show you a special yoga pose. I want you to remember this pose. Save that pose in your mind's eye. Now we are going to do some dancing (or other movement patterns such as jumping jacks) in our activity space. When you hear me clap three times, I want you to "freeze it," stop and do the special yoga pose you saved in your mind's eye and hold the pose without moving.

Finish

Bring students back to the circle. Ask students which yoga pose was their favorite. Discuss the importance of listening for the signal (e.g., the three claps) and remembering the saved poses.

Tree and Leaf Game

This movement activity connects yoga poses in sequences that can be repeated over and over.

Start

Child pose (students kneeling on floor, sitting back on heels with toes curled or flat, then folding themselves forward and laying their forehead on the ground in front of them with their arms laid alongside the body to form a seed or egg shape; see figure 5.3*a*)

Prompt

1. The child pose is also called the seed pose (see figure 5.3*a*). What does a seed need in order to grow into a beautiful, strong tree? (Pause for students to provide their ideas.) A seed needs rain or water, nourishing soil, sunlight, and time to rest. Take a few more deep breaths as you rest quiet and still in seed pose.

2. Start to move slowly from seed pose and grow into a seedling. (Pause.)

3. Continue to slowly grow. You are now a sapling, slowly growing into a young tree. (Pause, holding level 1 tree pose; see figure 5.3*b*.)

4. Reaching higher, you are now a tall, mature tree. (Pause, holding level 2 tree pose; see figure 5.3*c*.)

5. All the trees are a forest. Come together to make a circle and hold hands overhead while maintaining your tree pose.

6. Begin to move your tree in the gentle breeze. (Students continue to balance together in a circle.)

7. You are now a leaf, and the leaf drops from the tree and floats slowly and softly back to the earth into the seed or child pose. Remember to move as lightly as a leaf, gently floating to the warm earth. (Pause.) Rest in child pose.

Finish

Ask students to discuss why it is important to have plenty of rest along with physical activity as they grow.

Figure 5.3 *(a)* Child or seed pose, *(b)* level 1 tree pose, and *(c)* level 2 tree pose. A full description of tree pose is available in appendix B.

Sun Salutations

A sun salutation is a movement activity that connects a series of yoga poses in sequence. Repeated several times in a row, sun salutations can provide a challenging activity for students who may think that yoga is just about lying around.

Start

Standing in mountain pose (see figure 5.4a on page 118)

Prompt

1. Stand tall in mountain pose, keep your feet hip-distance apart and point your toes and knees straight ahead. Keep your knees slightly bent (soft or relaxed). Keep your legs, core muscles, and gluteus muscles (the muscles of your buttocks) strong. Keep your chest open and lifted. Now, move into the next pose.

2. Sun salutation pose 1: quarter moon pose (see figure 5.4b on page 118). From mountain pose, extend your spine long and straight while keeping your core strong and your feet firmly planted on the ground. Reach your arms overhead with your hands clasped together and your index fingers pointed together to make a steeple. Exhale. Stretch to the side and point the steeple toward the side wall. Check your breath to make sure it is full and deep, then find just the right amount of stretch. If your breath becomes tight at all, back off a bit. Inhale. Come back to arms overhead; keep your legs and feet firm. Exhale. Try the other side. Finish by moving back into mountain pose with your arms at your sides or your hands folded over your heart.

3. Sun salutation pose 2: forward fold pose (see figure 5.4c on page 118). From mountain pose, bring your arms up overhead and "touch the sky." Lift both arms toward the sky. Fold forward and dive forward, hinging at your hips and reaching your arms forward and then down. Let your arms and head hang down. Gently shake your head side to side so that your neck is released. Keep your knees bent so they are soft and relaxed. Hold onto each elbow; hold onto your legs or ankles or let your arms just hang like a rag doll. Finish by gently bending your knees even more and gently rolling up your spine with your head coming up last into mountain pose.

4. Sun salutation pose 3: chair pose (see photo 5.4d on page 118). From mountain pose, step your feet to hip-distance apart, keeping your feet and knees pointed straight ahead. Sit down as if sitting in an imaginary chair; keep your knees bent, drop your gluteus muscles down, and keep your tailbone pointing straight down at the ground. Reach your arms overhead and look at your fingertips. Lift your chest and relax your shoulders. Finish by holding the chair pose for five full, deep, relaxing breaths.

5. Sun salutation pose 4: rocket ship pose (see figure 5.4e on page 118). Start while you are still in the chair pose. Squat as far as possible in the chair, keeping your feet and knees straight ahead. Bring your hands in front of your chest in steeple position (hands clasped with index fingers pointed together). Count 1, 2, 3 and then shoot up into the air like a rocket. Touch the sky. Finish in mountain pose.

(continued)

Sun Salutations *(continued)*

Figure 5.4 *(a)* Mountain pose, *(b)* quarter moon pose, *(c)* forward fold pose, *(d)* chair pose, and *(e)* rocket ship pose.

Finish

This is a basic sun salutation. From here, other poses can be mixed in; see appendix B for more options. Ask students to discuss how a sun salutation is a great way to link poses together in a sequence to create a challenging cardiovascular activity.

Qigong

Qigong (pronounced "chee-gung") is an ancient system of stress management that allows for the balancing of physical and mental energy. The benefits of Qigong include strengthening and healing the body and mind, balancing emotions, and increasing energy. Qigong is just one of the many movement forms practiced extensively throughout the East and gaining popularity in the West. Like Tai Chi (another movement form), Qigong is founded on the concept that illness and disease result when chi or energy becomes blocked, choked, or stagnant. For example, when the body holds stress by tensing body parts, it blocks the flow of energy. However using a relaxed breath coordinated with flowing movement allows the flow of energizing and healing positive energy as well as the release and dissipation of stuck and negative energy. Qigong involves the components of focused breathing, visualization, posture, and specific body movements.

Diamond Breath

This Qigong-influenced activity uses movement to help students connect to and augment the lengthening of their inhalation and exhalation.

Start

Standing with arms at sides

Prompt

1. As you inhale slowly, move both of your arms out to the sides and in front to meet at eye level.
2. Bring your thumbs and index fingers together to form a diamond shape. Focusing on the diamond, slowly exhale as you bend your knees and slowly drop the diamond to your belly button.
3. Repeat 10 more times, remembering to slow down and maintain your focus on the diamond's slow movement from eye level to belly and back again.
4. Finish by coming into mountain pose and standing with your arms at your sides.

Finish

Ask students to share their experience with the moving of energy. Not all students will experience the movement of energy and that is fine as well.

Playing With Energy

This activity allows students to play with the idea of sensing and moving energy. It does not need to be taught in a big space. It can be practiced in the classroom as a great activity for indoor recess!

Start

Standing, with feet wider than hip-distance apart, knees slightly softened and adducted (toward the midline of the body), and core muscles engaged for a tighter, more stable center

Prompt

1. Bring both hands (one on top of the other) to contact with your lower belly. Feel your breath moving against your hands for six full, deep, diaphragmatic breaths. Inhale through your nose and exhale silently through slightly pursed lips.
2. Keeping your eyes closed, bring your hands in front of you and imagine you are holding a small round ball (about the size of a softball) in front of the center of your body (your lower belly). Notice the shape and color of this ball. Notice that your hands move with your breath.
3. Now, with each breath, allow the small round ball to gradually become bigger, as if you are making a huge snow ball. Notice the connection of your breath to the round

(continued)

Playing With Energy   *(continued)*

ball. Slowly allow the ball to expand into a larger and more colorful ball. What do you notice about the shape and color now? Remember to stand tall and allow your shoulders to relax. Make sure your breath is connected to making the ball bigger and more colorful.

4. Pull the ball into your center and again allow one hand to rest on top of the other on your belly. Feel your hands move with your breath. Continue these deep belly breaths for five more breaths.

5. Notice how you feel right now. What do you notice? Notice the energy in your body.

6. Release your hands to the sides of your body. Slowly allow your chin to drop into your chest, thus lengthening your cervical spine. On the inhalation, imagine that you are pulling the breath up from the center of your body, up your spine into your heart space, and continue to pull the breath up into your head. As you breathe out, direct the exhalation back toward the center of your body. Continue to pull the in-breath up your spine into your head and direct the out-breath back down into the core for five more breath cycles.

7. Come back to a regular, relaxed breathing pattern and slowly lift your head and stand in mountain pose. Slowly open your eyes.

8. With deep breaths, use cupped palms to gently tap your chest and now your scalp. Use your fingertips to gently tap around your eyes.

9. With your left cupped palm facing down, lightly tap from your right shoulder down your arm to your fingers with your palm facing down, then tap back up to your shoulder and tap around the right side of your neck. Do this two more times, then switch and repeat on the left side using the right cupped palm.

10. With both hands cupped, gently tap your kidney area, your hips, and on down your legs to your feet. Repeat this three more times.

12. Tap your head and then "sweep it off" with long strokes as if sweeping off bad energy.

13. Tap your chest and sweep off negative energy, then go through your arms and lower body, tapping and sweeping.

14. Return to standing with your hands positioned one on top of the other over your lower belly. Notice any changes in your body—any shifts in energy or sensation.

Finish

Students can share their experiences with the group, but make sure to emphasize that not everyone will have the same experience or sense the movement of energy.

Guided Creative Imagination Tools

With guided creative imagination, it is important to set up the exercises by encouraging students to use all five senses. This is why the tool is not called visualization; it connects to as many senses beyond sight as possible. There is no right or wrong way to do creative imagination—the key word is creative. It is also important to "act as if," which means to imagine the situation as if it is happening right now. The following methods can help you implement guided imagination with students.

- Help students get their creative juices flowing by spending a few minutes in relaxing breathing or doing a relaxation activity.

- Remind students to "act as if" by pretending that the situation in the creative guided imagining is happening in the present moment.

- Encourage students to make their guided imagination as rich as possible by including all of the senses.
- Help students feel the emotions elicited by the guided imagination. For example, what does it feel like to step onto the graduation stage and hold your diploma?

- The term *mind's eye* refers to a place in front of the space between the eyebrows. This is where we use our creative imagination. With eyes closed, imagine a large high-definition screen (like a screen at a movie theater). This very large white screen is called the mind's eye.

Guided Creative Imagination
Elementary through young adult
STANDARD 7—practicing health-enhancing behaviors

Birds in Flight

This is a guided imagination activity that allows students to imagine themselves flying on the currents of happy and peaceful thoughts.

Materials

Photographs of birds in flight

Start

Mindful sitting or relaxation pose on floor

Prompt

In your mind's eye, imagine that you are a bird perched on the ground. You are about to take flight, and your happy thoughts are the air beneath your wings. Think of things that help you feel happy and free. Let these wonderful thoughts fill up your wings. Watch as you slowly start to lift off the ground. Start to beat your wings and take flight as you climb higher and higher into the air. Keep sending the happy and contented thoughts to your wings so that they move strongly, smoothly, and with grace. Visualize and feel yourself as a bird soaring—gliding on the wind of these happy thoughts. (Pause.)

Look below you as you fly over beautiful and colorful scenes in nature: mountain peaks, magnificent oceans, emerald green forests. Finally, imagine yourself as a bird who has found a peaceful destination for landing. Slowly drift to this peaceful sanctuary in which you will rest. Allow yourself to slowly come to rest and nestle into this quiet and peaceful spot. (Pause.)

As you slowly come back to the awareness of this room, notice how you feel after doing this imagination activity. Think about how you can use the power of your imagination and creativity to bring on a sense of happiness and peace. Slowly sit up tall and take a big stretch.

Finish

Ask students to share with the group any details of how they felt as a flying bird. Ask them to describe what they flew over and where they landed for their restful destination. They can also share some of the happy thoughts that inspired their flight. Encourage students to use this activity when they need to redirect away from stressful situations. This restful destination is always ready for them to use.

Floating Bubbles

This activity uses images of bubbles to capture difficult emotions and let them float away. You can also provide soap bubbles and wands for students to use as visual aids for this activity; if you do so, ask students to blow their bubbles gently and slowly, since doing so encourages relaxed breaths.

Start

Mindful sitting or relaxation pose on floor

Prompt

1. Imagine that you are making bubbles with a bubble wand and soapy water. Take a few moments to think of some difficulties, troubling emotions, or concerns bothering you right now. (Pause.)
2. Take one of your concerns and put it inside a big soapy bubble. (Pause.)
3. Watch as the bubble starts to gently float away and then—pop! It is gone.
4. Keep inserting your troubles into bubbles and letting them float away.

Finish

Ask students to share their experiences with this activity and situations when they might use it.

Kick It to the Curb

Students can use stress balls in numerous ways (see the relaxation activities later in the chapter for more ideas). Stress balls provide a kinesthetic learning activity.

Materials

Provide a stress ball for each student and a basket. Stress balls can be purchased, or you can make them as a class project by filling sturdy balloons or surgical gloves with rice or small beans such as lentils. Use a funnel to fill up the balloons, then tie them off.

Start

Mindful sitting

Prompt

1. Take a moment to focus on all of the stress or worries you are concerned about right now.
2. As you slowly start to squeeze your stress ball with your nondominant hand, imagine your stress or concerns draining out of your hand into the stress ball.
3. Make sure you have emptied out all your stress by releasing it all into your stress ball. Now let go of all your stress and worries and "kick it to the curb" by gently tossing your stress ball back into the basket.

4. Take a few deep breaths and notice how it feels to let go of your stress and sit quietly in stillness.

Finish

Encourage students to use their stress balls in the classroom as a break during a challenging task such as a problem-solving assignment or before a test.

Guided Creative Imagination
Elementary through middle school
STANDARD 7—practicing health-enhancing behaviors

Glitter Jars

Glitter jars provide a visual and kinesthetic activity that enables students to creatively imagine feeling scattered and then allow their body and mind to settle down. (This activity can also be demonstrated with a jar of water mixed with baking soda.)

Materials

Light corn syrup, water, small glass jar with tight-fitting lid (e.g., baby food jar, canning jar), glitter or sequins, super-hold glue (optional: paints, paintbrush, food coloring)

Making the Glitter Jar

1. Mix corn syrup and water together and fill the jar about three-quarters full. For each quarter cup of corn syrup, add 1 tablespoon of water. Optional: If you want a colored mixture, add 1 drop of food coloring.
2. Add glitter and sequins.
3. Glue the lid securely onto the jar. Allow the glue to dry before using. Decorate the jar with paint.

Start

Mindful sitting

Prompt

When we feel anxious or overwhelmed by our thoughts, we can use the glitter jar as a reminder to settle down and relax. Shake up the jar and watch the glitter disperse all over the space. Set the jar down and watch carefully with each relaxing breath as the glitter begins to slowly drift down and settle at the bottom of the jar. We can do the same with our racing thoughts or worries in order to settle down. Sit tall and strong and with each breath feel your body and mind slow and settle down. (Pause.)

When we get upset, emotions can be like the glitter in the jar—"all shook up" and scattered. When we can slow down and allow things to settle by relaxing our breathing and our thoughts, we feel better. Just like the glitter in our jars, we can settle down and become still and quiet. Take a few more deep breaths to really experience the feeling of being settled and relaxed.

Finish

Ask students to discuss the imagery of the glitter falling as a metaphor for relaxing and becoming settled in their own bodies. Ask them if they can think of other images that fit in this metaphor (e.g., snowflakes or leaves falling).

Paint a Picture

Using creative imagination, students paint a familiar and comforting picture on a big screen in their mind. In this script, the school building will be used but it can be modified to any familiar scene, such as a house or park.

Start

Mindful sitting or relaxation pose

Prompt

Close your eyes and remember that your mind's eye is the spot right in front of your closed eyes. Imagine a huge white screen in this spot—very white and big like the ones at the movies. The picture we are going to paint is the front of our school. Paint the outline of the front entrance—all the doors. (Pause.) Add the windows, the roof, and the signs. (Pause.) Color in the picture you have created. (Pause.) Now, see the landscaping—shrubs, trees, pots of flowers. (Pause.) See the decorations in the windows of the classrooms. Paint in the school buses and the playground. (Pause.) It is time for recess. Watch the students as they line up to go out through the doors and into the playground to play with a ball and jump rope. (Pause.) Take three more deep breaths and notice how your body feels after doing this activity.

Finish

You can add to this scene by being flexible with it—that is, by not seeing the school as it is right now (e.g., in the spring with puddles on the playground and flowers in windows) but as it would look in another season, along with the changes brought on by the different season (e.g., the different clothes worn by students, the changed landscape). This activity helps students improve their power of imagination. Encourage students to write their own "painted picture" scripts to share with the class.

A Few of My Favorite Things

Students recall some of their favorite things as the focus for this guided imagination activity. Guide this creative imagination by making suggestions for students to use as their favorite things (e.g., the feeling of snowflakes on their faces, the smell of pizza, opening a new book, sitting in a comfortable easy chair, the crackle of wood burning in a fireplace, the rush of the wind against their faces when riding a bicycle, the feeling of a cat's tongue licking their fingers, the taste of their favorite kind of ice cream).

Start

Mindful sitting or relaxation pose

Prompt

Pick one of your favorite things and keep it in your mind's eye. Add not only the picture but also any sounds, tastes, feelings, smells, and textures associated with your favorite thing.

Finish

Students can share by writing their favorite things on index cards which you can then use to guide a creative imagination. Ask the students what it is like to experience their favorite things. How do they feel after using their creative imagination tools?

Our favorite things make for enjoyable memories and can provide material for use in imagining away our stress.

© Eyewire

Guided Creative Imagination

Elementary through young adult

STANDARD **7**—practicing health-enhancing behaviors

Brain Scan

This activity provides an opportunity for students to bring awareness to their senses and use their creative imagination to integrate and balance the right and left hemispheres of the brain.

Start

Mindful sitting or relaxation pose

Prompt

1. Take a few deep breaths. With your next breath, let go of any tension in your lower body. Now let go of any tension in your arms. With your next deep breath, let your heart and back relax. Take one more deep breath and let your whole body relax.

2. Picture in your mind's eye the left side of your brain. Color the left side of your brain blue. (Pause.) Erase the color and let it go. (Pause.) Now picture the right side of your brain and color it orange. (Pause.) Erase this color and let it go. (Pause.)

3. Switch to the left side of the brain and color it red. (Pause.) Erase it. Switch to the right and color it green. (Pause.) Erase it.

4. Take a deep, relaxing breath.

5. On the left side of the brain, imagine the experience of skiing down a steep ski slope. (Pause.) On the right side, imagine the experience of swinging a baseball or softball bat back and forth. (Pause.)

(continued)

Brain Scan   *(continued)*

6. On the left side of the brain, imagine that you feel the texture of soft rabbit fur. (Pause.) On the right side, imagine that you feel the texture of rough tree bark. (Pause.) On the left side, imagine that you feel smooth, slippery dolphin skin. (Pause.) On the right side, imagine that you feel the scratchy dry skin of an alligator. (Pause.)

7. On the left side of the brain, imagine that you smell buttery popcorn. (Pause.) On the right side, imagine that you smell the salty air of the beach. (Pause.)

8. On the left side of the brain, imagine that you taste a glass of cool lemonade. (Pause.) On the right side, imagine that you taste an apple. (Pause.) On the left side, imagine that you taste a sour pickle. (Pause.) On the right side, imagine that you taste a banana. (Pause.)

9. On the left side of the brain, imagine that you hear the soft trickling sound of water in a brook. (Pause.) On the right side, imagine that you hear the call of a songbird. (Pause.)

10. Sitting quietly, let go of all the senses and pictures we have created in our mind's eye. Focus on the feelings in your body. (Pause.) Focus on the feelings in your mind. (Pause.)

11. Take three more deep breaths. As I slowly count from five back to one, you will come back to this room wide awake and focused, as well as relaxed and grounded.

Finish

Ask students to share how using this activity might be useful before a challenging activity such as taking a test or a creative writing assignment.

Guided Creative Imagination

Middle school through young adult

STANDARD **7**—practicing health-enhancing behaviors

Spring Cleaning

This activity helps students tune into their senses. Each room in the house represents a different sense. The student cleans out negative images of clutter and dirt, thus leaving only clean, clutter-free, spacious rooms.

Start

Mindful sitting or relaxation pose

Prompt

1. Take a few deep breaths. With your next breath, let go of any tension in your lower body. Now let go of any tension in your arms. (Pause.) With your next deep breath, let your heart and back relax. (Pause.) Take another deep breath and let your whole body relax.

2. Using your creative imagination, picture a house in your mind's eye.

3. In front of you is a door to the first room in the house. It has a huge eye on it. Step into the first room in this house. This room is full of visual images. The room is stuffed full of junk, dirt, and spider webs. Imagine cleaning the room. Use cleaning supplies that you brought with you—vacuum, broom, soapy water, and sponges. Clean all the walls and floors. Dump out all the junk into a dumpster. The room is now shiny, clean, and fresh smelling. Take deep breaths, enjoying the sight of this sparkling clean room.

4. Walk down the hall and turn toward another door—this time with a huge ear on it. Open the door and step into this room. In this room, you hear loud, obnoxious sounds. This room is filled with noisy, clattering junk. As you clean it up, the sounds soften and disappear. Now the room is clean and neat. Open the window and hear the soft breeze of clean fresh air coming into the room. Listen to any sounds in the room right now. Listen to the soft ebb and flow of your breath. Take deep breaths, enjoying the soft peaceful quiet of this squeaky clean room.

5. Walk down the hall and notice another door. On this door is a huge nose. This must be the room of smells. As you step into this room, there is a terrible odor of rotting food and stinky, dirty clothes. Take some time to clean up all the surfaces of this room, using a sweet-smelling cleaner that reminds you of your favorite aromas. Make sure to really clean all the nooks and crannies so that this room is sparkling. Take a few deep breaths and enjoy the scent of this fresh, clean, and sweet-smelling room.

6. Again you are in the hallway. The next door you see has a big mouth on it. As you look into this room, it is a kitchen filled with food you really hate stacked high on plates and bowls all over the place. It is a mess, overflowing with dirty dishes full of nasty, yucky-tasting foods. Throw the dishes in the dishwasher and clean the counters. Make room for all your favorite foods. Picture plates and bowls of all the foods you enjoy. Taste a few small bites of these delectable foods, taking time to let the tastes linger on your tongue and in your mouth. Savor these wonderful tastes in this sparkling clean kitchen.

7. There is another room to explore. On its door is a hand. In it, there is so much scratchy junk and slimy garbage stacked high. As you clean out this room, you notice that your favorite textures start to appear from underneath all the debris you're clearing away. What are your favorite textures? The softness of your pet's fur, the smooth feel of a baseball glove, the cool hardness of a can of cold soda, the warm texture of freshly popped popcorn? Make sure to clean everything so that you can enjoy these textures in this super clean room.

8. There is one more room—with a heart on its door! In this room, there is even more clutter and debris. It is very dirty, and thick dust is everywhere. This room is for your sixth sense—your intuition, your ability to use your inner knowing, your gut feelings. Make this room gleaming and dirt free so your intuition can shine forth. Take a moment to sit quietly in this room and soak in what you know is in your heart and the truths deep inside you. As you leave this room and walk down the hall, recall all the rooms you have explored and cleaned.

9. Imagine leaving the house, shutting the door, and walking down the front walk and onto the sidewalk. Take three deep breaths and continue to sit or lie down quietly.

Finish

Ask students to share their experiences exploring and cleaning the different rooms. Did they have an easier or more difficult time in specific rooms? Ask them to reflect on why that might have happened.

Superhero

This activity allows students to imagine themselves as the hero of their own life!

Start

Relaxation pose

Prompt

Imagine that you are a super action hero who attracts super positive things like a strong magnet! Imagine yourself flying through the air as if you are a huge magnet attracting loving family and true friends, positive experiences, and happy times. (Pause.) Feel the energy of this attraction. Block out any negative experiences and feel the positive vibes flowing. Now, as we finish this superhero activity, take three deep, relaxing breaths. Gently roll onto your front. Stretch your arms out in front and point your toes as if you are a superhero stretched out and flying through the air!

Finish

Ask students to reflect on how it feels to be a magnet for positive energy. Ask them to suggest when they might use this tool (e.g., when working on a team project).

Rainbow Adventure

In this activity, students use colors to creatively imagine a powerful rainbow.

Start

Relaxation pose

Prompt

Imagine that you are walking on a quiet nature path after a rain shower. As the sun starts to come out, you step into each of the rays of a beautiful rainbow. Feel yourself bathed in each of the powerful, vivid, radiant colors of the magnificent rainbow. Take your time feeling and picturing the powerful energy of each color with deep relaxing breaths. Picture the rainbow's color of red (pause), orange (pause), yellow (pause), green (pause), blue (pause), indigo (pause), and violet (pause). Take three more deep breaths as you enjoy the beautiful rainbow you have created.

Finish

Ask students which color is their favorite? Ask them how it felt to be surrounded by the dazzling colors of a rainbow. Ask them to suggest when they might use this stress management tool.

Energizing With the Colors of the Rainbow

This activity uses the colors of the rainbow as metaphors for energizing various regions of the body.

Start

Relaxation pose (or mindful sitting)

Prompt

There are seven areas of the body that need to be continuously energized in order to maintain the best possible health and wellness. In this guided imagination activity, each area of the body is associated with a goal or intention and a color. We will establish and confirm these associations by using short statements called affirmations. As with any guided imagination activity, these are only suggestions—it is fine to change any of the ideas to reflect something that is more meaningful or a stronger image for you.

1. Find a comfortable position and set an intention to dedicate this time to relaxing and using your creative imagination. Focus your attention on your breath. Feel your belly rise with your next inhalation and as you exhale feel your whole body relax.

2. Imagine a ray of vivid, apple-red light shining from the base of your spine. This area of your body and the color red signify feeling strong, physically and emotionally stable, and firmly rooted in your environment. Take a slow, deep breath, and as you exhale imagine this ray of red light and say the following affirmation to yourself: "I feel connected." Take another relaxing breath and repeat this affirming statement.

3. Bring your attention to the center of your body—to the area a few inches below your belly button. From this area, imagine a bright orange ray of light radiating outward. This area of your body and this color stand for feeling centered. Feeling centered means focusing inward and keeping a healthy balance in your life. It also means feeling confident and experiencing feelings of self-respect. Imagine what it feels like to have a strong sense of confidence and respect. Take a slow, deep breath and as you exhale see this ray of orange light and say the following affirmation: "I feel centered and confident." Take one more calming breath and repeat this affirmation.

4. Bring your concentration to your upper abdominal area. From this area, imagine a ray of pure, sunshine-yellow light shining outward. This area and color symbolize the ability to receive love from family and friends. Take a slow, deep breath and as you exhale focus your imagination on this ray of yellow light and say the following affirmation: "I feel loved." Take another deep belly breath and repeat this affirmation.

5. The heart area represents your ability to be open to and share love—to share feelings of warmth, happiness, and caring. Imagine an emerald green ray of light beaming from your heart. Take a slow, deep breath into your heart and as you exhale focus on this green light and affirm to yourself: "I give love." Take one more deep breath into your heart and repeat this affirmation.

6. Bring your focus to the area surrounding your throat. From this area, imagine a ray of sea-blue light shining. This area and color signify having a voice and sharing this voice by having meaningful goals in your life. Think about what this means for you—the goals you want to accomplish and the determination and work needed to accomplish these goals. You have the power to reach these goals. Focus on these goals and on the sea-blue color. Take a full, complete breath and as you exhale repeat the following affirmation: "I have meaningful goals and will accomplish these goals." Take another full and complete breath and repeat this affirmation.

7. This next area represents understanding and insight. Focus on the area between your eyes. In order to make the best decisions for ourselves, we need to use both the right

(continued)

Energizing With the Colors of the Rainbow *(continued)*

(creative) and left (logical) hemispheres of the brain. Focus your attention on the area between your eyes and use your imagination to see the color of cobalt blue, the color of the sky at twilight, radiating outward. As you see this ray of cobalt blue, think of your ability to access your deepest knowing of what is best for you. Take a long and slow inhalation and as you exhale affirm the following statement: "I know what is best for me." Repeat this affirmation on your next exhalation.

8. From the top of your head, imagine a ray of light purple. This area of the body and this color represent your feelings of connection to the universe and of being at peace. Feeling connected is a vital aspect of your health and happiness. Focus on this color and imagine what it feels like to have a sense of connection and to feel at peace with yourself. Take a slow, deep breath and as you exhale visualize this color and say the following to yourself: "I feel a connection and am at peace with the universe." With your next exhalation, repeat this affirmation.

9. We will bring all the rays of the rainbow together to create a cocoon surrounding your entire body with diamond-bright white light.

10. Enjoy the feelings you have affirmed—connected, grounded, centered, confident, able to give and receive love, able to set meaningful goals, able to use your best thinking, and feeling a connection and at peace with the universe.

11. Take a full inhalation, then let all the air out on the exhalation by drawing your belly button toward your spine. Start to stretch, yawn open your body, and gently wiggle your fingers and toes.

12. Enjoy the feelings of calm and energy—ready to step back to the rest of your day.

13. Begin to become aware of your body and this room.

Finish

Ask students to share their experience with each of the seven areas. Was one area easier or more difficult to imagine and affirm? Ask students to think about one small aspect of this guided imagination activity that they might be able to bring to the rest of their day.

Adapted from Seward 2002.

Guided Creative Imagination

Elementary through middle school

STANDARD **7**—practicing health-enhancing behaviors

Flower Power Shower

In this activity, which is similar to the loving kindness meditation described in chapter 4, students use the power of their imagination and intention to wish others well.

Start

Relaxation pose

Prompt

Picture in your mind someone who is having a difficult time right now. This person can even be you. Picture the person in your mind's eye as vividly as possible. With sincere intention, imagine buckets of beautiful flowers pouring softly over the person. The power of the shower of flowers is helping this person become more relaxed and happy. See the person laugh out loud. Now, take a few deep breaths. Sit quietly and reflect on empathy—caring actively about another person's feelings.

Finish

Ask students to share what it was like for them to send someone empathy.

Wise Sage

This activity allows students to tap into their inner wisdom.

Start

Mindful sitting or relaxation pose

Prompt

1. Sit quietly and take a few relaxed breaths.

2. Focus on a problem you are working on.

3. Imagine a knock on the door. You open the door, and a trusted wise person is standing there. This trusted wise person is eager to help you with your problem. Invite him or her in and sit together for a few deep breaths.

4. Allow this wise person to help you with your problem—imagine handing it over to him or her. (Pause.) Listen to the advice he or she offers. The wise person hands the problem back to you, and you are ready to work on it. Walk the wise person to the door and thank him or her for visiting and helping you out.

5. As you sit back down, you realize you had the wisdom, the inner knowing, all along. You have the answers you need. Remember to take time to quiet down enough to listen to the answers that are best for you.

6. As you slowly come back to your chair and this room, take a few deep breaths.

Finish

Ask students to reflect on the answers they were given in their meditation and write about them.

Ordering a Pizza

This guided imagination activity involves the simple act of ordering a pizza. It may seem easy but there are many details students must focus on.

Start

Mindful sitting or relaxation pose. The creativity in this guided imagination comes from the students filling in the details from your cues about ordering a pizza.

Prompt

Take a few minutes to bring your awareness to the chair or the floor beneath you. Are you hungry? I am going to take you through the process of ordering a pizza. (Pause.) Take some deep relaxing breaths. (Pause.) It seems like a simple task but pay attention and focus on all the small details involved.

1. From which store will you order your pizza?

2. What kind of pizza do you want? Which toppings do you want on it?

3. How will you spend your time waiting for your pizza to be delivered?

4. How will you pay for your pizza? How much will you tip the delivery person?

(continued)

Ordering a Pizza *(continued)*

5. Where will you eat your pizza? How many slices will you have?

6. How will you clean up once you're done with your pizza?

Finish

The students can provide feedback on how being relaxed helps them to concentrate and focus. Ask students if you forgot anything in ordering the pizza.

Guided Creative Imagination

Middle school through young adult

Take a Hike in Soothing Nature

STANDARD **7**—practicing health-enhancing behaviors

In this activity, students imagine the soothing qualities of being outdoors during a hike.

Start

Relaxation pose

Prompt

1. Come into quiet, deep relaxed breathing. Invite your eyes to close.

2. We are going on a trip to a special relaxing spot. To get to our special relaxing spot, we need to get into our car and drive away from our school on a highway and then along a quiet country road. Notice that the sounds of the loud cars and trucks on the highway have changed to the quiet sounds of birds and the tires on the gravel of the country road.

3. As you get out of the car, you see a hiking path. Step onto this hiking path and, with each step, allow your thoughts to become calm and relaxed. Enjoy the quiet solitude of this hiking trail. Make a sincere effort to allow your mind to stop talking and find the peace deep within you.

4. As you continue on this hiking trail, you start to notice the quiet and peaceful sound of water moving over rocks. The sound of the water starts to become louder as you approach a waterfall. See the rainbow of light shining in the waterfall. The waterfall empties into a pool of water. There is a big flat rock in this pool.

5. Step onto the flat rock in the middle of the stream of water. As your breath becomes even more relaxed, imagine that you are part of this rock. As you sit quietly, notice the leaves and twigs floating by the rock. These leaves and twigs are like things going on in your life—your concerns. Imagine them passing by and floating away.

6. Notice your body and mind feeling grounded and alive. As you continue to sit quietly, feeling very safe and grounded, think of goals and dreams you might have in your heart. Using your courage and inner strength, imagine yourself accomplishing these heartfelt goals and dreams.

7. Taking some energizing breaths, stand up from the rock, and start to head back to the hiking trail and back to your day. Take a moment to affirm a positive outlook for your day and appreciate your skill of using your creativity and imagination to help you relax and focus on your heart's true goals and dreams.

8. Slowly start to stretch and gently move your fingers and toes. Take three more relaxing breaths, then gently sit up and open your eyes.

Finish

Ask students to share the most relaxing aspects of connecting with nature. Ask them to suggest ways they could be outdoors more (e.g., taking a walk in a park or reading a book under a tree).

Relaxation

Relaxation depends in part on body awareness, which allows a person to connect with and attend to sensations in his or her body. Under stress, it is common for us to contract or hold tension in muscles, but this tension has no useful function. If we repeatedly hold this kind of tension—tensing our shoulders while driving, furrowing our forehead when trying to recall someone's name or an important fact, gripping a pencil when taking a test—we may become unaware of or numb to the tension and the associated sensations.

Students can learn to pay attention to physical tension by practicing progressive muscle relaxation, in which they systematically contract and relax specific muscle groups. Students may not be aware of the tension they hold in muscle groups such as the neck and shoulder region or the forearms and hands. This tool allows them to build their awareness of the differences between tension and relaxation. Progressive muscle relaxation hinges on the idea that if our muscles are relaxed then our mind can relax as well. It is designed to be a kinesiological activity that relies solely on feeling tension and relaxation. However, for many of our students who have poor kinesthetic skills, you can augment the activity by using some visuals and imagination as well. The awareness of tension and relaxation is critical here. Prompt students to notice what tension feels like—for example, to compare one leg with the other by asking questions such as the following: Is it heavier? Does it tingle? Does it feel softer?

Relaxation

Progressive Relaxation Short Script

Early childhood education through middle school

STANDARD **7**—practicing health-enhancing behaviors

This stress management tool helps students build their awareness of the feelings of tension and relaxation in their body. During the activity, students focus on each region of the body and hold tension in that part for about 5 seconds. Then allow a long pause (20 to 30 seconds) of relaxation before moving to the next body region.

Start

Relaxation pose preferred but can be done seated

Prompt

1. Focus on your forearms and your hands. Imagine that you are squeezing a lemon, getting every last drop of juice out of it. Hold it (5-second hold). Now relax your whole arms and hands (long pause, approximately 20-30 seconds).

2. Focus on your upper arms and shoulders. Stretch your arms up as if you are holding onto a monkey bar. Continue to hold on (5-second hold). Drop your hands into your lap or to the sides of your body and let them totally relax. Take a few deep belly breaths (long pause, approximately 20-30 seconds).

3. Focus on your shoulders and scrunch them up to your ears and hold that position (5-second hold). Relax your shoulders down and shake them loose like you are fluffing up a pillow. Take a few deep belly breaths and completely relax your shoulders, arms, and hands. Is one arm more relaxed, heavier, or lighter? (long pause, approximately 20-30 seconds)

(continued)

Progressive Relaxation Short Script   *(continued)*

4. Focus on your jaw. Imagine that you are chewing a huge wad of bubble gum. Bite down and chew and chew. Hold the tension in your jaw (5-second hold). Relax your jaw, wiggle your jaw, separate your teeth slightly, and allow your tongue to relax as well (long pause, approximately 20-30 seconds).

5. Bring your focus to the area around your eyes. Squeeze your eyes tight and squint as if you have just stepped outside into bright blazing sunshine. Keep your eyes closed tight and hold them that way (5-second hold). Now soften the space around your eyes. Relax all the tiny muscles that surround each of your eyes (long pause, approximately 20-30 seconds).

6. Focus on your face and nose. Imagine that a fly is on your nose and wrinkle up your nose to swish it away. Now the fly is on your cheeks—swish it away. And now it is on your forehead—swish it away. Now the fly is gone, and you can relax your face. Let all the muscles soften and relax (long pause, approximately 20-30 seconds).

7. Focus on your stomach area. Imagine that a big hippo is sitting on your belly; hold the tension (5-second hold). The hippo has gotten off of your stomach, so you can let go of the tension and relax your belly. Take a few deep belly breaths (long pause, approximately 20-30 seconds).

8. Bring your focus to both of your legs: Imagine that you are walking through heavy, slushy snow. Your legs can hardly move, and all of the muscles in your legs are working and contracted. Keep walking through the heavy, wet snow. Now totally relax your legs. Wiggle them from side to side and let go of every last bit of tension (long pause, approximately 20-30 seconds).

9. Feel your whole body being relaxed. Scan your body, looking for any tension, and make an effort to relax every part of your body (long pause, approximately 20-30 seconds).

10. Take a few moments to notice how you feel when your body is relaxed. Slowly start to stretch and come back to this room— energized, awake, and ready to start our next activity.

Finish

Ask students to share one word that captures how they feel after completing progressive muscle relaxation. Ask them to suggest when they could use this activity (e.g., in bed if it is hard to fall asleep).

©Stewart Cohen/Digital Vision

Using examples of movements and experiences that most students will have experienced, like chewing bubble gum, helps them understand how to focus on different body parts and sensations in order to relieve the stress felt in their body.

Pay Attention to Me!

This activity involves a quick progressive muscle relaxation. Students hold muscle tension for 3 to 5 seconds, then practice relaxation for a longer (7- to 10-second) interval.

Start

Either seated or lying down (as long as students can fully relax specific body parts—some of which, such as the back and legs, may be easiest to relax when lying down)

Prompt

1. Make a frown and hold it. Now relax your face and let all the tension out (pause for 10 seconds). Take a big yawn and hold your mouth wide open. Hold it. Now relax your face again. Wiggle your jaws, separate your upper and lower teeth, and relax and soften your tongue. Let your face muscles become totally still and relaxed (pause for 7-10 seconds).

2. Raise the tops of your shoulders up to your ears and hold them there. With a big sigh, relax your shoulders down (pause for 7-10 seconds).

3. Lift up your chest, tighten your chest muscles, and hold this position. Let your chest drop and relax your heart and the core of your body (pause for 7-10 seconds).

4. Tighten your belly muscles as if you are putting on a pair of jeans that shrank in the wash and you can't button them. Hold this position. Now, relax your tummy and take a deep belly breath (pause for 7-10 seconds).

5. Lift your arms off of the floor (or off of your lap) and tighten your arms as if you are holding a heavy load of books. Hold it—don't let the books fall. Now, lower your arms to your lap (or the floor) and relax them completely (pause for 7-10 seconds).

6. Point your toes and lift your legs a few inches off of the floor (or ground). Keep pointing your toes—hold the position. Now, relax your legs (pause for 7-10 seconds).

7. Take a few moments to notice how you feel when your body is relaxed. Slowly start to stretch and come back to this room—energized and focused.

Finish

Ask students how they feel when they contrast tension and relaxation. Ask them to come up with situations in which they would use this tool (e.g., sitting for a long time while taking a test).

Autogenics

Autogenics can be understood by examining the two parts of the word. *Auto* means self, and *genics* means generating—thus self-generating. Relaxation can be brought about through self-suggestion by quietly talking to oneself about warmth and heaviness. The body feels warm and heavy when it is relaxed.

Start

Relaxation pose preferred but can be done seated upright

Prompt

1. I invite you to close your eyes and come into relaxed breathing. Imagine that you are lying down on the beach and the sun's rays are shining on your feet.

2. Repeat the following statement silently to yourself as you imagine the sun's rays warming your feet: "My feet are warm and heavy." Repeat the statement one more time: "My feet are warm and heavy." (Pause.) Imagine the sun's rays shining now on the calf muscles in your legs. Repeat silently to yourself: "My calves are warm and heavy."

3. (Continue to cue the students through the parts of the body—upper legs, hips, back, gluteus muscles, belly, and heart space—using the statement "My _____ is/are warm and heavy." Pause for 5 seconds after each part of the body.)

4. Take a few deep belly breaths, feeling very relaxed. Imagine your breath moving gently and slowly up and down your body like the waves on the beach. Feel your whole body being very warm and heavy. Your body is so heavy I could not pick up your arms or legs. (You can gently pick up students' legs or arms and encourage them to become heavier and more relaxed.)

5. Very gently come back to this space and wiggle your fingers and toes. Take a few more deep, relaxing breaths and slowly stretch like a cat waking up from a nap. Slowly sit up and let your head be the last part to come up.

Finish

Ask students to write or discuss with the class how it feels to use autogenics to relax the body.

Quick Minute of Autogenics

In this activity, students learn that when their hands are warm, their body is in a relaxed state.

Start

Mindful sitting or relaxation pose

Prompt

Close your eyes and relax your breathing. (Pause.) Imagine that you are holding a warm baked potato and allow your hands to become warm and heavy and your fingers to become slightly curled and relaxed. (Pause.) Say to yourself, "My hands are warm and heavy." (Pause.) Take a few deep, relaxing breaths while keeping your whole body still and quiet. Notice how it feels when your hands are warm and relaxed.

Finish

Ask students to suggest situations they could use this quick tool (e.g., before going up to bat in a baseball game).

Ball of Warmth

This activity uses both autogenics and creative imagination.

Start

Mindful sitting or relaxation pose

Prompt

Imagine that in your left hand a ball about the size of an orange is filling up your cupped palm with warmth and energy. Feel this ball of warmth and energy slowly radiate into your left pinkie finger, ring finger, middle finger, pointer finger, and thumb. Feel the weight of this ball of warm energy in your whole hand. Feel the warmth and energy of the ball traveling and moving into your wrist (pause), your forearm (pause), and your elbow (pause). Feel the ball of warm energy floating up your upper arm and into your shoulder (pause). Feel the warmth flow all the way from your fingertips to your left ear. (Repeat on the right side.) Now, take a few deep, relaxing breaths while keeping your whole body still and quiet. Notice how it feels when you use your creative imagination to create warmth and relaxation.

Finish

Ask students to think about why autogenics works—when they bring the suggestion of warmth to an area of the body, it relaxes.

Using Stress Balls

A pilot study was conducted by using stress balls with sixth graders, both in class and independently (Stalvey & Brasell, 2006). Although all types of learners benefited from using stress balls, kinesthetic learners used the stress ball more consistently and enjoyed subsequent increases in their attention spans.

Materials

Stress ball for each student

Start

Mindful sitting

Prompt

1. Hold the stress ball in the palm of your nondominant hand. Feel the weight of the ball resting in your hand. Relax your breathing and invite your eyes to close. Squeeze the stress ball with 100 percent effort and hold that position. Now release all the tension. Allow your hand, wrist, arm, and shoulder to completely relax. Continue to feel the tension flow out of your hand as you relax your breath even more (pause 10 seconds).

2. Now squeeze the stress ball with 50 percent effort. What does that feel like? Notice the tension in your hand, wrist, and arm and hold it at 50 percent tension. Now relax your entire arm and let your hand totally relax (pause 10 seconds).

3. Now squeeze the stress ball with such light tension that it is as if you are holding an egg and do not want to damage the fragile shell. Hold this light tension. Now, totally relax your whole arm and hand. Notice how this total relaxation feels (pause 10 seconds).

4. Put your stress ball down and take a few moments to soak in the relaxation you have created.

Finish

Ask students how this tool could be used for stressful situations such as taking a test.

Three-Minute Checkup

This quick activity allows students to become relaxed by paying attention to their thoughts, their breathing, and their bodies.

Start

Mindful sitting

Prompt

1. Close your eyes and sit quietly. Step inside your body and mind. Take an inventory of how you are feeling—your emotions—and your thoughts (pause for 30 seconds).

2. Find an anchor. This is a point in your breathing cycle that you can bring your attention to and focus on. This focus point could be your inhalation, the space between your inhalation and exhalation, your exhalation, or the space between your exhalation and the next inhalation. Find your anchor now (pause for 30 seconds).

3. Let's bring our focus to the whole body: Breathe in and out of your whole body. Notice how it feels to breathe with your whole body, as if each cell is opening and expanding with the inhalation and letting go of the breath with the exhalation. Let your whole body—every cell of your body—feel relaxed with each breath you take (pause 30 seconds).

4. Take a few deep, relaxing breaths while keeping your whole body still and quiet. Notice how it feels when you use your breath to bring calm to your body (pause 30 seconds).

Finish

These short duration tools are readily available to students. Encourage them to practice these tools often so they can utilize them when the going gets tough.

Relaxation

Elementary through young adult

STANDARD **7**—practicing health-enhancing behaviors

Beach Wave

This activity can be augmented by using a soundtrack of gentle waves.

Start

Relaxation pose

Prompt

Imagine that you are lying on a beach on a beautiful summer day. You are lying on your back at the edge of the shore where the waves move gently in and out. The water is warm, and the sand underneath is warm and soft. Imagine as you breathe in that your breath is like a wave washing up on the shore and gently flowing over your body. The first wave comes and washes over your toes and knees. Exhale, and the wave softly ebbs back into the ocean. (Pause.) The next wave gently flows over your whole lower body. Exhale, and the wave softly drifts back into the ocean. (Pause.) On your next inhalation, a gentle wave slowly washes right up to your collarbones. On the exhalation, it softly recedes. Your whole body feels surrounded by these waves. You float on these peaceful soothing waves. (Pause.) Take a few deep, relaxing breaths while keeping your whole body still and quiet. Notice how it feels when you use your creative imagination to create relaxation.

Finish

Ask students if there are other images of nature that allow them to relax.

STANDARD **7**—practicing health-
enhancing behaviors

Nature's Colors

This activity uses colors and peaceful images from nature to bring about relaxation. If students are not familiar with the colors of fall, you can use photographs of brilliantly colored trees to help them create images. This activity can also be modified for different seasons (e.g., walking in spring rain among beautiful flowers, walking in winter as snow falls).

Start

Relaxation pose

Prompt

1. Imagine that you are walking down a hiking trail on a crisp, sunny autumn day. The leaves offer a brilliant fireworks display of color—yellow, orange, red. You come to an open area surrounded by colorful trees. Sit down comfortably in the middle of all the beautiful colors, textures, and shapes.

2. Imagine that you are a leaf on one of the trees. Color your whole body with the color yellow. Watch the yellow leaf drop slowly to the ground, then watch it rest comfortably in a big pile of colorful leaves. Take a deep, relaxing breath.

3. Imagine that you are a leaf on a tree and color your whole body with the color red. Watch the red leaf float slowly to the ground, then watch it rest comfortably in a big pile of colorful leaves. Take a deep, relaxing breath.

4. Imagine that you are a leaf on a tree and color your whole body with the color orange. Watch the orange leaf glide leisurely to the ground, then watch it rest comfortably in a big pile of colorful leaves. Take a deep relaxing breath and enjoy and be grateful for the beauty of nature.

5. Take a few deep, relaxing breaths while keeping your whole body still and quiet.

Finish

Discuss with students the fact that nature can calm and soothe us. Ask if they have a favorite place outdoors that makes them feel calm and relaxed.

STANDARD **7**—practicing health-
enhancing behaviors

Relaxation
With Beanie Babies

The weight of a Beanie Baby serves as a nice cue to help students feel the breath in their belly.

Materials

One Beanie Baby per student

Start

Relaxation pose

Prompt

(The instructor places a Beanie Baby on the student's lower belly.) Without touching your Beanie Baby breathing buddy, watch it go and up down slowly with your relaxed belly breaths (long pause). Slowly curl up onto your side with your legs curled up comfortably toward your midsection in fetal pose with your breathing buddy and rest there while enjoying deep, full breaths.

Finish

Ask students how breathing with their Beanie Baby breathing buddy helps them to become calm and relaxed.

Relaxation

Early childhood education through elementary

STANDARD **7**—practicing health-enhancing behaviors

Starfish

This is a fun creative imagination activity in which students copy a starfish resting in the warm sand of a sunny tidal pool.

Start

Lying on back or front in the shape of a starfish

Prompt

You will use the next five exhalations to focus on relaxing a different part of your body; you will become relaxed, as if you are melting down into the floor.

> Exhalation 1. Melt your legs.
>
> Exhalation 2. Make your arms heavy.
>
> Exhalation 3. Soften your belly.
>
> Exhalation 4. Make your heart space peaceful.
>
> Exhalation 5. Relax your whole body.

Imagine that you are a starfish resting at the bottom of a tidal pool. It is very quiet, still, and peaceful here. Allow your body to find whatever shape best enables you to feel completely relaxed as you float on the gentle, warm, soft sand and feel the warm sun on your body. (Pause.) Take a few more breaths as you become even more relaxed.

Finish

Students can share how it felt to be restful and peaceful like a starfish.

Magic Freeze Wand

In this activity, students use their imagination to pretend that a wand has frozen their body.

Materials

A wand or wooden dowel

Start

Relaxation pose

Prompt

As I sweep the wand over your body, all the parts of your body will freeze. You then need to be quiet and still until I use the wand again to unfreeze your body. While you are frozen, continue to lie quiet and still with your eyes closed. Notice how it feels to be quiet and peaceful.

Finish

Ask students to share other ways they enjoy feeling quiet and peaceful.

Music Therapy

Music has been called the universal language, and it can serve as a powerful tool for stress management. The precise mechanism for its effectiveness is yet to be fully understood. Current theories focus on several aspects, such as the potential of sound vibrations to entrain or align the body's rhythms with the soothing pace of the music; the conversion of sound energy as a cause of biochemical changes in the body; or the possibility that music serves better than language does as a way to represent our emotional states.

Bat Ears

This activity encourages focus as students listen carefully to music that includes embedded sounds from nature (e.g., birdcalls, waterfalls, rain, and waves). Select soothing acoustic music with a slow tempo and without words. If students follow these guidelines, they can also make up their own playlists to share with the class for stress management.

Materials

Soothing music with nature sounds and music player

Start

Mindful sitting or relaxation pose

Prompt

We know that bats direct their movements by means of sound vibrations. We can use our own ears to pay special attention to special sounds in music. Listen to the music with your big bat ears and notice all the different sounds. You can share what you heard once the music has stopped. (Play the music and wait until it finishes before giving the next prompt.) Take a few deep breaths.

Finish

Ask students what sounds they heard. Invite them to share about other relaxing sounds they enjoy listening to.

Music Therapy

All levels

STANDARD **7**—practicing health-enhancing behaviors

Copycat

This activity can be led by you or by a student. The leader creates a special rhythm or pattern by clapping or slapping his or her thighs. The rest of the students then repeat the rhythm or pattern. Students can take turns serving as the leader and listening to each other's special sounds. The rhythm or pattern can also be made by using a musical instrument (e.g., shaker, drum, tambourine) or a plastic container (e.g., recycled yogurt container) with beans or sand (glue the lid's rim on so that the materials don't spill out!).

Start

Mindful sitting in a circle

Prompt

Listen carefully while I make a sound pattern, then repeat the pattern back to me. (Start off with simple patterns and gradually increase their difficulty.)

Finish

Ask students to identify their favorite pattern. Invite them to share about their reactions to sound patterns in nature or other aspects of their environment. Some people, for example, enjoy the sound of rain on the roof. Others might be soothed by the back and forth motion of a fan.

Drumming

Students enjoy this activity as an outlet for stress. The purpose is not to make music that is necessarily melodic but to focus on the rhythm and energy of the drums. A leader sets the rhythm, and the other students repeat it. This approach encourages active listening. Students take turns serving as the leader.

Materials

A drum for the instructor and each of the students. If the drums are larger, several students can share one drum.

Start

Mindful sitting with a drum

Prompt

Listen carefully while I play a rhythm pattern on my drum. Now it is your turn to repeat the pattern on your drum. (Start off with simple patterns and gradually increase their difficulty.) Now we will go around the room and each of you will have a chance to lead the class in drumming your favorite pattern.

Finish

Ask students to share the rhythm of their favorite song. Discuss situations in which it is important to listen carefully (e.g., asking directions, in class). Ask students how drumming might be an outlet for stress.

Expressive Art Therapy

Art therapy can be a wonderful tool for stress management, especially with younger students who may not have the vocabulary to express themselves or who have thoughts and emotions that are better expressed nonverbally. In such cases, a picture can indeed be worth a thousand words. These activities are not about producing a product (i.e., a work of art) but about the process itself. Students may scoff at their ability to do art, but you can emphasize that many of them do art all time in the form of doodling! Doodles and the consistent shapes such as curlicues or hearts that students gravitate toward can serve as powerful symbols for understanding and processing stress.

There is no right way to respond in expressive art therapy—it is all good. The interpretation that students give to a piece of art is the key, and it is a natural part of the process. Therefore, make sure to be inclusive of all students' work and ideas, avoid any competition, suspend judgment, and respect the right of a student not to share his or her work.

In our digital age of cutting and pasting images and clip art, we may have lost the chance to just draw! Make sure to offer a variety of color choices in as many media as possible, such as crayons, ink, colored pencils, paints, finger paints, and colored pastels. Another option is modeling clay. For paper, blank newsprint is economical and thus allows students to do as much as they want.

Art Therapy Topics to Explore (Level Depends on the Activity)

- Self-portrait. Who am I? To expand this topic, consider asking questions such as these: "What superhero ('To infinity and beyond!') would you be?" "What imaginary animal (e.g., Doctor Dolittle's pushmi-pullyu) would you be?"

- Peaceful scene or dream impression. Provide examples from the impressionist artists, who used large brush strokes and colors (e.g., red meaning strong emotion such as anger or blue meaning happiness) to give an impression but not an exact representation of an image.

- "My feelings are a work of art." This focus was used by the American Art Therapy Association (2010) as the theme for a recent National Children's Mental Health Awareness Day. Students can draw about how they are feeling right now. What do certain emotions (e.g., love, worry, shame) feel and look like?

- Mandalas. A mandala is a circle that includes sacred and other meaningful images (Cornell, 2006). You can find mandalas for students to look at on the web. See figure 5.5 for an example of a mandala activity.

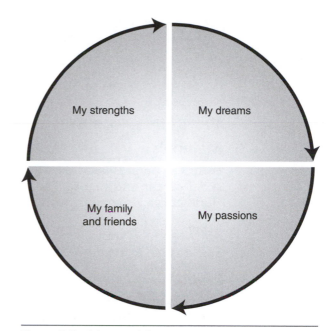

Figure 5.5 My mandala.

Puppets

Puppets provide a quintessential method for helping students express themselves. In this activity, students make their own puppets. Students can write their own puppet scenarios or use scenarios provided by you.

Materials

Puppets

Start

Students sitting in a circle

Prompt

One way to use puppets to address stress is to create scenarios in which a puppet character faces a stressful situation. The other puppets (friends) lead the stressed-out puppet in using a stress management tool such as progressive muscle relaxation or belly breathing or provide suggestions about effective ways to manage the stressful situation provided in the scenario (e.g., using assertive communication). Thus you can use this activity to practice teaching others how to use a stress management tool. In groups of 2 or 3, write a scenario involving a stressful situation and then use the puppets to act it out for the class.

Finish

Have students discuss the problem that the puppet had to solve. What other options did the puppet have? What consequences might result from the puppet's decisions? Did the puppet make health-enhancing decisions?

Jewelry

Making a friendship bracelet is a fun way to express what friendship means.

Materials

Beads can be purchased in bulk from online sellers or at a craft or discount store; charms and shells can also be used. The objects can be strung on stretchy elastic or leather strings. Students can also make earrings.

Start

Students sitting at large tables with beading supplies available

Prompt

Make a card that shows what each bead and charm you use symbolizes for you. For example: "This friendship bracelet was made especially for you. The blue beads say thanks for listening to me when I was blue!"

Finish

Students can put on a fashion show and share their works of art. Ask students to share how using their hands in making a craft can be a stress management tool and how their jewelry can serve as a reminder of the important support factors in their lives such as friends.

Dealer's Choice

This activity recycles an old deck of cards into a stress management tool.

Materials

Deck of cards (each student using as many as five cards, depending on how much time is available); art supplies including markers and other coloring materials

Start

Students seated at tables

Prompt

Cover your cards with stickers, paper, or white mailing labels to make new cards on which you can draw ways to relax. Here are some examples: reading a book, taking deep relaxing breaths, going for a walk, calling a friend, listening to music, drawing a picture, writing a story, and doing yoga poses.

Finish

Students can bring their cards home and deal themselves a card each day as a stress management activity. Another way to use the card deck is for students to pick one card as their personal stress management activity for a Stress Less Hour on a Friday afternoon, during which the entire class engages in a stress management activity.

Journaling

Journals can be purchased in bulk so that each student has a designated place for writing. Hand-writing the journals is preferred over word-processing them because writing by hand takes longer, thus allowing more time for thinking. It also provides a tactile activity in which students can engage mindfully by allowing them to disengage from technology and take time to be present with the paper, the pen, and their thoughts. Journals can be collected and kept in a secure place so the entries remain private and confidential. It is important in all journaling activities to emphasize honest disclosure, self-respect, and confidentiality.

Here are some examples of ground rules for journaling:

- Take time to become centered by taking several deep breaths.
- Date each entry.
- Be spontaneous and uncensored while still emphasizing self-respect.
- Keep this journal private—only the instructor and you will read your entries, and you will both approach them with confidentiality and respect.
- Open and close your journal quietly and with care to set a tone for reflection.
- Allow for enough time to write—don't be in a hurry.

Journaling

Elementary through young adult

STANDARD 7—practicing health-enhancing behaviors

This Is My Life!

This activity enables students to look at their life in the form of a screenplay written from someone else's perspective; it should include details and directions.

Start

Make sure that each student has a good place to write (supplied with paper and a writing utensil). Set a timer for 30 minutes of writing time.

Prompt

Start your screenplay with the location and circumstances of your birth. For example, do you know the length of your mother's labor or your birth weight? Next, address your first day of school, a favorite summer vacation, a time you fell in love, a sad time, a funny occurrence, or your favorite accomplishment. You can write about all of these events or just pick one or two. In this first round, we will just write for 30 minutes. As you work on your screenplay, you will remember more and more details, but as with any fabulous movie script you may need to leave out some scenes.

Finish

Students can work on their projects over a long period of time (e.g., a school term or several weeks). They can also act out and video their screenplays. Ask students to share the significance of the events in their lives and what it was like to capture them in writing or on video.

Unsent Letters

In this activity, students will write a letter to someone to whom they would like to describe a situation or tell a story about an issue or problem they are facing. The letter will not be sent; rather, it serves as a vehicle for getting thoughts and emotions out and down on paper, and is used as an outlet to relieve difficult emotions.

Start

Each student should have paper and a writing utensil.

Prompt

Think of someone you are having a problem with. You will write that person a letter detailing the concerns and emotions you have as a result of the situation or problem. In this activity, we will use *I-statements* as much as possible—that is, statements that start with "I" and state what your concern is, how you feel about the concern, and a request of what you want the person to do to resolve the problem as well as what you will do yourself to help the situation improve. Make sure to express your concerns, how you feel, and what you both can do to resolve the situation.

Finish

Ask students to discuss how it felt to be able to write down their emotions about a difficult situation involving someone else. Invite them to share about situations in their lives where using *I-statements* could be helpful.

My Dreams

In this activity, students recall and journal about dreams they have had. They can also write about dreams in a different sense—dreams as goals—and about actions they can take in order to realize these dreams.

Start

Mindful sitting at tables with journals

Prompt

Today we are going to journal about dreams, both life dreams and dreams you have while you sleep. It has been said that goals are dreams with deadlines. The following questions can help you to start writing about your dreams, messages you can take from your dreams, and goals for the future:

* Do you have any recurring dreams?
* Can you speculate about these dreams' messages?
* What are some of your life dreams or goals?
* What are some action steps you can take to move in the direction of your life dreams?

Finish

Students can do research and present their critical thoughts about dream interpretation. Several websites offer dream interpretations; in addition, here are a few relevant books:

* *The Complete Idiot's Guide Dream Dictionary* by Eve Adamson and Gayle Williamson
* *The Dream Book: Symbols for Self Understanding* by Betty Bethards
* *Dream Dictionary: An A to Z Guide to Understanding Your Unconscious Mind* by Tony Crisp

Journaling

Elementary through young adult

STANDARD **7**—practicing health-enhancing behaviors

Fill in the Blank!

This creative writing activity allows students to use a prompt and then continue journaling about their statement.

Start

Students choose from a variety of prompts for the fill-in-the-blank activity. Prompts can be written on the board or on handouts that the students fill out. See the Fill-in-the-Blank! worksheet (page 225 of appendix A) for examples of prompts. Students can help by brainstorming other fill-in-the-blank statements. Allow students to work on one statement at a time. During a session, students might work on as many as three statements.

Prompt

On the board or on your paper, you will find several prompts or beginnings of statements. Choose one of the prompts and fill in the blank. Write as much as you can to completely finish the prompt.

Finish

Encourage students to share their fill-in-the-blank compositions and how they relate to practicing healthy behaviors.

Name _____   Date _____

Fill in the Blank!

1. I am unique because _____
2. I am diverse because _____
3. The accomplishment I am most proud of is _____
4. My dream for the future is _____
5. I take time to relax and become centered by _____
6. I enjoy movement each day by doing _____
7. My nutrition habits are _____
8. I feel connected to _____
9. I creatively express myself by _____
10. The way I define my spirituality is _____

From N.E. Tummers, 2011, *Teaching stress management: Activities for children and young adults* (Champaign, IL: Human Kinetics).

My Accomplishments

This activity uses lists rather than prose to brainstorm accomplishments in each student's life. Students also reflect on what led to this accomplishment (e.g., studying, practicing, working as a team, getting up at 6 a.m.).

Start

Students use the My Accomplishments worksheet (page 226 in appendix A).

Prompt

(Distribute the worksheet.) In the first column, titled My Accomplishments, write down as many of your accomplishments as you can think of. Come up with at least six accomplishments that you would like to investigate today. Now, take time to reflect on each accomplishment—what you accomplished and what actions you took that helped you complete it. List these actions in the next column, titled Steps to Success. When you have finished with the two columns, review your steps to success and identify any common words or themes that highlight how you were able to be successful.

Finish

Lead a discussion about the common themes identified by students—for example, practice, perseverance, and discipline—and how students can use those same qualities when they are stuck or frustrated with their progress toward their current goals.

Name _____   Date _____

My Accomplishments

List your accomplishments below.   Steps to success

1. _____
2. _____
3. _____
4. _____
5. _____
6. _____

From N.E. Tummers, 2011, *Teaching stress management: Activities for children and young adults* (Champaign, IL: Human Kinetics).

A Reflection on the Serenity Prayer

God, grant me the serenity
To accept the things I cannot change;
Courage to change the things I can;
And wisdom to know the difference.

Reprinted from Niebuhr. Available: http://en.wikipedia.org/wiki/Serenity_Prayer

This verse, referred to as the Serenity Prayer, is generally attributed to Reinhold Niebuhr. It has been adopted by Alcoholics Anonymous and can also serve as a powerful affirmation or motto for anyone trying to deal with stressors in health-enhancing ways.

Start

Mindful sitting at tables with My Reflection on the Serenity Prayer worksheet (page 227 of appendix A)

Prompt

Reflect on the Serenity Prayer and answer the first five questions on the worksheet. Then reflect on your answers and your life and use the last two questions to create your own personal motto.

Finish

Students can share their reflections and their mottoes. This activity can be expanded to include printing T-shirts that display students' favorite mottoes.

Name _____ Date _____

My Reflection on the Serenity Prayer

1. What are my strengths? _____
2. What are my challenges? _____
3. What areas in my life can I change? _____
4. What areas in my life can I improve upon? _____
5. What are areas I need to accept? _____
6. After exploring this motto in depth, take a look at all of the answers you have given. Think about your own life. What are some wisdoms that are important to you? Write them here: _____
7. What do you think a good motto for yourself would be? _____

My wise person motto: _____

From N.E. Tummers, 2011, Teaching stress management: Activities for children and young adults (Champaign, IL: Human Kinetics).

An Expansion of the Serenity Prayer

Middle school through young adult

STANDARD 6—goal setting and 7—practicing health-enhancing behaviors

This activity, suggested by Jay Winner in *Take the Stress Out of Your Life* (2008), involves expanding the Serenity Prayer with the following line: "Please give us the understanding that change often takes time and the wisdom to enjoy the process of change" (p. 24).

Serenity Prayer

God, grant me the serenity

To accept the things I cannot change;

Courage to change the things I can;

And wisdom to know the difference.

Reprinted from Niebuhr. Available: http://en.wikipedia.org/wiki/Serenity_Prayer

Start

Mindful sitting at tables with journals

Prompt

Think about the Serenity Prayer and the additional line provided by Winner. Reflect on the extended prayer and on ways in which you might become more understanding of change and more able to enjoy the processes involved in change. Now, reflect on a major change that you have faced. Did it take time to accomplish the change? In hindsight, was it a positive change?

Finish

Students can share their reflections on setting goals toward positive change with the group.

Adapted from Winner 2008.

Sharing My Stress Strategies

This journaling activity can provide an icebreaker for students who might serve as peer mentors or be mentored by another student or an adult. See chapter 6 for more information on mentoring.

Start

Each student will have a Sharing My Stress Strategies worksheet (page 228 in appendix A).

Prompt

Fill in the statements on the worksheet by reflecting on the variety of influences on your stress management practices, then share your reflection statements with a partner or mentor.

Finish

Students can analyze similarities and differences in the influences on their stress management practices. Students can help each other in adopting healthy behaviors or serve as mentors to younger students.

Name _____ Date _____

Sharing My Stress Strategies

1. When I am bullied, I _____
2. When I am the center of attention, I _____
3. When I feel awkward, I _____
4. When my feelings are hurt, I _____
5. When someone puts me down, I _____
6. When I am under a lot of stress, I _____
7. I fear _____
8. One way I relax is _____
9. My favorite stress management tool is _____

From N.E. Tummers, 2011, *Teaching stress management: Activities for children and young adults* (Champaign, IL: Human Kinetics)

My Favorite Ways to De-Stress

In this activity, students promote and encourage positive stress management practices among their peers. They start the activity by journaling and then take their ideas one step further by creating slogans and visual messages that make a clear point: It is time to de-stress!

Materials

Large newsprint or posterboard and markers

Start

Mindful sitting at tables with large newsprint or posterboard and markers for each student. Students will have time to journal about their favorite ways to de-stress.

Prompt

Addressing each of your senses, write about ways to use your senses in order to de-stress. Here are some examples:

* Sight: reading, doodling, viewing art, watching movies, doing crossword puzzles
* Smell: cooking, enjoying nature, aromatherapy
* Sound: listening to music or nature sounds

* Feeling: exercising, taking hot bubble baths, feeling a cat's soft fur
* Taste: eating fresh baked cookies or hot oatmeal on a cold winter day

Use your written thoughts as raw material for creating a poster that features visuals and slogans to encourage other students to adopt healthy de-stressing tools.

Finish

The posters can be displayed around the classroom or school to advocate that everyone in the learning community take time to de-stress! Students can assess each other's posters to make sure they conveyed healthy de-stressing messages with passion and conviction.

Journaling
Elementary through young adult
STANDARD 6—goal setting

Brief Grief

This activity gives students an opportunity to appropriately and healthily acknowledge a loss, disappointment, or failure. Experiencing the emotions of grief enables us to eventually let these losses go and move on by setting and pursuing health-enhancing goals.

Start

Mindful sitting at tables. Give each student a copy of the Steps for Goal Setting worksheet (page 229 in appendix A).

Prompt

Today you will set a goal which will focus on something you felt to be a loss, disappointment, or failure in the past. Take a moment to think about this, then write about a situation where you experienced a loss, disappointment, or failure which you would like to change into a goal. (Provide time for students to write.) Closing your eyes and sitting quietly, take a few moments to acknowledge how it felt to experience this loss. (Long pause.) Use the Steps for Goal Setting worksheet to set a goal and determine the action steps that you can take to come to terms with this situation.

Finish

Students can continue to journal about their progress toward their goal. Doing so is a key part of the process of working toward a health-enhancing goal. We all face setbacks, and students need time to reflect on their progress or lack thereof. It is crucial that students develop the ability to set goals and continually track and evaluate their progress toward meeting those goals.

Name _____

Date _____

Steps for Goal Setting

1. What is your long-term goal? Is it measureable? Is there a deadline—a time by which you want to achieve it? How will you know if you have achieved this goal? How will you celebrate the accomplishment of this goal?

2. Where are you now? Are you doing things to move toward the goal? Are you doing things that compromise your progress toward the goal?

3. What resources and support do you need in order to achieve this goal?

4. What are attitudes and other obstacles you need to overcome in order to make progress toward this goal?

5. Break the goal down into small action steps that you can do and set a deadline for each one of these action steps.

From N.E. Tummers, 2011, *Teaching stress management: Activities for children and young adults* (Champaign, IL: Human Kinetics).

Storytelling

Morris, Taylor, and Wilson (2000) support the use of children's stories to promote social skills. In fact, bibliotherapy is defined as a strategy that helps people cope with a variety of developmental concerns through the use of literature (Stamps, 2003). Books and stories can provide opportunities for teachers to model problem-solving and conflict resolution skills. Students can identify with characters by seeing them gain insight as they resolve a challenge.

Storytelling

Elementary through young adult

STANDARD **2**—analyzing influences

Retelling a Story From a New Perspective

We have witnessed the popularity of classic tales rewritten from the perspective of another character. For upper elementary, *The True Story of the Three Little Pigs,* by Jon Scieszka, tells the story from the perspective of the wolf. For young adults, Gregory Maguire's *Wicked: The Life and Times of the Wicked Witch of the West* retells *The Wizard of Oz* from the perspective of the witch, now named Elphaba.

This activity allows students to analyze the influences—family, peers, culture, media, technology, and other factors—on the health behaviors of characters from their favorite stories.

Start

Students can select their own stories or use classic stories provided by the instructor.

Prompt

Rewrite the story from a different perspective that includes both internal factors (e.g., feelings, moods) and external factors (e.g., media, family, friends) that influenced the chosen character's health behavior. Make sure this different perspective shows a health-enhancing outcome. For example, imagine *Little Red Riding Hood* retold from the perspective of the wolf! What if the wolf had been given lessons in conflict resolution? What if Little Red Riding Hood had ventured out with her friends instead of going alone? What if Little Red Riding Hood had befriended the wolf?

Finish

Students discuss this activity and bridge to situations from their own experiences that could have been resolved with a health-enhancing outcome.

Storytelling
Elementary through young adult
STANDARD ❷—analyzing influences

Stress Management Heroes

Students investigate examples of role models for stress management from media, culture, friends, and family members.

Start

To help students get started, share examples of a variety of healthy influences for modeling stress management, such as characters (from books, television, and the movies), community members, friends, and family members. This approach can also be a great way to infuse other academic topics (e.g., literature) into your work with stress management.

Prompt

Recall a favorite character in a book or film. Discuss (or write about) what you most admire in this character's response to a stressful situation. For example, the character might have asked for help when he or she didn't know how to solve a problem.

Finish

Students can reflect on times when they have used their role model's stress management tool and brainstorm ways in which they could use it in the future.

Humor

Using humor to deal with stress is part of human nature. When introducing the activities in this section, you can share with your students the story of Dr. Norman Cousins as it is told in his book *Anatomy of an Illness as Perceived by the Patient* (1991). Cousins emphasizes the importance of laughter—he loved to watch Marx Brothers comedy routines—in his recovery from serious illness. In fact, his practice of using laughter to heal himself formed a case study in a major medical journal! A good belly laugh can be seen as an internal workout that decreases stress hormones, improves the immune system, oxygenates the blood, and gives the diaphragm and abdominal muscles a good workout.

Before doing the activities presented in this section, emphasize to your students that jokes are not funny when they make fun of a specific group, seek laughs at someone else's expense (thus increasing that person's stress), or are geared merely at helping the teller feel superior. Make clear that anything done in the humor activities should be shareable with the rest of the group—no private jokes.

Sometimes laughter really is the best medicine.

© Andres Rodriguez/fotolia.com

Humor Scrapbook

A humor scrapbook collects a student's best ways to laugh and keep a sense of humor during stressful circumstances. For example, a student might collect funny jokes, videos, movie quotes, and photos. Students can use the handout for this activity to make up their own funny materials and be creative at the same time!

Start

Student can each have a notebook or file (hard copy or electronic) where they keep their humor scrapbook. The Tickle My Funny Bone worksheet (page 230 in appendix A) provides some ideas for helping students get their creative juices flowing.

Prompt

Your humor scrapbook is a collection of funny material (e.g., photos, videos, quotations, jokes, puns, situations) that you have created or collected to tickle your funny bone. Fill out the worksheet to help create your scrapbook.

Name _____   Date _____

Tickle My Funny Bone

1. Make up oxymorons. An oxymoron is a combination of two words that form a contradictory message such as "living dead."

2. Make up puns. A pun is a form of word play. For example, "Did you hear about the guy whose whole left side was cut out? He's all right now."

3. Write absurd headlines for a tabloid newspaper. For example, "Cat Eats Balloons and Floats Away to California Coast."

4. Complete this sentence. For example, "You know you are really stressed when you are wearing two different socks." You know you are really stressed when . . .

5. Take an ordinary photograph and create a caption that makes the pictured situation funny.

From N.E. Tummers, 2011, *Teaching stress management: Activities for children and young adults* (Champaign, IL: Human Kinetics).

Finish

Students can share their scrapbooks, and a joint collection of the best of all the students' scrapbook items can be put together by the entire class and shared with other classes or the entire school. Students can view the group scrapbook during stressful situations (e.g., as a reward during state testing).

Joke of the Day or Week

This activity provides a nice ritual for starting class in a health-enhancing way. It can be done either daily or weekly.

Start

Students take turns being in charge of the joke of the day or week.

Prompt

When it is your turn to be in charge of the joke of the day or week, you are responsible for bringing in or writing your own joke to share with the class.

Finish

Students can discuss how humor or seeing things from a humorous point of view help them manage their stress (e.g., they might take things less seriously). Students can collect all the jokes used during the school year to create a book.

Stand Up for Humor

In this activity, students demonstrate the power of humor as a stress management tool by encouraging others to handle stressful situations by making positive health choices.

Start

Students brainstorm stressful situations their peer group is facing (e.g., moving up to high school, taking state tests, facing the holidays, having to wear school uniforms). Then either you or the class can choose one of the situations to address in this activity.

Prompt

You and your classmates will hold an open-mike time in class during which you share funny stories or haikus, comic skits, or made-up fortune cookies messages that use humor to help your peers practice healthy behaviors when faced with stressful situations. You may work on your own or in small groups.

Finish

Students can perform their open-mike messages at a school meeting or assembly. Open-mike sessions can also be video-recorded for sharing.

A Funny Thing Happened on the Way to . . .

This activity helps students hone their ability to notice humor and be on the lookout for the funny or absurd moments that are out there if you just look!

Start

You can provide situations or photos to help students get started.

Prompt

Write a short story about something funny that you have seen in the last week. You can use thought bubbles to show someone having funny thoughts in a photograph (materials for doing this can be purchased at scrapbooking supply stores) or use pictures to illustrate your story.

Finish

Ask students how looking at the humorous perspective of everyday situations helps them to manage their stress. Students can collect their best humor stories and photos and publish them in the student newspaper.

Silly Movie Fest

In this advocacy activity, students serve as their own funny movie film directors, actors, and producers. It is crucial that you set clear boundaries for this activity—no one should get hurt or be made to feel stupid or otherwise bad.

Start

Students need access to video recorders; small digital cameras can be used if they have a video function.

Prompt

Either write a script for acting out funny situations or capture video of other students doing something funny (e.g., telling a joke). You should avoid doing physical comedy in which you could hurt yourself or others. Remember your project needs to advocate for humor as a positive and powerful stress management tool.

Finish

Students can share their videos, give awards, and even hold a film festival complete with a red carpet!

Writing Funny Greeting Cards

In this activity, students design greeting cards to advocate for healthy humor.

Start

Students can select a group of peers, older adults, or younger students and design funny stress-reducing cards for this group. Students should make sure they know their intended audience (e.g., older adults may not understand cultural references the students' peer group would relate to).

Prompt

Create funny cards to lift someone's mood or to celebrate April Fools' Day or a holiday that you make up for fun (e.g., Funny Daze). Use thought bubbles to show someone having funny thoughts. Materials for doing this can be purchased at scrapbooking supply stores.

Finish

Students can deliver their funny cards and share some laughs with members of the group for whom they chose to advocate using humor as a stress management tool.

Silly Word Games

This a fun and quick activity that lets you take a break and laugh a bit with your students.

Start

You can make up index cards with one word written on each card. Deal each pair of students 5-10 cards.

Prompt

Select from the cards you have been dealt and choose two words that you can pair together to make up new words—for example, belly + button = belly button!

Finish

Students share their funny word combinations. Have students discuss how looking at humor in everyday situations can help them to manage their stress.

Other Stress Management Tools

There are a great many stress management tools that we can share with our students. Many of them depend on your own comfort level in sharing with your students. For example you may feel comfortable teaching breathing exercises but not yoga. Good sources for increasing your knowledge and experience include: community college classes, adult education programs, books, and the web. I also encourage you to practice using stress management tools in your own life in order to be able to share your experiences using the tools with students. For example in teaching meditation, it is helpful to share with students how you use meditation (e.g., setting a timer for 5 minutes of meditation each morning).

Massage

According the American Massage Therapy Association (2010), massage is a medically established stress management tool. Among its many benefits are decreased pain and tension and improved circulation and relaxation. The activities presented here involve self-massage. Students can also do hand massages, and foot massage can be offered to young children after a yoga session. It is important to emphasize respectful touch if students are massaging each other and students need to communicate if the touch is too hard or uncomfortable in anyway.

Face Massage

This activity helps students become aware of how much stress can be held in their face. Often, we can tell when a person is stressed simply by noticing his or her facial expression.

Start

Mindful sitting

Prompt

1. Wiggle your eyebrows and allow them to relax. Soften your forehead, as if it a smooth piece of ribbon. Use your fingertips to gently smooth your forehead area with light pressure.

2. Take in a big breath of air and puff out your cheeks. Now pucker up your lips and let all the air out of your lungs. Use your fingertips to gently massage the cheek bone area with small circles.

3. Smile a big smile, making your mouth as wide as possible. Now relax your mouth and wiggle your jaw. Massage your jaw joints with light pressure from your fingers moving in small circles.

4. Bring your hands together and rub them together to warm them up. Place your hands over your closed eyes and let them rest there for five deep, relaxing breaths.

5. Massage your earlobes with your thumb and forefinger.

6. Bring your forefinger and middle finger to the spot between your eyes and apply steady downward pressure to release tension. Hold for five deep, relaxing breaths.

7. Imagine a chalkboard right in front of your nose. Draw big slow circles with your nose on the chalkboard. Now, reverse and make big slow circles going in the other direction. Reach over and massage one side of your neck. (Pause.) Switch sides.

8. Reach across and massage the top of the shoulder area with gentle squeezes, circles, and downward pressure. (Allow enough time for students to work on one shoulder and then switch.)

9. Sit quietly and take five deep, relaxing breaths and notice how you feel after your massage.

Finish

Students can share how using self-massage to relieve tension in the neck, shoulders, and face is helpful to them as a stress management tool.

Tennis Ball Massage

Using tennis balls can provide enough pressure to relieve tension in muscles. It is a fun way for students to use an inexpensive item as a stress management tool.

Start

Mindful sitting against a wall. This activity can be done lying down, but it is easier to control the pressure of the ball when sitting up and using the wall. Alternatively, instead of moving the ball, the student can place it anywhere on the back where there is tension and hold it in place for 30 to 60 seconds.

Prompt

Place a tennis ball behind you, just below shoulder level so that the ball is held between your back and the wall. If the ball slips down, you can place it in a sock and hold onto the end of the sock to keep the ball in place. With the tennis ball held against the top or mid level of your shoulder blades, slowly start to move the ball across the back of your body, up and down the sides of your spine, and in slow circles. If you discover a knot, gently lean back against the tennis ball to apply pressure to the tense area for about 30 seconds. After students are finished use the tennis ball, they can continue to sit quietly with their back against the wall reinforcing a tall posture.

Finish

Ask students how using the tennis ball to massage their back is an effective stress management tool. Remind them that they can use the same method to massage their feet and hands.

Acupressure

Acupressure is used in Traditional Chinese Medicine and other Asian health modalities (Culbert & Kajander, 2007). As in Qigong (discussed earlier in the chapter), the concept of energy mobilization comes into play in acupressure as well. By applying steady pressure, stuck or blocked chi (energy) can be released, thus decreasing pain and increasing energy. There are hundreds of acupressure points, and the following activity offers a simple way to share this approach with students.

A Little Pressure Can Be Good!

In this activity, students experiment with applying steady pressure to pressure points in order to release tension.

Start

Mindful sitting

Prompt

1. Take deep belly breaths. We will use steady medium pressure with your middle three fingers for 30 to 60 seconds right between your eyes. Take five deep breaths.

(continued)

A Little Pressure Can Be Good!   *(continued)*

2. At the center of your sternum or breastbone, apply steady medium pressure in a small circular motion with your middle three fingers of both hands. Continue for 30 to 60 seconds. Pause and take five deep breaths.

3. Find the spot about 1.5 inches (4 centimeters) up from your wrist crease on your forearm with your palm facing up. This pressure point helps slow down racing thoughts. Apply steady medium pressure in a small circular motion with your middle three fingers at this spot for 30 to 60 seconds. Pause and take five deep breaths. Switch arms and repeat.

4. Find the spot 1 inch (2.5 centimeters) from the curve of your thumb (between your thumb and forefinger). Apply steady medium pressure with your first two fingers on the palm side of your hand and your thumb on the other. Continue for 30 seconds and then switch hands and repeat.

Finish

Ask students to discuss how it felt to use pressure to relieve tension. Invite them to share about situations in their lives where this tool might be helpful.

Aromatherapy

Aromatherapy uses the sense of smell to provide a tranquil stress management tool. Essential oils or original scent (e.g., pine needles, dried rosemary leaves) are preferable to synthetic ones which can lose their aroma quickly and do not provide the true essence of the smell. Essential oils can be purchased in health food stores and craft departments.

Students can make their own sachets or use ones made by the instructor. Apply a few drops of the oil to a cotton ball, then place a few of the cotton balls at the middle of a piece of cloth that is 4 inches (10 centimeters) square. Fold the corners into the middle of the cloth and tie them securely with a piece of ribbon or yarn. When not in use, the cotton balls can be stored in separate plastic bags; simply reapply the oils the next time they are used. If the sachets are kept together, they tend to take on each other's scents, thus losing their own distinct aroma. Do not allow the oils to be applied directly to the skin, which can cause allergic reactions.

Here are some suggested oils and their uses:

Foot Scrub and Soak Recipe

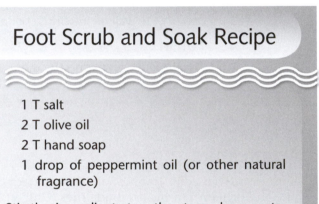

1 T salt

2 T olive oil

2 T hand soap

1 drop of peppermint oil (or other natural fragrance)

Stir the ingredients together to make a paste. Place your feet in a tub of warm water and let them soak for 5 minutes. Massage the scrub into your bare feet. Place your feet back in the warm water and let them soak for 5 to 10 more minutes. Rinse your feet and towel them dry.

- For calming: lavender, vanilla, sandalwood
- For waking up: peppermint (see the sidebar for a foot scrub using peppermint oil), dried rosemary, dried lemon or orange peel
- For soothing: ginger, pine needles

Smelling Fans

Students use inexpensive plastic fans that have been sparingly sprinkled or sprayed with scented essential oils. The gentle waving movement of the fan near the nostrils is a relaxing and calming activity.

Start

Mindful sitting

Prompt

Select a scented fan. Settle quietly into mindful sitting and gently move the fan back and forth in front of your face. Keeping your mouth sealed, slowly "sip" in the scent of the fan on your inhalation and slowly relax your breath out through your nose on the exhalation. You can try other fans with various scents.

Finish

Students can discuss their favorite scents presented in this activity and how they felt while using aromatherapy. They can also share about everyday smells that calm and relax them, such as freshly mowed grass, peppermint sticks, or hot chocolate.

Sand Garden

Sand gardens, in which one creates patterns in sand, are used in the East as a relaxing activity and a meditation focus tool. To give students ideas, you can display photographs of sand gardens. This activity can be done as a class (and the final product can be placed on the peace table; see chapter 6 for more) or as an individual project in which each student makes his or her own sand garden.

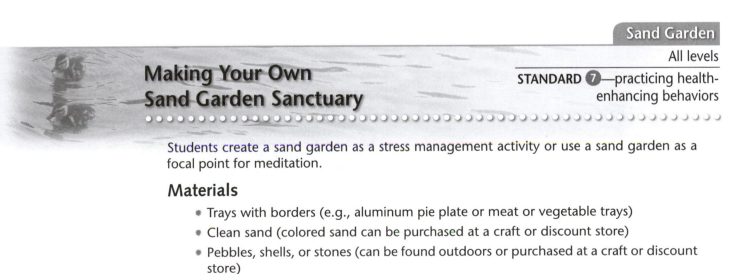

Making Your Own Sand Garden Sanctuary

Students create a sand garden as a stress management activity or use a sand garden as a focal point for meditation.

Materials

* Trays with borders (e.g., aluminum pie plate or meat or vegetable trays)
* Clean sand (colored sand can be purchased at a craft or discount store)
* Pebbles, shells, or stones (can be found outdoors or purchased at a craft or discount store)
* Rake (plastic fork or recycled forks purchased from tag sales)

(continued)

Making Your Own Sand Garden Sanctuary   *(continued)*

Start

Each student has his or her own tray with sand, a fork, and supplies (e.g., rocks, small pinecones, trinkets). Show examples of sand gardens to help students get an idea of possible shapes and placement of objects. Each student should pour about 0.5 to 1 inch (1 to 3 centimeters) of sand into his or her tray.

Prompt

Place pebbles or stones in an interesting pattern. Use the rake gently to make patterns in the sand. Imagine that you are sitting in this sand garden. In your mind's eye, you are sitting tall and strong in this beautiful garden. Take a few relaxing breaths. Imagine the gentle patterns in the sand washing over your relaxed body.

Finish

Invite students to share their sand gardens. They can talk about what is special about the shapes and patterns they made that were soothing and relaxing for them? They can also discuss other places where they spend time that could be made more soothing and relaxing (e.g., a small area in their bedroom).

Nature Table

The nature table holds various objects that the instructor or students bring in to observe. It can provide a quiet space where students select an object and reflect on the qualities of the natural objects and stress management. For example, students can share how they could emulate the various qualities of the natural objects, such as a rock being smoothed by water, a willow tree branch being flexible, or the possibilities of the many facets of a crystal.

You can also put a new object on the table and invite everyone to explore it and consider ways in which it symbolizes stress management. This activity could form a ritual in the classroom; as students arrive at class each day, they would know that it is time to be quiet, go to the nature table, and investigate what is new there.

© Elenathewise/fotolia.com

Nature offers us not just beauty but also opportunities for stress relief.

Exploring the Nature Table

Students explore items from nature to use as stress management objects.

Materials

Various objects from nature (e.g., rocks, water, willow tree branch, shells, nuts, pine cones, crystals—most anything from nature can be used)

Start

Students can select an object, investigate several objects and come up with a theme, or study one object presented for everyone at the nature table.

Prompt

Look for qualities of stress management tools within the objects on the nature table. For example, consider a bottle of water: If we heat it up, it can boil, just like when our feelings get heated up and out of control. With enough persistence and patience, water can smooth a rough object like a rock; similarly, we can learn to go with the flow. (Pause to allow students to continue thinking about water and stress management. The list of possibilities is endless! Students can write, draw, ask questions, or conduct research about the objects on the nature table.)

Finish

Students can share with each other how the nature object symbolizes stress management and how they could incorporate these concepts into their lives—for example, "I can sit quietly and listen to my water fountain when I get stressed."

Creative Ways to Build Students' Stress Management Skills

In solitude we give passionate
attention to our lives, to our memories,
to the details around us.

Virginia Woolf

Much of our education in the United States focuses on comprehending facts, which sometimes leaves but little time for students to apply these facts to their lives in authentic and meaningful ways. We need to provide as much opportunity as possible for students to practice skills that promote healthy behaviors. Doing so builds students' confidence in their ability to use stress management tools when they are needed.

Our task as instructors is to creatively provide many activities for students to practice stress management tools. This work begins with setting up the learning environment. We need to be thoughtful in setting up activities, deciding what language to use, and arranging the physical aspects of the activity room. When handled well, all of these factors help increase students' ability to practice stress management tools.

This chapter offers lesson and project ideas to infuse stress management concepts into curricula and after-school programs. It also discusses methods shown to engage students with other students through the work of mentoring.

Facilitating Stress Management Practice for Our Students

In the case of stress management, instructors should practice what they teach—the more you explore and practice the wide variety of stress management skills, the better. Students tend to be astute when it comes to figuring out whether an instructor walks the walk or just talks the talk. Stress management activities often go beyond students' comfort zones, and an instructor who has experienced the process as a beginner can be more empathetic in introducing tools to students. These activities may at times seem corny or weird to the Western mentality that focuses on always producing something. This unfamiliarity may be especially apparent in light of the United States' education expectations of accountability and deliverables (e.g., higher test scores preferred over lifelong skills). However different it may seem, stress management is an important practice; it is, in fact, something that we should practice continually in order to improve the quality of our lives. In this light, we are teaching process. As instructors we may never witness the behaviors of our students that result from what they learn with us. For example, we may not know if they decide not to smoke because of the breathing technique they learned. Our task is to offer as much practice in as many tools as we can so that students can take responsibility for their personal stress management. By modeling an intention of being open to trying out all the various tools, we can hope to encourage students to become creative in their own adoption of what works best for them.

Allowing for Student Choice

We should not expect that students will embrace and fully implement all of the stress management tools presented to them, but these activities give students the opportunity to try things and find out what works best for them. When faced with students who might resist trying these tools, you might think of your job as simply giving them a taste. Be grateful for slight shifts in their attitudes and for those times when you are privileged to witness an "aha" moment. Offer your students the intention of being open to the experience without forcing it. Emphasize that they have the option not to participate (as an alternative, they could choose to simply sit quietly). At all times, though, the hope is that the student will take what he or she needs, leave the rest with respect, and respect other students' rights to practice their choices.

Reflection

In order to best help our students become lifelong learners who practice stress management throughout their lives, we must give them opportunities for reflection. When we ask our students to reflect, they use introspection to process what they have learned and experienced in a given activity. Reflection may involve making connections with past knowledge and experiences; making and examining observations about knowledge and experiences; looking for personal meaning; developing theories or ideas; and deciding how to apply what has been learned to future choices.

Using Invitational Language

We need to set the bar high for our students, and the best way to do this is to use invitational language. Doing so means rephrasing from commanding language to affirming language, turning complaints into requests, being specific when offering compliments, and using words that allow students to make their own decisions by providing choices. Use statements that include words and phrases such as the following: consider, I suggest, would you like to help me out, help me understand, can we agree, get curious about, and explore. Here are some examples of invitational language:

- I invite you to close your eyes or soften your gaze, whichever is best for you.
- I know you are mindfully sitting when you are sitting tall and strong and looking at me with your mouth closed.
- When you are ready, slowly begin to stretch and make your way back to your seat. Can you be so quiet that no one hears you get up and move?
- If it interests you, explore the possibility of making your letter shape bigger—or choose to keep still, holding your yoga pose.

Creating a Calm Environment

Take a moment to observe your own teaching space and ask yourself the following questions (Northeast Foundation for Children, 2010).

- Is it conducive to helping students stay focused and on task?

- Do students have opportunities to self-monitor or peer-monitor? Do they know, for instance, that they can take a time-out and go to the peace table?
- Can students help or coach each other in learning stress management activities? For example, students might remind each other to take a deep breath.
- Does this space create a positive climate? Is the room arranged for inclusivity and cooperation?
- Are students responsible for their own experience and self-assessment?
- Are procedures in place so that students know, for example, what is expected when starting their day, making transitions (e.g., for lunch or emergency drills), when asking for help, and when using the bathroom?
- Do students know what behavior is expected for the task they are doing (e.g., total silence, quiet sharing, or use of indoor voices)?

For ideas about setting the stage for optimal stress management experiences, see the sidebar titled Setting Up the Environment for Practicing Stress Management Skills.

Setting Up the Environment for Practicing Stress Management Skills

- Modulate your voice to be soothing and relaxing.
- Practice script prompts beforehand to ensure that the language is developmentally appropriate and comprehensible for your students' learning level. Use words that are comfortable to you. If you are not comfortable with the jargon used in this book, make sure to adapt to meet the needs of your intended audience.
- Use lighting to enhance the experience. Fluorescent lighting is harsh and can undercut a relaxation experience. Electric candles and natural sunlight work well.

- Be firm, fair, and friendly in your expectations for the class. Students with behavioral issues probably need practice in stress management the most!
- Make the activities student-centered and student-directed. Have students volunteer to lead activities or suggest good times for the class to take a Stress Less break.
- Notice the environment of your teaching space. Is it cluttered, disorganized, distracting? Spend the time needed to clean up and de-stress the space. Schedule a clean-it-up session during which the entire class cleans and then takes ownership of the decluttered space.

(continued)

(continued from previous page)

- Work with what you have. Your school may not have a quiet yoga studio. Students may be wearing street clothes. There may be only 10 minutes for an activity. Be creative and flexible in finding ways to infuse stress management!

- Model stress management skills within your students' learning experiences—not just during concerted stress management time. For example, if a student is stressing over an assignment, encourage him or her to do belly breaths.

- Use a variety of learning experiences that incorporate the various senses as well as engaging multiple learning styles.

- For ESL students, consider researching the appropriate words for discussing stress management in other languages.

- Allow students to express their feelings in appropriate ways using the many activities in chapter 5 and modeling for students correct ways (e.g., soften your tone, use respectful language).

- Be cognizant of students who may need a referral for stress symptoms or disruptive behavior. Follow up on these referrals.

- Less is more. Allow enough time to introduce activities, practice, finish, return students' energy to the teaching space, and process the activity. In stress management, we want to create an atmosphere of patience and enough time—not being in a hurry.

- Allow for students to provide feedback to you about the activities by means of a suggestion box or by leaving enough time for students to process and assess the outcomes of the activities.

- Use reflection as much as possible. It allows students to witness their own skill development. Process beyond what students might think you want to hear. For example, instead of settling for "it was relaxing," follow up by asking, "What did you do to help you relax?"

- Establish rituals that students look forward to. For example, use the singing bowl to start quiet reading time or designate part of your Friday afternoons as the Stress Less Hour.

- Allow for silence. It is okay not to fill up every moment with instruction. Take pauses and observe your students.

- Use music to drown out distracting noise and drapes, sheets, or the like to darken the room during stress management activities.

- Use artwork, flowers, or other natural objects to transform a classroom into a stress management oasis.

- Change the pace by turning an activity in which students usually talk to each other (e.g., snack time) into a silent retreat.

- Be patient. Not all students will participate at any given time. Respect their choices but also enforce their obligation to respect your right and that of other students to practice.

- Be willing to honor and hold the space. Awkward or difficult topics and moments may arise. Allow students to process what is happening.

- Make sure that your students take care. Empower them with permission to stop an activity at any time, open their eyes, and sit quietly or find a place of refuge (e.g., peace table).

- Use word banks to provide students with the vocabulary to connect feelings to words. Examples include bumpy, smooth, exhausted, curious, impatient.

Here are some activities to help students start processing the meaning of stress in their lives. The activities can be done in succession so that students build their knowledge and skills from one to the next.

Think, Pair, Share:
Let's Talk About Stress

This activity allows students to recognize their individual signs of and reactions to stress. It also helps them think about how such signs might be manifested in other people. In this three-part activity (think, pair, share), students first think on their own, then pair up, and finally share with the whole group.

Start

Seated at tables

Prompt

Write down your own answers to the prompt questions, then pair up with another student to discuss your answers. Finally, we will come together as a whole group and share our responses.

Here are the questions:

* What stressors do you typically experience?
* What are the signs or symptoms of stress that you exhibit or experience?
* Does everyone react to the same stressors in exactly the same way? Provide some examples.
* What healthy stress management tools do you use?

Finish

Have students fill out an "exit ticket" listing three common stressors and three common stress symptoms. Each student hands in an exit ticket at the end of the class period. The information you gather from the tickets allows you to determine whether or not students learned the session's core concepts: sources of stress, signs and symptoms of stress, and responding to stressors and stress management tools. (The exit ticket approach can be used at any time to assess whether or not the health-enhancing messages of a given activity have been learned.)

Wellness Checkup

This activity allows students to reflect on how they respond to stressful situations.

Start

Students are seated at tables, and each has a pen and a Wellness Checkup worksheet (page 231 of appendix A).

Prompt

Complete the Wellness Checkup worksheet.

Finish

Students can share their responses to the various statements in parts I and II with a partner, small group, or the entire class. They can also offer additional statements that reflect on stress and stress management in their lives.

Name _____ Date _____

Wellness Checkup

Part I

1. Place a check mark next to the statements that apply to you.

   When I am stressed, it is hard for me to:

   ☐ concentrate on homework or projects

   ☐ enjoy doing fun things with my family or friends

   ☐ go to school or other normal activities

   ☐ play or hang out with my friends

   ☐ talk to my teacher or a trusted adult

   ☐ relax

   ☐ eat

   ☐ exercise or workout

   ☐ sleep or get out of bed

2. Now write another sentence or more to continue your thoughts concerning the statement(s) that you checked in number 1 about your stress.

   _____

3. Check in: On a scale of 1 (not well) to 5 (very well), how are you feeling?

Date:	1	2	3	4	5	Reflection
Emotionally						
Spiritually						
Socially						
Intellectually						
Physically						(continued)

From N.E. Tummers, 2011, *Teaching stress management: Activities for children and young adults* (Champaign, IL: Human Kinetics).

© Photodisc

Sometimes students handle stress by withdrawing from social circles. Students should learn to recognize this tendency and strategize healthier ways to manage their stress.

Partner Case Studies

This activity allows students to use a case study to practice looking objectively at a stressful situation.

Start

A case study is a short description of a stressful situation; examples are included in the Partner Case Studies worksheet (page 233 of appendix A). You can generate additional case studies based on your students' experiences of stressful situations either by writing them yourself or by having students provide them.

Prompt

Working with a partner, examine each case study for stressors, stress signs and symptoms, a negative stress management response, and a proactive stress management response. Then share your responses with the rest of the class.

Finish

Ask students to identify and discuss both positive and negative methods for stress management.

Name _____ Date _____

Partner Case Studies

- You are pitching in tomorrow's baseball game. What are some ways in which you can manage your stress and do your best? _____

- A friend wants you to do something that your parents have told you not to do. How could saying no help you manage your stress? _____

- The science fair is coming up, and you must design the project as well as explain the results to a judge. What goal could you set so that you are successful in your project? _____

From N.E. Tummers, 2011, *Teaching stress management: Activities for children and young adults* (Champaign, IL: Human Kinetics)

Stand Up for Stress Management

This activity allows students to learn about protective factors in stress management and discover other students who use them.

Start

Seated in a circle

Prompt

I am going to read, one item at a time, a list of protective factors for stress management (see the Protective Factors for Stress Management handout on page 234 of appendix A for suggestions). After reading each item, I will ask you to stand up if you use this protective factor—for example, "Stand up if you take time to practice gratitude." If you do practice that protective factor, stand up at that time. After each item, ask students to evaluate how each stress management activity is a tool for decreasing or managing stress.

Protective Factors for Stress Management

- Taking time to be grateful
- Practicing active listening
- Planning for a goal
- Planning one's schedule in order to take breaks
- Taking responsibility for one's actions
- Maintaining an internal locus of control
- Confiding in a trusted adult or friend
- Enjoying solving problems
- Reflecting or thinking back on a situation and knowing how to do it differently next time
- Being empathetic
- Being self-aware
- Having a plan for the future
- Feeling connected
- Being optimistic
- Being creative
- Having a sense of humor
- Going with the flow
- Being generous
- Avoiding drama
- Avoiding gossip
- Being a good friend
- Volunteering to do things for others

From N.E. Tummers, 2011, *Teaching stress management: Activities for children and young adults* (Champaign, IL: Human Kinetics)

(continued)

Stand Up for Stress Management   *(continued)*

Finish

Discuss with the group how they might incorporate one or more of the protective factors into their lives. Emphasize to the group that they do have these protective factors and to try as often as possible to include them in their lives (e.g., talking to a trusted adult).

Stress Management Bingo

Elementary through young adult

STANDARD **1**—core concepts and
7—practicing health-enhancing behaviors

This activity is a variation on Stand Up for Stress Management. It serves as an icebreaker that helps members of the group get to know each other and see how others use various stress management methods.

Start

Students are seated in the learning area, each with a Stress Management Bingo card (page 235 of appendix A) and a pen.

Prompt

Your bingo card lists various proactive stress management methods (e.g., talking with a trusted adult). For each method listed, find another student in the class who uses that stress management method, then write that student's name in the designated square. You can use each student's name only once per card.

Finish

Process this activity by asking each member of the group to introduce another member by stating his or her name and the activity that he or she practices. Students can then discuss the ways in which members of the group practice proactive stress management. To help students connect the tools to stress management, you can lead a discussion about how the tools work. For example, how exactly does physical activity help improve mood and decrease anxiety and depression? After discussing this question, students can brainstorm ways to increase their own physical activity and make it enjoyable.

Stress Management Bingo

Reads for pleasure	Takes bubble baths	Takes naps	Walks for fitness
Laughs a lot	Does yoga	Uses a planner	Listens to music
Enjoys being outdoors	Likes time alone	Tells all to best friend	Prays or meditates
Sews, cooks, bakes	Does puzzles	Volunteers	Dances

From N.E. Tummers, 2011, *Teaching stress management: Activities for children and young adults* (Champaign, IL: Human Kinetics).

Are You Someone Who . . .?

The following activity is a variation on Stress Management Bingo.

Materials

Nonstick circles or poly spots (one per student)

Start

In a learning area big enough for students to move around in, place poly spots on the floor (one fewer spots than the number of students participating). Whichever student does not have a spot to stand on will serve as facilitator for the next round of the activity.

Prompt

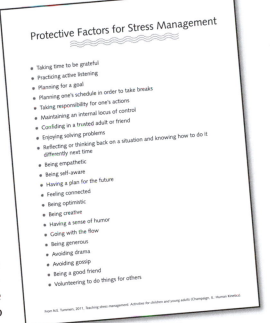

1. When the facilitator names a specific tool from the Protective Factors for Stress Management handout (page 234 of appendix A), you will respond in one of two ways. If you have not used the tool, you will stay put on your spot; if you have used the tool, you will find another spot to stand on (only one person per spot). If you are the student who does not have a spot to stand on, you will serve as facilitator for the next round of this activity. (Serve as the first facilitator and start the activity by saying, "Are you someone who . . .?" and name a protective stress management tool while moving to a spot left empty by a moving student.)

2. The next facilitator, says "Are you someone who . . .?" and names a protective stress management tool not yet mentioned. The game continues until everyone has had a chance to be the facilitator.

Protective Factors for Stress Management

- Taking time to be grateful
- Practicing active listening
- Planning for a goal
- Planning one's schedule in order to take breaks
- Taking responsibility for one's actions
- Maintaining an internal locus of control
- Confiding in a trusted adult or friend
- Enjoying solving problems
- Reflecting or thinking back on a situation and knowing how to do it differently next time
- Being empathetic
- Being self-aware
- Having a plan for the future
- Feeling connected
- Being optimistic
- Being creative
- Having a sense of humor
- Going with the flow
- Being generous
- Avoiding drama
- Avoiding gossip
- Being a good friend
- Volunteering to do things for others

From N.E. Tummers, 2011, *Teaching stress management: Activities for children and young adults* (Champaign, IL: Human Kinetics).

Finish

Help students process the wide variety of protective stress management tools. Emphasize that not all may seem to be a good stress management tool to everyone but to appreciate and respect individual preferences.

Techno Logs

In this project, students investigate their own technology habits—that is, the ways in which they use electronics for entertainment—which can act as stressors due to wasted study time, physical inactivity, and miscommunication. The Center for Screen-Time Awareness (www.screentimeinstitute.org) is an advocacy group that works to raise awareness of the effects of excessive screen time on students, as well as measures to reduce screen time in society as a whole.

Start

Each student will maintain a log which can be a general journal or photocopied sheets with specific data items to be included such as date, time of day, mode of electronic use, and duration of time using.

Prompt

For 1 week, you will keep a daily log of the time you spend connected to electronics for entertainment purposes (not for schoolwork). Activities to log include television watching, digital games, web surfing, social networking, and texting. You should also write a daily reflection on how technology affects your stress.

Next, set a goal and collect data for the following week in an effort to reduce your screen time to less than your current use per day and substitute alternative activities instead (e.g., reading, going outside, shooting hoops).

Finish

At the end of the 7-day trial period, have students share their experiences and reflect on their goals. Send a letter or e-mail to parents to invite them to participate in this project as well; for example, a parent could also set a goal to reduce screen time to less than their current use per day for entertainment purposes.

Stress Management Projects

Group projects encourage cooperative learning by giving students the chance to work in collaboration toward shared goals. Projects allow students to apply the strengths-building skills of problem solving, decision making, active listening, sharing responsibility, cooperation, and accountability. Building this skill set can help students be proactive in stress-inducing situations.

Positive Eggs

In this activity, students write positive or inspirational statements that will be delivered to another class or group. They could also lead a stress management activity—for example, a quick session on relaxed breathing—with their chosen audience.

Materials

* Plastic eggs that open and close (often available at discount stores)
* Slips of paper that can be folded into the eggs

Start

Students each receive a plastic egg and a slip of paper.

Prompt

1. For this project, we will create positive stress management messages. Your egg's message should address your intended audience (e.g., a first-grade class, adults at a senior center) and show conviction—we really believe in the importance of this stress management message. Here are two examples to get the ball rolling: "If there is to be peace in this world, it begins with me." "The force is with you—what are you going to do with it today?"

2. The eggs will then be delivered by the students (using an egg carton or basket) to their intended audience to enjoy and use as a stress management tool.

Finish

This stress management activity could include journaling about the statements they created or brainstorming how they can use the statements' messages in their own lives.
In this project, students work in pairs and demonstrate the ability to investigate community resources for stress management.

Scavenger Hunt

Start

Students need web access, phone books, and community resource literature (e.g., pamphlets) in order to access valid and reliable resources for information about stress management.

Prompt

1. Working with a partner, search for and investigate resources for stress management in our community.

2. Once you have investigated various resources, share with the group the value of the resources you found, what services those resources provide, and any other relevant information. Examples include the skate park, the library, the farmers' market, yoga classes, volunteer opportunities, parks, art classes, music venues, poetry readings, comedy clubs, and counselors.

Finish

Students can make a bulletin board or web page describing good stress management resources.

Stress Management Brochure

In this project, teams of 2 or 3 students design brochures to advocate the practice of stress management by members of a target audience.

Start

To help students envision their brochures, show examples of effective brochures and not-so-effective ones. Discuss the key elements of the well-designed brochures. The target audience for the brochures can be selected either by you or by the students; good examples include the students' own peer group, students in younger grades, and adults in the community.

Prompt

Your brochure should feature a clear health-enhancing message, be supported by relevant information, show awareness of your intended audience, encourage healthy choices for stress management, and be passionate and convincing (Joint Committee on National Health Education Standards 2007).

Finish

Have students make copies of the brochures to deliver to their target audience.

Nature Connection Space

In this activity, students design natural stress management spaces for themselves or other groups. Older students might use the activity as a service-learning project to help another group (e.g., members of an assisted-living home or an elementary school class).

Although we depend on nature for our lives—think of food grown in fields and water coming from reservoirs—students today spend a great deal of time shut off from nature. They are often inactive, sitting for long periods of time while being entertained by a screen, perhaps in the absence of any natural light. Indeed, students spend entire school days in artificial environments such as overheated school rooms illuminated by florescent lights. Students also consume volumes of artificially colored foods that are manufactured or over-processed. Perhaps by introducing students to more natural stress management spaces, we can advocate for all to enjoy the stress-reducing effect of being outdoors.

Start

This project may be hard to conceptualize unless students are provided with models. You can show pictures or videos of natural stress management spaces. You may have an idea for the project (e.g., a butterfly garden), or you can have students come up with an idea of their own.

Prompt

In this project, the class will be a design team. The team will design an outdoor learning area where students (or another intended audience) can read, study, or practice stress management activities. Here are some possibilities:

* Research and design a labyrinth.

* Design a nature trail.

* Research and design a parcourse—a trail featuring fitness stations embedded into natural surroundings.

* Design and plant a healthy school garden.

* Design an outdoor reflection space that includes flowers, other plants, and a water fountain (inexpensive solar-powered fountains are available).

Finish

Students can establish a visitor log inviting comments by users in order to evaluate possible revisions or additions for the space. Students can also survey visitors about the effectiveness of using their nature connection space as a stress management tool.

Stress Management Toolbox

In this project, students create a stress management toolbox by selecting stress management tools and either collecting the necessary materials or making the tools for others to use.

Start

Sample projects can be shown to help students generate ideas—for example, a stress management toolbox could be an inexpensive plastic tub containing spa materials (e.g., aromatherapy candles or oils, relaxing music recordings, and instructions for giving someone or oneself a face massage).

Prompt

In teams of 3 or 4, students plan and design stress management toolboxes. Here are some ideas for stress management tool boxes:

* Design a peaceful stress management toolbox. The toolbox could be a plastic bin kept at a designated table space in the classroom that contains stress management tools and activities, such as earphones for listening to relaxing music, stress balls, puzzles, and beanbags to sit on while doing relaxed breathing.

* Design a stress management toolbox that includes activities for a Stress Less Day (e.g., DVDs of funny movies, instructions for relaxation activities, and a gift certificate for a chair massage therapist to provide massage sessions).

* Design and sew a peace quilt. For example, students could design and make quilt blocks for a homeless shelter or a family in need. Quilt themes could involve using stress management tools, such as "things to do to feel peaceful" with depictions of pleasure reading, yoga, or being outdoors on the quilt squares.

Finish

Students could use their projects as sources for fundraising. For example, parents could buy a stress management toolbox for their students before final exams. The resulting revenue could be donated to charitable organizations or used to purchase supplies for future service learning projects for people in need.

Curriculum Infusion

Curriculum infusion involves integrating the concepts and skills of stress management across the curriculum into all subjects or individual classes in the learning community. This integration might take the form of the entire student body actively using stress management tools in team-building activities or a schoolwide town hall meeting. It could also involve individual instructors planning lessons on stress management (e.g., Stress Less sessions on Friday afternoons) or infusing content and skill into standard subjects such as reading.

Healthy and Happy Learning Community Meeting

For the town hall meeting activity, students will take part in a meeting attended by the entire learning community, including administrators. Students need the opportunity to interact in learning community experiences in order to understand and feel connectedness. Although the town hall meetings are usually moderated by the teachers and administrators, in upper grades the class president could be the moderator with adult guidance.

Start

Students should arrive at the meeting prepared with agenda items to bring up and should be ready to contribute suggestions for solutions to agenda items submitted by others. These agenda items should include issues that affect the happiness and health of the campus or learning community (e.g., students leaving garbage in the hallways or being disrespectful of visitors to the school by booing other athletic teams).

Prompt

1. Attend the town hall meeting.
2. Follow the Learning Community Meeting Guidelines:
   * Everyone is greeted by name with a handshake and eye contact.
   * All members of the group are encouraged to take responsibility for sharing and contributing.
   * The group enjoys a group activity such as yoga, singing, or dancing (see also the activity named Genevieve's Happy Teachers Retreat Day described later in this chapter).
   * Both good and "needs work" news is shared.
   * All members of the learning community check in—that is, state their name and express any feelings or thoughts they would like to share in one sentence: "My name is Jasmine, and I am tired today." While Jasmine speaks, no one else interrupts or comments; the speaker owns the space.

   Adapted from the Northeast Foundation for Children Responsive classroom. Available: www.responsiveclassroom.org/about/research.html.

3. Suggest your agenda items. The student body should take responsibility to get the problem solved. For example, if an agenda item addresses the state of the cafeteria, all members of the learning community will work together to come up with a solution to the problem.
4. Effective meetings lead to meaningful action that resolves issues. You are accountable for taking the necessary steps to implement these solutions. Note action steps to be reviewed at the next meeting.

Finish

After the meeting, lead a discussion about the meeting. Ask students how it went, what they learned, and how they feel about the issues that were brought up. Help students process the information for possible future topics at future meetings.

STANDARD **7**—practicing health-enhancing behaviors

Suggestion Box

This activity encourages students to take action to voice a solution to problems in the classroom.

Start

Students write suggestions to problems in the classroom and include their names. Suggestions should be reviewed by the instructor before the class meeting in order to make sure that they constitute suggestions that are both legitimate and appropriate for class discussion.

Prompt

1. I will read a suggestion out loud to you. The suggestor then has 1 minute to speak about his or her suggestion without interruption.

2. Each of you then offers suggestions out loud or writes one or two additional resolutions to the problem to be shared with the class.

3. Then, as a class, we will decide which suggested resolution is the best and select the necessary action steps to implement the suggestion.

4. At the end of the session, the student(s) who had the most suggestions chosen will be recognized as the peacekeeper(s) until the suggestion box is opened again.

Finish

It is important for students to follow up on the effectiveness of their action steps. Have students discuss revisions to be implemented when necessary.

STANDARD **7**—practicing health-enhancing behaviors

I Have a Question Box

In our classrooms, students may have questions but feel embarrassed to ask them. Often, students do not want to be singled out if they have personal questions but in fact other students are often wondering about the same things such as school issues they are experiencing. This activity provides a chance for students to ask questions anonymously. It also gives the instructor time to prepare an answer.

Start

The instructor reads students' questions ahead of time in preparation for answering appropriate questions at a class meeting.

Prompt

1. If you have a question that you are embarrassed to ask out loud, you can ask it anonymously by writing it down on a piece of paper and putting it into the I Have a Question box.

2. Periodically, I will read a question from the I Have a Question box to the class. After I have shared some of my thoughts about the question, I will ask you to share your

ideas as well. (For example, if elementary students are concerned about transitioning to middle school, the teacher and students can make suggestions on how to make this transition less stressful.)

Finish

This activity can be used as a jumping-off point for more discussion and reflection by students. Some questions may have simple answers, whereas others may require more time to process (e.g., why are there bullies?).

Genevieve's Happy Teachers Retreat Day

This idea came from one of my undergraduate students who remembered doing this activity in high school. It calls for teachers in the school to provide stress management activities in which they actively participate and want to share with students. An afternoon could be set aside in which the entire school participates in a stress management activity of their choice.

Materials

As needed for each teacher's special activity (e.g., cooking ingredients and utensils, yarn and knitting needles, various other craft supplies)

Start

Students choose from a menu of teacher-led stress management activities. First pick might be awarded by means of a lottery or as a reward for academic achievement or good behavior for individual students or classrooms. Possible activities include knitting, listening to music, doing yoga, taking a nature walk, playing basketball, meditating, and cooking healthy snacks.

Prompt

Choose one of the teacher-led stress management activities you would like to participate in. Practice this activity with the teacher to learn more about it and how it relates to stress management.

Finish

Students can write thank-you notes to the presenting teacher in which they describe their experience of the activity as an effective stress management tool.

Tokens of Appreciation

This activity uses tokens to reward a classroom of students when they practice proactive stress management tools such as volunteering to help another student, or sitting quietly during quiet time. Tokens could also be credited toward a reward such as a Stress Less afternoon or time in the outdoor stress management space.

Materials

Good supply of poker chips and a large container to collect them in

Start

Teachers observe student behavior during everyday class activity.

Prompt

You will be given a poker chip when I "catch" you doing a proactive stress management activity (e.g., complimenting another student, taking belly breaths when frustrated, using I-messages). I will state exactly what you did to earn the token. At the end of each day, I will collect all the tokens handed out and put them into a jar. This way, you will work together as a class to increase your overall token count each week.

Finish

All members of the staff are encouraged to use the tokens of appreciation and to "catch" students in areas where interpersonal stress, such as pushing and shoving, can occur (e.g., in school bus areas, at recess, in the cafeteria, and in hallways).

Circle of Respect

In this activity, students use role playing to demonstrate positive ways to resolve conflict.

Start

Put students into teams to act out role-play scenarios. The scenarios can be written by you or by the students in order to better capture the specific stressful situations that arise in their lives, schools, and communities. The situations should address physical bullying, as well as other issues (e.g., prejudice, coercion, gossiping).

Prompt

In this activity, you will analyze a situation by paying attention to both internal and external influences. You will then role-play the situation to demonstrate positive methods for achieving a resolution.

Finish

Students can use a scorecard to list the positive methods used by the actors in their role playing.

Team-Building Activities

Stress management concepts and skills form an important part of team building. The following activities focus on helping students engage with their peers in order to help them. Most of these activities are done in small groups. The atmosphere is low pressure so that students can feel comfortable and safe in exploring the sometimes difficult tasks of building trust and working together cooperatively. Use reflection prompts to help students process the team-building aspects of the activity. Here are some examples:

- What roles did the different members of your group take on to complete this activity?
- How well did you communicate with each other?
- What happens when too many team members try to take over the team—or when no one steps up?
- Did all team members contribute ideas and participate in this activity? How could the team have worked better together?
- What are some ways in which we can communicate trust and cooperation?

Team Building

Middle school through young adult

STANDARD ④—interpersonal communication and ⑦—practicing health-enhancing behaviors

Zany Scavenger Hunt

In this activity, students work cooperatively in a team to find objects from a scavenger hunt list provided by another student team. You can make suggestions or rules about the kinds of objects that students can put on their list (e.g., nothing stolen or disrespectful). You can also determine the designated limitations—for example, search within a designated area, for a specified amount of time, and without asking for help from anyone outside the team.

Start

Divide the class into teams.

Prompt

1. Work with your team to make up a list of clues to locating or collecting designated items.
2. Exchange clue lists with another team.
3. Work with your team to follow the clues to search for the items on the list you received from the other team. The entire team must work and stay together at all times. When you are done or the time limit is up, return to this room.

Finish

Teams can share about the methods they used to work cooperatively together.

Team-building activities, such as scavenger hunts, allow students to build the rapport, trust, and interpersonal skills needed in order to create a social support system that can help them during stressful times.

Making a Cup of Hot Chocolate

This activity helps students see how important it is to use clear and precise language in building team cooperation and communication. The prompt is for making a cup of hot chocolate but can be modified for other common snacks students might make (e.g., making popcorn).

Materials

Cups, hot chocolate mix, spoons, access to hot water

Prompt

1. Working individually, write a recipe for making a cup of hot chocolate. Your recipe should specify the exact steps in the right order.

2. Now, watch as a student volunteer tries to make a cup of hot chocolate by following one of the recipes chosen at random. The student volunteer must follow the recipe exactly as it is written. If the directions do not provide exact directions (e.g., open the packet of hot chocolate), the student will not fill in the gaps.

3. We will then work together as a whole group to write more precise directions as needed.

Finish

Students can process ways to help each other communicate better. They can also identify situations in which clear, concise communication is useful or necessary.

Color Me Awesome

Students work together to create art that infuses positive messages about each other.

Materials

Large rolls of newsprint, paint, markers

Start

Students are formed into teams that are set up in large work areas.

Prompt

Have one member of your team lie down on a large piece of newsprint. Have another team member trace the body outline of the student who is lying down. (Once the outline has been drawn, the student in question can stand up.) Then each member of your team should identify a part of the body that the student who was outlined uses to make a positive contribution to the team or classroom and then colors in the body part he or she specified. For example, the mouth could symbolize smiling, joking, or speaking the truth. Each member of the team contributes to coloring in positive characteristics and attributes of the student who has been outlined. Do the same for each member of your team.

Finish

Teams can share each student's body portrait and the important characteristics each member of a team contributes.

Team Architects

Team members work together cooperatively and creatively to build sculptures with their bodies.

Start

Gymnastics mats or carpeting are useful for this activity. It is imperative to emphasize safety and cooperation so that all team members are safe and included.

Prompt

Your team will make a sculpture by using your bodies as the clay or marble. Your sculpture must include everyone in your group. Here are some sculpture ideas: a bicycle, a bird's nest in a tree, a computer screen and keyboard with a mouse and hard drive. Be aware of the importance of safety and cooperation in doing this activity (e.g., not forcing any student into difficult or unstable sculptures).

Finish

Have students process the steps for working together in building their sculpture and how they ensured all participants are included and safe.

Supreme Team Challenge

In this activity, each team is challenged to pay attention and communicate clearly.

Start

You will need an activity area and an adjacent area that is closed off and private.

Prompt

In this challenge, your team is charged with replicating a specific sculpture or puzzle; however, only one team member at a time can look (for 10 seconds) at the design of the sculpture or puzzle. That team member must then report back to your whole team what the team needs to do to copy the design. Your team then has 30 seconds (or an appropriate length of time) to try copying the design. If your result is incorrect, another team member is sent to look at the original sculpture or puzzle for 10 seconds and then report back to the team—and so on, until your team duplicates the design correctly.

Finish

Students can process the steps necessary for working together in this challenge so that all were included and safe.

Air Traffic Control

This activity challenges the team to pay attention to each member.

Start

Students are grouped in teams of four or more in a large activity area that is carpeted or protected with gymnasium mats.

Prompt

In this activity, one member of your team serves (blindfolded) as a helicopter pilot, another team member serves as an air traffic control tower, and the rest of your team members act as obstacles around the landing spot. The air traffic controller verbally guides the blindfolded pilot to walk unassisted to the landing spot while the rest of your team members stand in various spots to form obstacles (e.g., trees, boulders). The pilot has to safely guide the helicopter to the exact landing spot without touching the obstacles.

Finish

Students can process how making clear and direct communication is important in working together.

Dream Team Newspaper or Web Page

In this activity, teams write newspaper articles featuring stories about individual members or about instances of team members working together.

Start

Students need pens and paper or access to word processing software.

Prompt

In this activity, you will work in teams to write feature articles or columns about projects you have worked on as individuals or in teams or about job descriptions for your dream job. You could also write Dear Editor letters to share team members' achievements or personal dreams. You can also use other typical sections of a newspaper, such as personals, sport briefs, comics, art, and advertisements.

Finish

Students can display their newspapers throughout the school or sell copies and donate the proceeds to a charity. Alternatively, they could exchange copies of the newspaper for cans of food to donate to a local food bank.

Team Building
Middle school through young adult
STANDARD **2**—analyzing influences
and **8**—advocacy

News 24-7

Students develop a news story in which their team members identify another team's positive characteristics and accomplishments. This could be a great activity after the class has been working in teams for a while (i.e., at the end of the school year) to provide recognition of each team's accomplishments and their members' contributions.

Start

Pens and paper for each team

Prompt

Working with your team, write a news story using all the names of another team's members. Include their assets, contributions to their team, and other positive characteristics. You will then read aloud or publish your story to share with all the teams.

Finish

Students can discuss the important assets of good team members. Students can explore the outstanding characteristics that play important roles in their stories. They could also read their stories to students in younger grades to inspire them to cultivate these assets and become good team members.

Team Building
Middle school through young adult
STANDARD **7**—practicing health-
enhancing behaviors and **8**—advocacy

Team Video

Students recognize each team member's unique contributions to the team and address them in a short video.

Start

Teams need access to video or audio recording equipment, as well as a quiet area in which to make their recordings. This activity uses small teams of four to six students.

Prompt

In this activity, your team will design a short video of about 2 minutes to be presented without editing. Your team will develop your video to include a news flash about each member of your team. These news flashes can include the team member's achievements or something else about him or her that is woven into a typical news report (e.g., weather, traffic, sports). All members of your team must contribute to your video.

Finish

Students can share their creations with younger students and explore with them the important characteristics of teamwork.

Meaningful Mobiles

This activity asks students to create symbols that represent their contributions to the team.

Start

Students need craft materials and other supplies (e.g., magazines, string or yarn, coloring supplies) for this activity. In addition, each student needs a clothes hanger or two wooden chopsticks.

Prompt

A one-dimensional presentation of a person's strengths, support, goals, and dreams is known as a vision board. In this activity, you will construct a *multi*dimensional and multimedia mobile. Using string and either a clothes hanger or chopsticks connected to form a hanger, you will attach objects to represent your strengths and contributions to your team. The objects should be personal and meaningful to you (e.g., a feather representing the lightness you bring to dark and difficult situations).

Finish

Students share their mobiles with the group, explaining the important aspects of their team building mobile symbols.

Advocating for Stress Management

Mentoring, peer mentoring, service learning, and after-school Stress Less clubs all offer creative and authentic ways to help students become advocates for stress management—both for themselves and for others. These methods can be used individually or in combination. This section provides an example of an after-school Stress Less club that uses mentoring and service learning.

Mentoring

Mentoring typically involves an older student mentoring a younger student. It is valuable for mentor pairs to use various activities presented in the preceding chapters as learning experiences for both the mentor and the mentee. One excellent model for mentoring is provided by Big Brothers Big Sisters (BBBS) where mentors meet with their mentee weekly and participate in activities provided by the BBBS as well as activities on their own. Another example is provided by the Sisterhood Project (featured in an after-school program described at the end of this chapter), in which university students mentor at-risk high school students. The college students gain valuable experience as mentors and also learn about and participate along with their little sisters in stress management activities that they can use as tools in their own busy lives. In the Sisterhood Project, students of all ages realize the common bonds they share as they address similar stressors (e.g., relationship troubles, heavy schoolwork load). They also spend time together practicing the stress management tools in a supportive and safe atmosphere and sharing about those experiences.

Take Your Little Brother or Sister to School Day

In this mentoring activity, younger students (little brothers and sisters) spend a day or half-day at school with older students (big brothers and sisters). This approach can work for elementary students shadowing middle schoolers, middle school students shadowing high schoolers, and high schoolers shadowing college students.

Start

Permission is needed from parents of the littles.

Prompt

In this activity, your little brother or sister spends a day or half-day shadowing you in order to learn the routine of their future school and see the school from your perspective as a mentor. You can give the littles some helpful advice or even conduct short workshops on topics such as getting involved in school activities, selecting courses, and establishing good study habits. Share with your little sister or brother some of the stressors you might encounter such as homework, balancing school work and athletics, and fitting in with your peers. Ask your little brother or sister about their stressors and suggest ways they might prepare for and handle these stressors (e.g., having a day planner or joining a club).

Finish

Both mentors and mentees can come together after the time spent together and process the stressors and stress management tools they would utilize. Mentor pairs can continue to do activities together, and the littles can stay in touch with their bigs and ask questions as they arise.

Dear Little Sibling

In this activity, the little sibling receives a letter from the big sibling prior to the start of the mentoring project. A photo can be attached in order to put a face with the name and the information about the big sibling.

Start

The big sibling fills out the Dear Little Sibling worksheet (page 236 of appendix A). The letters will be sent to the little prior to the first meeting.

Prompt

At the first meeting, the little and big sibling pair up and share more about their interests. A Dear Big Sibling worksheet can be created for the little siblings to fill out. This activity is

(continued)

Dear Little Sibling

My name is _____, and I like to be called _____.

My major is _____, and when I graduate I hope to _____.

1. My favorite artist is _____
2. Something you can't tell by looking at me is _____
3. I am most scared about _____
4. My favorite snack is _____
5. I am the most worried about my _____
6. I have a dream, which is _____
7. My biggest button pusher is _____
8. What stresses me the most is _____
9. My favorite way to chill is to _____
10. My friends say this about me _____

From N.E. Tummers, 2011, *Teaching stress management: Activities for children and young adults* (Champaign, IL: Human Kinetics).

Older students can mentor younger students by talking about their experiences, their stressors, and the ways in which they relieve their stress.

a nice icebreaker to facilitate bonding between the big and little siblings.

Finish

Pairs can share with the group what surprised them and what they learned about their new siblings. This activity helps both little and big siblings to realize they have a lot in common when it comes to stressors and stress management.

Peer Mentoring

Peer mentoring has been defined as involving an "effective, personalized relationship where peers support each other to take action toward specific goals" (Burak, 2002, p. 8). The benefits of the mentoring model have been cited in the literature for various professions and populations (Guetzloe, 1997). In this mentoring relationship, peers learn about and practice lifelong skills, such as interpersonal communication, problem solving, decision making, and self-care in a nonjudging and supportive atmosphere. The inclusion of peer mentoring approaches in the curriculum also helps address diverse learning styles because of the hands-on approach as students spend time working together one on one. Peer mentors can use many of the activities presented in the previous chapters (e.g., decision making, goal setting, practicing active listening) to enhance the mentoring process.

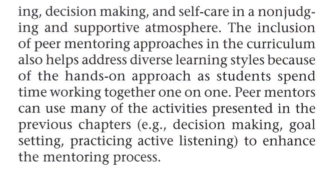

Peer Mentoring

Elementary through young adult

STANDARD **4**—interpersonal communication, **6**—goal setting, and **7**—practicing health-enhancing behaviors

Peer Problem Solving

In this peer mentoring activity, pairs of students encourage each other in setting a stress management goal.

Start

It is best to assign pairs randomly to avoid the pitfall of having students pick friends who may not keep them on task or be honest about their progress toward their goal. This activity can last from 5 to 15 weeks.

Prompt

In this activity, you will work with a partner to help each other write a personal, clear goal for stress management. Each week, you and your partner will meet to process your progress toward your personal goal. You will demonstrate active listening and make suggestions to help your partner focus on achieving his or her goal.

Finish

Peer pairs can share with the group the ways in which they help each other move toward their goals. At the end of the project, students can reflect on their peer mentors and on the mentoring process, as well as their progress toward meeting their stress management goal.

Service Learning

Students can experience the empowering quality of wellness education for both themselves and others through service learning. The goal is to provide students with the opportunity to explore the relevance of classroom subject matter to the real needs of the community and to work collaboratively with their peers. In service learning, the community site identifies critical needs, and the service project is designed by students to meet those needs. This process allows students to see the reality of a community's stress management needs, as well as issues that the students may not have experienced before. Often, the cooperating community site does not have the time or resources to stay current with research or best practices, and the students who participate in service learning projects are often seen as role models who are young and enthusiastic. In addition, the information and skills conveyed by the older students may have a broader appeal and effect on younger community members as they look up to positive role models closer to their age rather than adults.

Service learning differs from volunteering. A service learning project involves a partnership between students and another group in the community, such as an elementary class, a senior citizen group, or participants in an after-school program. Let's say that some high school students enrolled in a health education class are studying stress management. For their service learning project, they could plan and implement stress management activities for elementary students who are experiencing anxiety and behavior problems during test taking. For example, they could lead a 30-minute session for elementary school students that included breathing exercises, a relaxation activity, and a guided imagination activity for test taking.

Service learning also involves a reflection component, which allows students to increase their knowledge on the subject and develop their skills in problem solving and teamwork. Reflection also enables students to appreciate how the process brings about changes in their perceptions of themselves, of their work with peers, and of their connection and relationship with the community.

You can find ideas for service-learning lesson plans and projects from around the country at Learn and Serve America's National Service-Learning Clearinghouse (www.servicelearning.org/what-service-learning).

Service Project for Stress Management

In this service learning activity, upper-grade students (e.g., high school seniors) plan and implement a stress management activity for a target group (e.g., incoming first-year students).

Start

You will need to carefully address logistics, including the project's duration, the needs (and number of members) of the target group, and any needed supplies and space.

Prompt

In this activity, you will plan and implement a stress management activity for a target group. To help you do this, we will address the specific stress management needs of your intended audience, possible stress management activities to include in your projects, and planning and implementing the project.

Finish

Help students reflect on their service learning project. Here are some sample reflection questions:

* What insights did you gain about your target group?
* What insight did you gain about yourself?
* What benefits did members of the target group gain?
* What benefits did you gain?
* How might you plan and implement this project better next time?
* What perceptions did you have about service learning before doing this project? And now?

After-School Programs: Starting a Stress Less Club

The Stress Less club can either be open to everyone or restricted to students who are recruited or advised to join. All students can benefit from stress management activities. However, with recruited students (e.g., students struggling with test anxiety), the activities can be chosen to address more specific needs. The club should meet at least once a week, depending on interest and the availability of space and supervision. The club's leaders might be high school students taking responsibility for their club with guidance and advice from a faculty advisor. Leaders can also be recruited from local colleges or the community at large. The club can invite appropriate community members (e.g., yoga instructors, massage therapists, biofeedback therapists) to speak about stress, lead activities, and provide services. It is suggested that all participants—including mentors, volunteers, and guest speakers—sign confidentiality pledges so that trust will be honored. The confidentiality pledge can include language which clearly states that members of the Stress Less club will not share information disclosed by other members of the club. Here is a good ground rule: What happens in the Stress Less club stays in the Stress Less club!

Greeting to Know Each Other

This icebreaker can be used at the first meeting of the Stress Less club. Students form a circle and step forward if they practice a particular stress management tool called out by the instructor. Students can also share their names and answer questions about their participation.

Start

Standing in a circle

Prompt

Step forward and share details if you do the following (pause after each to allow for responses):

* Have a hobby or craft (What is it?)
* Play an instrument (What kind?)
* Read for pleasure (What is your favorite book?)
* Watch funny movies (What is your favorite?)
* Do something for others or volunteer (What is it?)
* Listen to relaxing music (What artist?)
* Confide with your best friend (How are you a good friend?)
* Spend time outdoors and in nature (Doing what?)

Finish

Students can share more strategies that they use to manage stress in a positive way.

Example of an After-School Program

The Sisterhood Project is an after-school program that provides stress management and mentoring services for "at risk" urban high school females. Students deemed at risk for stress face a broad spectrum of situations, including but not limited to poverty, family situations, exposure to crime, truancy, failing grades, pregnancy, substance abuse, physical and emotional harassment, isolation, depression, aggression and other poor coping behaviors, anxiety, and physical illness. The school district recognized a critical need to provide these students with effective stress management programs.

The 8-week program involved physical, cognitive, and experiential methods for stress management and reduction. The "big sisters" who served as wellness mentors were female college student volunteers. Reported measures of awareness about stress and use of stress management techniques were assessed before and after participation in the program. Significant improvements were seen in the at-risk students' abilities to seek out supportive peers and adults who listened and supported their positive health choices (Tummers 2009).

Thus this project empowered at-risk students by providing them with cultural and social experiences and helping them build their stress management skills. In addition, by participating in the Sisterhood Project on a college campus, they were engaged in positive mentoring relationships and given a chance to see college as an option in their own futures. For the college students, this partnership with the community allowed them to experience the powerful effect of wellness. They were also able to see opportunities for possible future roles in working with at-risk youth through community organizations and nonprofits. Another Sisterhood Project was conducted at a residential facility

(continued)

(continued from previous page)

for incarcerated 14- to 16-year-old females. In this version, volunteer female college students served as mentors to the girls at the locked-down facility. Due to confidentiality issues, research was not conducted with this cohort, but anecdotal evidence confirmed the incredible power of mentoring and stress management programs for both the college students and the at-risk girls. See table 6.1 for a sample unit plan.

Table 6.1 Eight-Week Unit Plan for Stress Less Club

Week and topic	Social and emotional or life skill emphasis	Breath exercise	Stress management activity	Journal activity	Materials needed
Week 1: sharing	• Dear Big/Little Sibling • Sharing about ourselves	• Belly breath • Mantra breath	• Journaling • Breaking the ice and getting to know my sister	What surprised you about this connection activity and about meeting your sister?	• Journals, pens • Activity space • Chairs
Week 2: stressors	• What are your top five stressors? • Share similarities and differences in your stressors and those of your sister.	• Mindful breathing • Singing bowl	Mindfulness activities: body scan, autogenics, eating a raisin	What are some things you can do to help you feel better when faced with stressors?	• Activity space • Journals, pens • Raisins
Week 3: sadness	Understanding and discussing sadness (activity)	Counting the breath	Chilling out! Progressive muscle relaxation	What are ways for you to express yourself when you feel sad?	• Script for relaxation • Journals, pens • Relaxation space
Week 4: compliments	Students select M&M's candy and make a statement depending on the color: • Red: compliment the person on your right • Blue: state something you like about personality in general • Yellow: state something you like about your style • Brown: compliment someone in the group who does positive actions	Dragon breath	• Yoga to calm and relax • Guided imagination: rainbow activity	How does it feel to say something positive about yourself and hear it from others?	• M&M's • Rainbow activity script • Yoga space, mats • Journals, pens
Week 5: anger	Recognizing anger and proactive anger management	Coloring the breath	Yoga to energize: active yoga poses	What are some healthy ways to handle your anger? Who are people you can talk to when you get angry?	• Yoga space, mats • Journals, pens

(continued)

Table 6.1   (continued)

Week and topic	Social and emotional or life skill emphasis	Breath exercise	Stress management activity	Journal activity	Materials needed
Week 6: stressful situations	• What situations can we avoid? • What situations can we learn to accept? • In what ways can we adjust our attitudes?	Noisy breath	Art therapy: Mandalas, photo collage	• How is your portrait or art piece different from the image you project to others? • How does your mandala represent your dreams or your journey in life? • What did you learn about stress management today?	• Mandala outlines • Newsprint and paints • Magazines, scissors, glue sticks • Arts and crafts space with tables and chairs
Week 7: affirmations	Writing affirmations	Affirmation breath	• Spa day • Aromatherapy • Massage therapy • Music therapy	What are some ways in which you can combat negative thinking with positive thinking?	• Pedicure supplies • Aromatherapy supplies • Music and player • Index cards • Relaxation space
Week 8: support system	Students write on construction paper the names of trusted and loved adults, helpful adults for assistance and support, trusted friends, and items and activities that provide relief from stress and promote positive thoughts. The papers will be posted in the activity area.	Count to 10 activity	• Random acts of kindness: students select one random act of kindness to do in the next week. • Final party	• When is it most important for you to remember your support system for stress management? • What is your random act of kindness?	• Construction paper • Journals • Drinks, cookies • Tables, chairs

Adapted, by permission, from J.V. Taylor and S. Trice-Black, 2007, *Girls in real life situations. Group counseling activities for enhancing social and emotional development* (Champaign, IL: Research Press).

Reproducibles

Contents

Name _____   Date _____

Mindful Work Habits

Describe your work space at home or where you study.

1. Is it absolutely quiet? _____

   _____

2. Are you alone or are others there? _____

   _____

3. Are you sitting? On a chair or couch? On the floor? _____

   _____

4. What is the best time for you to work? After school, after you have done physical activity? Or later at night? _____

   _____

5. How do you break up your study time? Fifteen minutes and then a stretch, or longer periods of time? _____

   _____

6. When reading, how long can you focus on the materials in one sitting?

   _____

7. How do you decide what you will study? Do you use a to-do list or a day planner? _____

   _____

8. What are some ways in which you could make your study habits more mindful? _____

   _____

From N.E. Tummers, 2011, *Teaching stress management: Activities for children and young adults* (Champaign, IL: Human Kinetics).

RU Listening Script

Student 1: I'm frustrated; my pencil broke.

Student 2: I like strawberries.

Student 1: I need to find a pencil sharpener.

Student 2: It's my birthday next week.

Student 1: I can't finish my worksheet.

Student 2: Why can't you finish your worksheet?

Student 1: Because my pencil broke.

Student 2: Oh, your pencil broke. Here, I have an extra one.

From N.E. Tummers, 2011, *Teaching stress management: Activities for children and young adults* (Champaign, IL: Human Kinetics).

Name _____   Date _____

Hardiness Discussion and Writing Exercises

Write about each of the qualities of hardiness.

1. When have you shown these qualities in your own life? _____

_____

_____

2. When have you observed these qualities in others? What were the specific situations? _____

_____

3. How could you cultivate these qualities more in your daily life? _____

_____

_____

4. Consider your connectedness. Who do you feel connected to? _____

_____

_____

5. Think about two ways you can improve your connectedness. _____

_____

_____

6. What do you feel is your dharma—or your life purpose—and what can you do now to help you move toward and realize this life purpose?

_____

_____

7. What does self-responsibility mean? How does self-responsibility relate to dharma?

_____

_____

From N.E. Tummers, 2011, *Teaching stress management: Activities for children and young adults* (Champaign, IL: Human Kinetics).

Name _____   Date _____

Stress Detective Log

Stressor	Situation and time	Proactive response or activity
(Example) Can't find homework.	3 minutes before the bus is picking up for school. Mom is yelling at me to be ready for school bus.	Take a few deep breaths. Take 5 minutes before going to bed to set up backpack each night—making it a habit.
(Example) Too tired, too much homework.	8 p.m. After dinner and basketball game.	Organize study area—shut off phone. Use study hall time to study and not socialize.

From N.E. Tummers, 2011, *Teaching stress management: Activities for children and young adults* (Champaign, IL: Human Kinetics).

Name _____   Date _____

Wellness Brainstorm

1. What are the personal strengths from each of the areas of the wellness model?

_____

_____

_____

2. What are your challenges in each of these areas? _____

_____

_____

_____

3. Do you see change or setback as a challenge or as a stumbling block where you quit or give up? _____

_____

_____

(continued)

From N.E. Tummers, 2011, *Teaching stress management: Activities for children and young adults* (Champaign, IL: Human Kinetics).

4. Think of two examples of stressful changes or setbacks that have happened recently. For each, write a strategy that you could use to change your "frame of mind" or attitude and view the situation as a positive challenge. _____

_____

_____

_____

_____

5. How important are your lifestyle choices? _____

_____

_____

_____

_____

6. Think of two areas in your lifestyle you could change. _____

_____

_____

_____

_____

From N.E. Tummers, 2011, *Teaching stress management: Activities for children and young adults* (Champaign, IL: Human Kinetics).

Name _____   Date _____

Gratitude Journal

I am grateful for _____

_____

_____

_____

I am appreciative of _____

_____

_____

_____

I am so fortunate to have _____

_____

_____

_____

Thank you for _____

_____

_____

_____

From N.E. Tummers, 2011, *Teaching stress management: Activities for children and young adults* (Champaign, IL: Human Kinetics).

Name _____ Date _____

Wise Owl Checklist

☐ Is this the right time to speak?

☐ Have you listened carefully and thought about what you want to say?

☐ Have you found the right words to say so that you're saying what you really mean, or should you take a quiet moment to think about it some more?

☐ Are your words kind?

From N.E. Tummers, 2011, *Teaching stress management: Activities for children and young adults* (Champaign, IL: Human Kinetics).

Name _____   Date _____

What Pushes Your Angry Buttons?

Review the following list of frustrating situations and make a check mark by any that you have experienced. You can also write in any additional ways you react when angry.

☐ Being late

☐ No money

☐ Friends gossiping

☐ Parents' expectations

☐ Parents fighting

☐ Slow computers

☐ Boring classes

☐ Forgetting something important

☐ People who interrupt

☐ People who are rude

☐ Your boss

☐ Waiting for downloads

☐ Losing stuff

☐ Disorganized people

☐ Long lines

☐ People changing plans at the last minute

☐ Friends who won't stop texting you

☐ Rules

☐ Losing an important game

☐ Group work

☐ Being ignored

☐ Being treated unfairly

☐ Being disrespected

☐ Being lied to

Other button pushers (list):

_____

_____

_____

_____

_____

From N.E. Tummers, 2011, *Teaching stress management: Activities for children and young adults* (Champaign, IL: Human Kinetics).

Name _____   Date _____

Dealing With Difficult Situations

Work on your own and check off the methods that you use to deal with difficult situations.

☐ Walk away

☐ Just be nice

☐ Be direct

☐ Take turns

☐ Hang out with someone else

☐ If I can't say something nice, just be quiet

☐ Come up with a solution

☐ Use an I-message

☐ Set a boundary

☐ Be clear and stick to my word

☐ Ignore them

☐ Step into their shoes

☐ Ask them questions

☐ Ask a friend or trusted adult for an objective point of view

☐ See the situation from a different point of view

☐ Take calming breaths and ask for what I need

☐ Make a choice not to be influenced by this situation—try to keep your emotions separate from the situation so that you can look at it objectively

☐ Tell the person I don't know and will get back to them

☐ Agree to disagree

☐ Affirm that I can only change my point of view, not theirs

Other ways to deal with difficult people (list):

_____

_____

_____

_____

_____

From N.E. Tummers, 2011, *Teaching stress management: Activities for children and young adults* (Champaign, IL: Human Kinetics).

Stop, Drop, and Be Calm

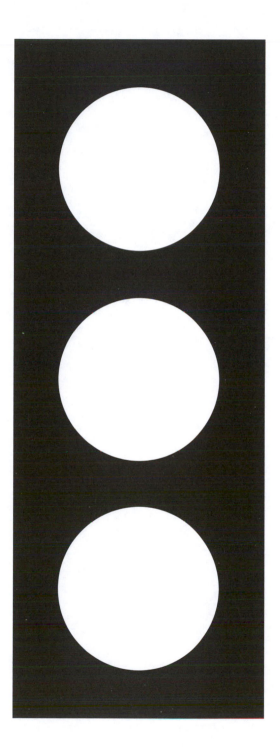

From N.E. Tummers, 2011, *Teaching stress management: Activities for children and young adults* (Champaign, IL: Human Kinetics).

Stop, Breathe, and Act Smart

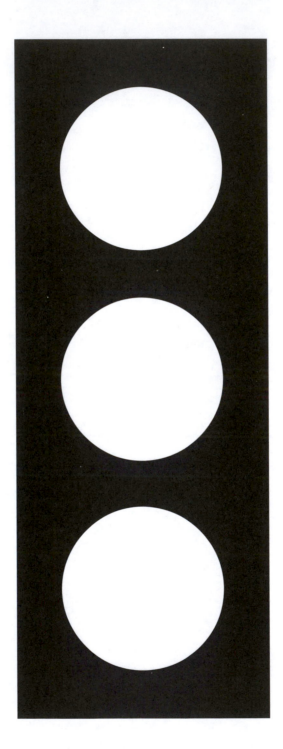

From N.E. Tummers, 2011, *Teaching stress management: Activities for children and young adults* (Champaign, IL: Human Kinetics).

Name _____ Date _____

Strong Feelings Log

Strong feeling situation	Physical reaction	Emotions	Thoughts

From N.E. Tummers, 2011, *Teaching stress management: Activities for children and young adults* (Champaign, IL: Human Kinetics).

Name _____   Date _____

Problem Diary

~~~~~~~~~~~~~~~~~~~~~~~~~~~~~~~~~~~~

1. How are you feeling? _____

_____

_____

2. What is the problem? _____

_____

_____

3. What are some actions you can take to solve this problem? _____

_____

_____

4. What might be some of the consequences of these actions? _____

_____

_____

5. What is the best solution, and what is your plan? _____

_____

_____

6. Reflect on your plan. What worked? What would you change?

_____

_____

_____

From N.E. Tummers, 2011, *Teaching stress management: Activities for children and young adults* (Champaign, IL: Human Kinetics).

Name _____   Date _____

Finding the Calm

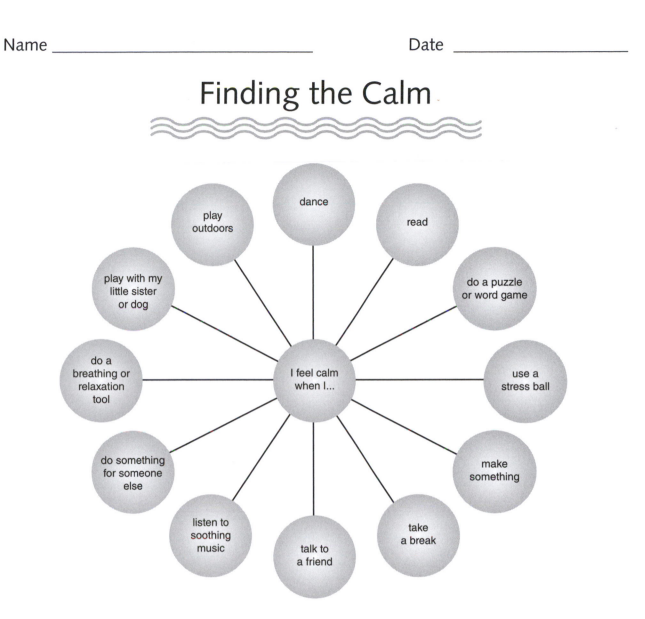

1. Brainstorm a list of tools that you can use to help yourself calm down.

_____

_____

_____

_____

_____

_____

_____

_____

(continued)

From N.E. Tummers, 2011, *Teaching stress management: Activities for children and young adults* (Champaign, IL: Human Kinetics).

2. You can create some drawings or develop your own mind map to help yourself remember what helps you find your calm.

Temperature Rising and Chilling Out

Start at the bottom of the thermometer with the words "no problem," then work your way up the thermometer using words that describe yourself as you get more upset. The top of the thermometer is boiling mad!

On the bottom of the worksheet are ice cubes where you can write things you can do to cool off. For example, you could write, "I know I can choose to be cool" or "I can feel myself relax and calm down."

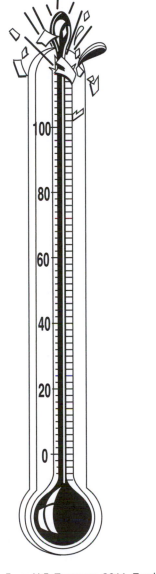

From N.E. Tummers, 2011, *Teaching stress management: Activities for children and young adults* (Champaign, IL: Human Kinetics).

Active Listening Topics

1. Tell me about the funniest situation you have ever experienced. _____

_____

_____

_____

2. Tell me about a person you admire and why you admire him or her. _____

_____

_____

_____

3. Tell me about the proudest moment in your life. _____

_____

_____

_____

4. Tell me about your dream career. _____

_____

_____

_____

5. Tell me about your favorite memory. _____

_____

_____

_____

6. Tell me the hardest thing about romance. _____

_____

_____

From N.E. Tummers, 2011, *Teaching stress management: Activities for children and young adults* (Champaign, IL: Human Kinetics).

Name _____   Date _____

The Straight-Talk Building Blocks

Rewrite your dialogue situation using the straight-talk building block procedure shown below. Examples of dialogue to rewrite:

* Your mom keeps yelling at you over little things.

* You text and leave messages for your friend, but he or she never texts or calls you.

* Your big brother keeps telling you what to do and annoyingly play-punching you.

* Your boyfriend is ignoring you and pays more attention to his friends than to you.

* A kid you don't even know keeps calling you names in the hall.

1. State what is happening objectively. _____

_____

_____

_____

2. Explain how it makes you feel—not putting down the other person by telling them how they should feel, but stating how you feel. _____

_____

_____

_____

3. State specifically what you want in the form of a request. _____

_____

_____

4. Invite the person to respond to your request and ask for agreement. Example: "I feel (what you are feeling) when you (what the person did). I want (what you want the person to do)." Then ask for agreement. _____

_____

_____

From N.E. Tummers, 2011, *Teaching stress management: Activities for children and young adults* (Champaign, IL: Human Kinetics).

Compliment Categories

The way the
person behaves:
"I appreciate it
when you take turns."

The way the person is:
"I like that you smile all the time."

What the person does:
"That is awesome you can roller skate."

What the person has:
"Those are cool shoes."

How the person looks:
"I like your smile."

From N.E. Tummers, 2011, *Teaching stress management: Activities for children and young adults* (Champaign, IL: Human Kinetics).

Name _____   Date _____

Good Decision Checklist

≈≈≈≈≈≈≈≈≈≈≈≈≈≈≈≈≈≈≈

☐ Can this decision be made on my own, or do I need help? What kind of help is best for this situation?

☐ What are the healthy options in this situation? What is best for me and my family? Did I consider all of the options and possible consequences for each option?

☐ What are the potential outcomes in both the short term and the long term for each of the healthy options?

☐ How effective was my decision? What could I do different next time to make it healthier?

Scenarios

Pair up with a partner and generate solutions for the following situations:

1. Provide an example of a not-so-good decision you made in the past. Use the Good Decision Checklist to decide which step you skipped or did not fully execute.

   _____

   _____

2. Provide an example of a decision that you made impulsively without thinking through all the steps. _____

   _____

3. Provide an example of a time when a decision was needed but you procrastinated until it was too late to make a good or achievable decision. _____

   _____

   _____

4. Provide an example of a situation in which you did not give your opinion and others made the decision for you. _____

   _____

   _____

From N.E. Tummers, 2011, *Teaching stress management: Activities for children and young adults* (Champaign, IL: Human Kinetics).

Name _____   Date _____

Formula for Goal Setting

1. Awareness: Think about what you want and brainstorm or research things that will help you to accomplish that. For example, you might think about a problem you are having and think about what, specifically, could help make the situation better. List those thoughts, ideas, and possible resources here. _____

_____

_____

2. Own it: Many times, goals are expectations created by parents, teachers, or coaches. In order to achieve goals, it is critical to exercise self-responsibility and make sure that it is a personal goal and under your control. When the goal is seen in a positive light—this is what I want—it is more likely to be achieved than when it is seen as a punishment and forced upon you. My goal is: _____

_____

_____

3. Action: What are the specific steps for action? Break the goal down into bite-size pieces known as action steps and set a deadline for each step. My action steps are: _____

_____

_____

4. Specific measures: Often, we don't really know what we want, and thus the goal is ambiguous or vague, which makes it difficult to know what we need to do. Action steps need to involve specific, measurable actions. The ways that I will objectively measure or evaluate progress towards my goal include: _____

_____

_____

_____

From N.E. Tummers, 2011, *Teaching stress management: Activities for children and young adults* (Champaign, IL: Human Kinetics).

Name _____   Date _____

Steps for Disputation

~~~~~~

1. Look at the evidence (the facts) to support stressful thoughts. Look for assumptions—conclusions made without sufficient information. When approaching challenging beliefs, beware of the tendency toward tunnel vision; it is better to widen the focus instead. _____

_____

_____

2. See if there is a positive explanation for the situation. _____

_____

_____

3. Put the situation in perspective. How important will this be tomorrow or next week? How can the situation be viewed in a more holistic and healthy way? Try to change your framing of the situation and use less dramatic or less emotionally packed language to describe it. _____

_____

_____

4. If you are not part of the solution, the problem will remain. What proactive actions could you take in this situation rather than dwelling on the problem—chewing and stewing—which perpetuates the stress cycle? Set an intention of not allowing the disturbing thought to override your best response to the situation.

_____

_____

_____

From N.E. Tummers, 2011, *Teaching stress management: Activities for children and young adults* (Champaign, IL: Human Kinetics).

Debbie Downer or Polly Positive Scenarios

* Ashley gets a C on her English paper.

* José misses the bus for school.

* Phillip gets put on the JV baseball team rather than varsity.

* Keisha doesn't get invited to a popular girl's party.

From N.E. Tummers, 2011, *Teaching stress management: Activities for children and young adults* (Champaign, IL: Human Kinetics).

Mind Map

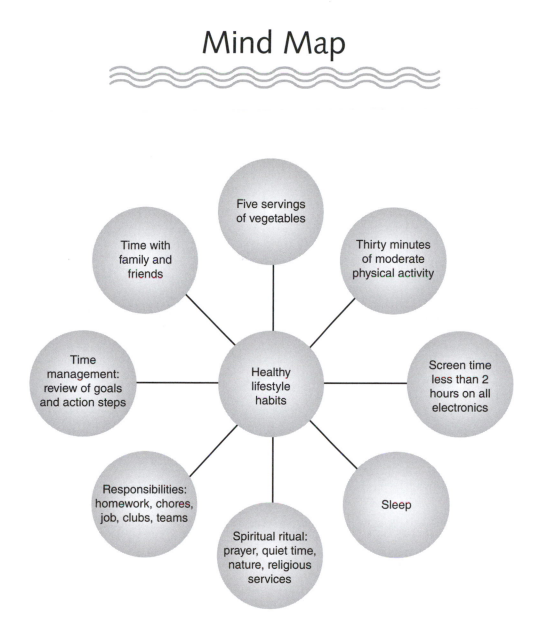

From N.E. Tummers, 2011, *Teaching stress management: Activities for children and young adults* (Champaign, IL: Human Kinetics).

Name _____   Date _____

Physical Activity Challenge Calendar

Day ____	Day ____	Day ____	Day ____	Day ____	Day ____	Day ____

Name _____   Date _____

Fill in the Blank!

~~~~~~~~~~~~~~~~~~~~~~~~~~~~~~~

1. I am unique because _____

_____

2. I am diverse because _____

_____

3. The accomplishment I am most proud of is _____

_____

4. My dream for the future is _____

_____

5. I take time to relax and become centered by _____

_____

6. I enjoy movement each day by doing _____

_____

7. My nutrition habits are _____

_____

8. I feel connected to _____

_____

9. I creatively express myself by _____

_____

10. The way I define my spirituality is _____

_____

From N.E. Tummers, 2011, *Teaching stress management: Activities for children and young adults* (Champaign, IL: Human Kinetics).

Name _____   Date _____

My Accomplishments

List your accomplishments below.   *Steps to success*

1. _____   _____

   _____   _____

   _____   _____

2. _____   _____

   _____   _____

   _____   _____

3. _____   _____

   _____   _____

   _____   _____

4. _____   _____

   _____   _____

   _____   _____

5. _____   _____

   _____   _____

   _____   _____

6. _____   _____

   _____   _____

   _____   _____

From N.E. Tummers, 2011, *Teaching stress management: Activities for children and young adults* (Champaign, IL: Human Kinetics).

Name _____   Date _____

My Reflection on the Serenity Prayer

1. What are my strengths? _____

_____

2. What are my challenges? _____

_____

3. What areas in my life can I change? _____

_____

4. What areas in my life can I improve upon? _____

_____

5. What are areas I need to accept? _____

_____

6. After exploring this motto in depth, take a look at all of the answers you have given. Think about your own life. What are some wisdoms that are important to you? Write them here: _____

_____

_____

7. What do you think a good motto for yourself would be? _____

_____

_____

My wise person motto: _____

_____

_____

From N.E. Tummers, 2011, *Teaching stress management: Activities for children and young adults* (Champaign, IL: Human Kinetics).

Name _____   Date _____

Sharing My Stress Strategies

1. When I am bullied, I _____
   _____

2. When I am the center of attention, I _____
   _____

3. When I feel awkward, I _____
   _____

4. When my feelings are hurt, I _____
   _____

5. When someone puts me down, I _____
   _____

6. When I am under a lot of stress, I _____
   _____

7. I fear _____
   _____

8. One way I relax is _____
   _____

9. My favorite stress management tool is _____
   _____

From N.E. Tummers, 2011, *Teaching stress management: Activities for children and young adults* (Champaign, IL: Human Kinetics).

Name _____   Date _____

Steps for Goal Setting

1. What is your long-term goal? Is it measureable? Is there a deadline—a time by which you want to achieve it? How will you know if you have achieved this goal? How will you celebrate the accomplishment of this goal? _____

   _____

   _____

   _____

2. Where are you now? Are you doing things to move toward the goal? Are you doing things that compromise your progress toward the goal? _____

   _____

   _____

   _____

3. What resources and support do you need in order to achieve this goal?

   _____

   _____

   _____

4. What are attitudes and other obstacles you need to overcome in order to make progress toward this goal? _____

   _____

   _____

5. Break the goal down into small action steps that you can do and set a deadline for each one of these action steps. _____

   _____

   _____

   _____

From N.E. Tummers, 2011, *Teaching stress management: Activities for children and young adults* (Champaign, IL: Human Kinetics).

Tickle My Funny Bone

1. Make up oxymorons. An oxymoron is a combination of two words that form a contradictory message such as "living dead." _____

   _____

   _____

2. Make up puns. A pun is a form of word play. For example, "Did you hear about the guy whose whole left side was cut out? He's all right now." _____

   _____

   _____

   _____

3. Write absurd headlines for a tabloid newspaper. For example, "Cat Eats Balloons and Floats Away to California Coast." _____

   _____

   _____

   _____

4. Complete this sentence. For example, "You know you are really stressed when *you are wearing two different socks.*" You know you are really stressed when . . . _____

   _____

   _____

   _____

5. Take an ordinary photograph and create a caption that makes the pictured situation funny. _____

   _____

   _____

From N.E. Tummers, 2011, *Teaching stress management: Activities for children and young adults* (Champaign, IL: Human Kinetics).

Name _____   Date _____

Wellness Checkup

Part I

1. Place a check mark next to the statements that apply to you.

    When I am stressed, it is hard for me to:

    ☐ concentrate on homework or projects

    ☐ enjoy doing fun things with my family or friends

    ☐ go to school or other normal activities

    ☐ play or hang out with my friends

    ☐ talk to my teacher or a trusted adult

    ☐ relax

    ☐ eat

    ☐ exercise or workout

    ☐ sleep or get out of bed

2. Now write another sentence or more to continue your thoughts concerning the statement(s) that you checked in number 1 about your stress.

    _____

    _____

3. Check in: On a scale of 1 (not well) to 5 (very well), how are you feeling?

Date:	1	2	3	4	5	Reflection
Emotionally						
Spiritually						
Socially						
Intellectually						
Physically						

(continued)

From N.E. Tummers, 2011, *Teaching stress management: Activities for children and young adults* (Champaign, IL: Human Kinetics).

Part II

Complete the following open-ended questions:

1. At school, I do my best when _____

   _____

   _____

   _____

2. At school, the areas in which I need to improve are _____

   _____

   _____

   _____

3. My friends and family would say that I am _____

   _____

   _____

   _____

4. I am proud of _____

   _____

   _____

   _____

5. I get upset when _____

   _____

   _____

   _____

From N.E. Tummers, 2011, *Teaching stress management: Activities for children and young adults* (Champaign, IL: Human Kinetics).

Name _____   Date _____

Partner Case Studies

~~~~~~~~~~~~~~~~~~~~~~~~~~~~

* You are pitching in tomorrow's baseball game. What are some ways in which you can manage your stress and do your best? _____

_____

_____

_____

_____

* A friend wants you to do something that your parents have told you not to do. How could saying no help you manage your stress? _____

_____

_____

_____

_____

* The science fair is coming up, and you must design the project as well as explain the results to a judge. What goal could you set so that you are successful in your project? _____

_____

_____

_____

_____

From N.E. Tummers, 2011, *Teaching stress management: Activities for children and young adults* (Champaign, IL: Human Kinetics).

Protective Factors for Stress Management

* Taking time to be grateful

* Practicing active listening

* Planning for a goal

* Planning one's schedule in order to take breaks

* Taking responsibility for one's actions

* Maintaining an internal locus of control

* Confiding in a trusted adult or friend

* Enjoying solving problems

* Reflecting or thinking back on a situation and knowing how to do it differently next time

* Being empathetic

* Being self-aware

* Having a plan for the future

* Feeling connected

* Being optimistic

* Being creative

* Having a sense of humor

* Going with the flow

* Being generous

* Avoiding drama

* Avoiding gossip

* Being a good friend

* Volunteering to do things for others

From N.E. Tummers, 2011, *Teaching stress management: Activities for children and young adults* (Champaign, IL: Human Kinetics).

Stress Management Bingo

Reads for pleasure	Takes bubble baths	Takes naps	Walks for fitness
Laughs a lot	Does yoga	Uses a planner	Listens to music
Enjoys being outdoors	Likes time alone	Tells all to best friend	Prays or meditates
Sews, cooks, bakes	Does puzzles	Volunteers	Dances

From N.E. Tummers, 2011, *Teaching stress management: Activities for children and young adults* (Champaign, IL: Human Kinetics).

Dear Little Sibling

My name is_____, and I like to be called

_____.

My major is_____, and when I graduate I hope to

_____.

1. My favorite artist is _____

2. Something you can't tell by looking at me is _____

_____

3. I am most scared about _____

_____

4. My favorite snack is _____

5. I am the most worried about my _____

_____

6. I have a dream, which is _____

_____

7. My biggest button pusher is _____

_____

8. What stresses me the most is _____

_____

9. My favorite way to chill is to _____

_____

10. My friends say this about me _____

_____

From N.E. Tummers, 2011, *Teaching stress management: Activities for children and young adults* (Champaign, IL: Human Kinetics).

Additional Yoga Poses

The following yoga poses are appropriate for early childhood through adulthood. They can be interspersed within the sun salutations after the forward fold or done as stand-alone yoga poses.

Adapted, by permission, from N. Tummers, 2009, *Teaching yoga for life: Preparing children and teens for healthy, balanced living* (Champaign, IL: Human Kinetics), 108, 109, 110, 115, 123, 130, 131, 132, 133, 138, 148, 151, 152.

Downward Facing Dog Pose

This pose may not look at first like a relaxing one, but as the students become familiar with it they will love hanging out in the down dog! In teaching the down dog, ask students to imagine themselves as an upside-down V. Students tend to do the down dog like a push-up, with all their weight over their arms and wrists, rather than by pressing their hips up to the sky and pressing their heart space back toward their legs.

1. Start in a forward fold pose and come into table pose (on all fours).

2. Place your hands flat on the floor straight ahead with your fingers spread wide and strong.

3. Tuck your toes under and balance on the balls of your feet while keeping your feet hip-distance apart.

4. Straighten your legs and lift your hips into an upside down V shape. Lift your gluteus muscles high and back (dog tilt). Your heels do not need to touch the ground.

5. Relax your head and look toward your knees; press your chest back toward strong legs.

6. Finish: Gently release both legs, coming back into table pose.

Upward Facing Dog Pose

You may notice that animals naturally move from down dog into upward facing dog. Make sure to encourage students to keep their shoulders and shoulder blades down and their heart lifted when doing upward facing dog.

1. Start in downward facing dog pose.
2. Stretch forward onto your toes and hands and make a big happy puppy grin. Move back and forth from down dog to up dog a few times and then rest in child pose.
3. Finish in table pose (on all fours).

Cobra Pose

This pose is a core strengthener. Infants do the cobra in order to gain enough core strength to be able to start creeping and crawling. In cobra, the hands are not doing the work but are used more for balance.

1. Start prone, lying flat on the floor on your belly.
2. Bring your legs together like the tail of a snake. Keep your lower body strong and grounded on the floor.
3. Place your hands at the chest line under your shoulders with your fingers pointed forward and your elbows bent and close to the sides of your ribs.
4. Press your hands into the floor and gently lift your chest with your head in line with your spine (not extended back). Feel the stretch in your back.
5. Keep your lower body strong and grounded into the floor; keep your back fluid and keep the front of the body open and spacious.
6. Finish by gently coming out of cobra but continue to lie on the floor for a few relaxing breaths.

Warrior I Pose

Warrior is a total body strengthening exercise. The legs hold the pose, the arms reach overhead, and the core is engaged to keep the pose steady and the spine strong.

1. Start in mountain pose.
2. Take a big step back into lunge with your left foot while keeping your right foot straight ahead with the knee bent; turn your left foot slightly out to the side. (Your right foot is at 12 o'clock, and your left foot is at 9 or 10 o'clock.)
3. Square shoulders and hips to the front.
4. Reach overhead, keeping a strong straight back leg.
5. Finish by stepping back into mountain pose.

Warrior II Pose

Warrior II is a great pose for building confidence; it is an affirming pose that students love.

1. Start in mountain pose.
2. Jump into wide leg stance.
3. Turn both feet to face the right.
4. Bend your right knee and keep your left leg strong and straight.
5. Arms in airplane—hold arms straight at shoulder height positioned over legs and look over the right finger tips.
6. Turn and square your shoulders and hips to the side.
7. Keep tailbone pointing straight down. Your right foot is at 3 o'clock, and your left foot is at 12 o'clock.
8. Finish by returning to a wide leg stance and reverse your feet to practice warrior II pose to the left.

Reverse Warrior Pose

This pose allows for a modified side bend and opens up the ribs and chest.

1. Start from warrior II pose and drop your back arm to your back leg and hold.
2. Your front arm reaches to the sky—look at your front hand and feel your heart area open and a slight side bend. You can move from extended side angle pose (see the next pose description) to reverse warrior pose, moving like a teeter-totter.
3. Finish in mountain pose.

Extended Side Angle Pose

This pose engages the whole body as the legs are engaged and strong and the top arm is reaching up and over the head.

1. Start in warrior II pose.
2. Bend your right knee, let your right forearm rest on the bent knee, and extend your left arm up to sky, looking up at your hand. To advance, reach your left arm over your head.
3. Keep your left leg strong; press your left foot into the floor.
4. Finish by pressing your legs firmly into the ground; slowly come up and reverse.

Triangle Pose

The triangle pose is challenging, but students love to make these geometric shapes!

1. Start in mountain pose.
2. Jump out into wide leg stance about as far as one big walking step.
3. Turn one foot to point to the right and the other slightly to the right with both legs strong and straight.
4. Hips and shoulders square to side with arms straight over legs at sides (airplane arms).
5. Reach your right arm to the side, hinge at the hip, reach to the side wall, and hold onto your shin or ankle; left arm reaches up to sky (look at it or at floor).
6. Gently come back up and reverse feet (point them to the left) and reach your left arm out to triangle on the left.

Tree Pose

This is a quintessential balancing pose that looks easy but can be a challenge!

1. Start in mountain pose.
2. Stand tall and strong and place your weight on one leg. Pretend that your standing foot has grown roots into the earth below and that the top of your head is reaching to the sun.
3. Now bring the sole of your other foot to rest on the inner calf muscle or on the top of the supporting foot.
4. Bring your hands to your heart space and slowly grow the branches of the tree (reaching your arms up to the sky or out to the sides).
5. Make sure to breathe and keep your eyes glued to a spot in front of you. Hold your tree pose strong and proud! Switch feet and remember to use a chair or the wall for help in balancing.
6. Rest hands on hips or clasped at chest or reach overhead like limbs of a tree.
7. Finish in mountain pose.

Butterfly Pose

Butterfly is a hip-opening pose.

1. Start seated on the floor.
2. Hold onto your feet and bring the bottoms of your feet together. Turn the soles of your feet to face the ceiling, open your knees out like butterfly wings, and let them gently flap like a butterfly on the breeze.
3. Fold forward from hips and hold.
4. A variation is Half Butterfly Pose, in which one leg can remain straight while the other knee drops into butterfly.
5. To finish, gently stretch and shake out both legs.

Turtle Pose

This pose offers a good way to illustrate the fact that a turtle does not go fast but is steady in pursuing its goal!

1. Start by sitting on the floor and separating your feet about as wide (2 to 3 feet or 0.6 to 0.9 meter) as the yoga mat.
2. Reach forward and hold onto your toes, shins, or ankles. Your knees should be kept soft (more bent) as needed.
3. Lift your head and stretch your face and neck like a turtle head coming out of its shell!
4. Finish by gently bringing your legs back together and shaking them out.

Seated Twist Pose

This pose allows the spine to be gently twisted—a great antidote to being seated for a long time.

1. Start seated on the floor with your legs straight out in front.

2. Keeping one leg glued to the ground and sitting tall, bend your other knee and cross that leg over the straight leg, drawing it close to your chest, and hug the bent knee.

3. Turn your belly button toward your bent knee. Bring your opposite elbow across your body, hook it on the outside of your knee, or turn and hug the outside of your knee.

4. Come back to center. Switch legs.

5. Finish by gently bringing your legs together in front of you and shaking them out.

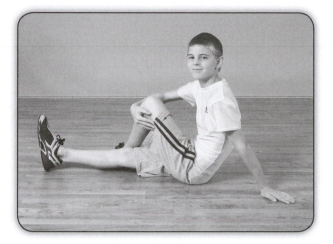

References and Resources

References

Abascal, J, Brucato, D & Brucato, L. (2001). Stress mastery. *The art of coping gracefully*. Upper Saddle Ranch, NJ: Prentice Hall.

Action for Healthy Kids. (n.d.). www.action-forhealthykids.org/.

American Art Therapy Association. (2010). National Children's Mental Health Awareness Day. www.arttherapy.org/chmad.asp.

American Massage Therapy Association. (2010) Massage Therapy Industry Fact Sheet. www.amtamassage.org/articles/2/PressRelease/detail/2146.

Anderson, K. (2010). Divinity in disguise. www.divinityindisguise.com/meditation.html.

Arck, P., Slominski, A., Theohardies, T, Peters, E. & Paus, R. (2006) Neuroimmunology of stress: Skin takes center stage. *Journal of Investigative Dermatology 126*, 1697-1704.

Arnold, L.E. (1990). Stress in children and adolescents: Introduction and summary. (pp. 1-19). In L.E. Arnold (Ed.), *Childhood stress*. New York: Wiley.

Association for Supervision and Curriculum Development. (2004a). Health and learning [ASCD adopted position]. www.ascd.org/news-media/ASCD-Policy-Positions/ASCD-Positions.aspx.

Association for Supervision and Curriculum Development. (2004b). *The whole child* [ASCD adopted position]. www.ascd.org/news-media/ASCD-Policy-Positions/ASCD-Positions.aspx.

Bagdi, A., & Pfister, I. (2006). Childhood stressors and coping actions: A comparison of children and parent's perspectives. *Child & Youth Care Forum* [online], 35(1).

Barnes, V.A., Bauza, L.B., & Treiber, F.A. (2003). Impact of stress reduction on negative school behavior in adolescents. *Health and Quality of Life Outcomes, 1*(10), 1-7.

Barton, M.L., & Zeanah, C.H. (1990). Stress in the preschool years (pp. 193-215). In L.E. Arnold (Ed.), *Childhood stress*. New York: Wiley.

Benson, H. & Proctor, W. (2010). *Enhancing your personal health through the science and genetics of mind-body healing*. New York, NY: Scribner.

Benson, H., Wilcher, M., Greenberg, B., Huggins, E., Ennis, M., Zuttermeister, P., Myers, P., & Friedman, R. (2000). Academic performance among middle school students after exposure to a relaxation response curriculum. *Journal of Research and Development in Education, 33*(3), 156-165.

Big Brothers Big Sisters. (n.d.). www.bbbs.org/.

Bothe, D., & Olness, K.A. (2006). The effects of a stress management technique on elementary school children. *Journal of Developmental & Behavioral Pediat*rics, *27*(5), 429-430.

Bradley, T. (2006). Chill out! Helping gifted youth deal with stress: What are some specific, practical ways to teach stress management? *Understanding Our Gifted, 18*(2), 9-12.

Brain Gym. (n.d.). www.braingym.org/.

Broderick, P.C., & Metz, S. (2009). Learning to BREATHE: A pilot trial of a mindfulness curriculum for adolescents. *Advances in School Mental Health Promotion, 2*(1), 35-46.

Burak, E. (2002). *College student's guide to peer wellness mentoring: Mentoring for lifestyle success*. Dubuque, IA: Kendall/Hunt.

Burns, J.W. (1990). *An evaluation of the Make Your Day program of student management*. Unpublished doctoral dissertation, Northern Arizona University, Flagstaff.

Catalano, R.F., Haggerty, K.P., Oesterle, S., Fleming, C.B., & Hawkins, J.D. (2004). The importance of bonding to school for health development: Findings from the Social Development Research Group. *Journal of School Health*, 74(7), 252-262.

Center for Mindfulness in Medicine, Health Care and Society. (n.d.) University of Massachusetts Medical School. Major Research Findings. www.umassmed.edu/Content.aspx?id=42426.

Center for Screen-Time Awareness. (n.d.). www.screen-timeinstitute.org

Centers for Disease Control and Prevention (2008a). National Center for Chronic Disease Prevention and Health Promotion, Division of Adolescent and School Health. www.cdc.gov/healthyyouth/healthtopics/.

Centers for Disease Control and Prevention. (2008b). Coordinated school health program. www.cdc.gov/healthyyouth/cshp.

Centers for Disease Control and Prevention (2009a). National Center for Chronic Disease Prevention and Health Promotion, Division of Adolescent and School Health. www.cdc.gov/HealthyYouth/mentalhealth/index.htm.

Centers for Disease Control and Prevention. (2009b). School connectedness. www.cdc.gov/healthyyouth/AdolescentHealth/connectedness.htm.

Centers for Disease Control and Prevention. (2010a). Youth violence: Risk and protective factors. www.

cdc.gov/ViolencePrevention/youthviolence/risk-protectivefactors.html.

Centers for Disease Control and Prevention. (2010b). YRBSS: Selected health risk behaviors and health outcomes by race/ethnicity—National. YRBS: 2009. www.cdc.gov/HealthyYouth/yrbs/pdf/us_disparity-race_yrbs.pdf.

Centers for Disease Control and Prevention. (2010c). YRBSS: Youth risk behavior surveillance system. www.cdc.gov/HealthyYouth/yrbs/index.htm.

Centers for Disease Control and Prevention. (2010d). Youth Risk Behavior Surveillance—United States, 2009. Summaries, June 4, 2010. MMWR 2010; 59, SS-5.

Childre, D., & Martin, H. (1999). *The HeartMath solution*. San Francisco: HarperCollins.

Chopra Center. (n.d.). www.chopra.com/.

Christakis, D., & Zimmerman, F. (2007). Violent television viewing during preschool is associated with antisocial behavior during school age. *Pediatrics, 120*(5), 993-999.

Collaborative for Academic, Social, and Emotional Learning (CASEL) (2003). Social and emotional learning and student benefits [Brief]. www.casel.org/downloads/EDC_CASELSELResearchBrief.pdf.

Committee for Children. (2010). Second Step research and results. www.cfchildren.org/programs/ssp/research/.

Copeland, W., Keeler, G., Angold, A., & Costello, J. (2007). Traumatic events and posttraumatic stress in children. *Archives of General Psychiatry, 64*, 577-584.

Cornell, J. (2006). *Mandala: Luminous symbols for healing: 10th anniversary edition with a new CD of meditations and exercises*. Wheaton, IL: Quest Books.

Cousins, N. (1991). *Anatomy of an illness as perceived by the patient*. New York: Bantam Books.

Covey, S. (1989). *The seven habits of highly effective people*. New York: Fireside Books.

Covey, S. (1998). *The seven habits of highly effective teens*. New York: Fireside Books.

Covey, S. (2005). *The 8th habit: From effectiveness to greatness*. New York: Free Press.

Culbert, T., & Kajander, R. (2007). *Be the boss of your stress*. Minneapolis: Free Spirit.

Desrochers, J.E., Cowan, K.C., & Christner, R.W. (2009, April). These tough economic times. *Principal Leadership*, pp. 10-14. www.nasponline.org/educators/NASSP_Supporting_Students_Econ_Crisis_Apr_09.pdf.

Edwards, O.E., Mumford, V.E., Shillingford, M., & Serra-Roldan, R. (2007). Developmental assets: A prevention framework for students considered at risk. *Children & Schools, 29*(3), 145-153.

Find Youth Info. (2010). How can positive youth development be integrated into programs? http://findyouthinfo.gov/topic_pyd_integration.shtml.

Fox, A., & Kirschner, R. (2005). *Too stressed to think? Teen guide to staying sane when life makes you crazy*. Minneapolis: Free Spirit.

Fulkerson, J.A., Story, M., Mellin, A., Leffert, N., Neumark-Sztainer, D., & French, S.A. (2006). Family dinner meal frequency and adolescent development: Relationships with developmental assets and high-risk behaviors. *Journal of Adolescent Health, 39*, 337-345.

Gillham, J.E., & Reivich, K. (2004). Cultivating optimism in childhood and adolescence. *Annals of the American Academy of Political & Social Science, 591*(1), 149-163

Gillham, J.E., Reivich, K., & Shatté, A. (2002). Positive youth development, prevention, and positive psychology: Commentary on positive youth development in the United States. *Prevention & Treatment*, 5, (18).

Gonzalez, L., & Sellers, E. (2002). The effects of a stress-management program on self-concept, locus of control, and the acquisition of coping skills in school-age children diagnosed with attention deficit hyperactivity disorder. *Journal of Child and Adolescent Psychiatric Nursing, 15*(1), 5-15.

Grosswald, S., Stixrud, W., Travis, F., & Bateh, A. (2008, December). Use of the Transcendental Meditation technique to reduce symptoms of attention deficit hyperactivity disorder (ADHD) by reducing stress and anxiety: An exploratory study. *Current Issues in Education* [online], *10*(2). http://cie.ed.asu.edu/volume10/number2/.

Guetzloe, E. (1997). The power of positive relationships: Mentoring programs in the school and community. *Preventing School Failure, 41*, 100-105.

Henderson, N., Bernard, B., and Sharp-Light, N. (Eds.) (2007). Resiliency in action. Practical ideas for overcoming risks and building strengths in youth, family, and communities (2nd ed.). Ojai, CA: Resiliency in Action.

Hendren, R.L. (1990). Stress in adolescence (pp. 247-262) .In L.E. Arnold (Ed), *Childhood stress* (pp. 247-263). New York: Wiley.

Horowitz, J.L., & Garber, J. (2006). The prevention of depressive symptoms in children and adolescents: A meta-analytic review. *Journal of Consulting and Clinical Psychology, 74*(3), 401-415.

Huesmann, L. (2007). The impact of electronic media violence: Scientific theory and research. *Journal of Adolescent Health, 41*(6), S6–S13.

Humphrey, J.H. (1993). *Stress management for elementary schools*. Springfield, IL: Charles C. Thomas.

Illinois State Board of Education. (2010). Illinois learning standards: Social/emotional learning (SEL). www.isbe.net/ils/social_emotional/standards.htm.

Institute of HeartMath. (n.d.). www.heartmath.org/.

Jensen, E. (2005). *Teaching with the brain in mind* (2nd ed.). Alexandria, VA: Association for Supervision and Curriculum Development.

Joint Committee on National Health Education Standards. (2007). *National Health Education Standards: Achieving excellence* (2nd ed.). Atlanta: American Cancer Society. www.cdc.gov/healthyyouth/sher/standards.

Jordan, J., McRorie, M., & Ewing, C. (2010). Gender differences in the role of emotional intelligence during the primary–secondary school transition. *Emotional & Behavioral Difficulties, 15*(1), 37-47.

Karren, K.J., Smith, L., Hafen, B.Q., & Frandsen, K.J. (2010). *Mind/body health: The effects of attitudes, emotions, and relationships* (4th ed.). San Francisco: Benjamin Cummings.

Kimchi, J., & Schaffner, B. (1990). Childhood protective factors and stress risk (pp. 475-495). In L.E. Arnold (Ed.), *Childhood stress*. New York: Wiley.

King, K.A., Vidourek, R.A., Davis, B., & McClellan, W. (2002). Increasing self-esteem and school connectedness through a multidimensional mentoring program. *Journal of School Health, 72*(7).

Klimas, N. (2003, February 17). Yoga for youngsters. *Advance for physical therapists and PT assistants.* http://physical-therapy.advanceweb.com/Article/Yoga-for-Youngsters-8.aspx.

Knox, R. (2010, March 1). The teen brain: It's just not grown up yet. National Public Radio. www.npr.org/templates/story/story php?storyId=124119468&sc=emaf.

Kobasa, S.C. (1979). Stressful life events, personality and health: An inquiry into hardiness. *Journal of Personality and Social Psychology, 37*, 1-11.

Kragg, G., Zeegers, M.P., Kok, G., Hosman, C., & Abu-Saad, H.H. (2006). School programs targeting stress management in children and adolescents: A meta-analysis. *Journal of School Psychology, 44*(6), 449-472.

Krovetz, M.L. (2008). *Fostering resilience. Expecting all students to use their minds and hearts well* (2nd ed.). Thousand Oaks, CA: Corwin Press.

Lantieri, L. (2008). *Building emotional intelligence: Techniques to cultivate inner strength in children.* Boulder, CO: Sounds True.

Lazar, S., Kerr, C., Wasserman, R., Gray, J., Greve, D., Treadway, M., McGarvey, M., Quinn, B., Dusek, J., Benson, H., Rauch, S., Moore, C., & Fischl, B. (2005). Meditation experience is associated with increased cortical thickness. *Neuroreport, 16*(17), 1893-1897.

Learn and Serve America's National Service-Learning Clearinghouse. (n.d.) www.servicelearning.org/what-service-learning.

Levine, S. (1983). A psychobiological approach to the ontogeny of coping (pgs. 107-132). In N. Garmezy & M. Rutter (Eds.), *Stress, coping, and development in children*. New York: McGraw-Hill.

Lyubomirsky, S. (2007). *The how of happiness: A scientific approach to getting the life you want.* New York: Penguin Books.

Maguire, G. (2004). *Wicked: The life and times of the Wicked Witch of the West.* New York: Harper.

McCraty, R., Atkinson, M., Tomasino, D., Goelitz, J., & Mayrovitz, H.N. (1999). The impact of an emotional self-management skills course on psychosocial functioning and autonomic recovery to stress in middle school children. *Integrative Physiological & Behavioral Science, 34*(4) 246-268.

McEwen, B., & Seeman, T. (2009, August). Allostatic load and allostasis. San Francisco: University of California, San Francisco (MacArthur Research Network on Socioeconomic Status and Health). www.macses.ucsf.edu/research/allostatic/allostatic.php.

McGrady, A. (2007). Psychophysiological mechanisms of stress. A Foundation for Stress Management Therapies. (pp. 16-36) In *Principles and practice stress management* 3rd ed. Lehrer, P, Woolfolk, R & Sime, W. Eds. New York, NY: Guilford Press.

Merikangas, K.R., Burstein, M., Swanson, S.A., Avenevoli, S., Cui, L., Benjet, C., Georgiades, K., & Swendsen, J. (2010, October). Lifetime prevalence of mental disorders in U.S. adolescents: Results from the National Comorbidity Study—Adolescent Supplement (NCS-A). *Journal of the American Academy of Child and Adolescent Psychiatry, 49*(10), 980-989.

Middlebrooks, J.S., & Audage, N.C. (2008). *The effects of childhood stress on health across the lifespan.* Atlanta: Centers for Disease Control and Prevention.

Morris, V.G., Taylor, S.I., & Wilson, J.T. (2000). Using children's stories to promote peace in classrooms. *Early Childhood Education Journal, 28*(1), 41-50.

Munsey, C. (2010) The kids aren't all right. *Monitor on Psychology: A Publication of the American Psychological Association, 40*(1), 12. www.apa.org/monitor/2010/01/stress-kids.aspx.

Nation, M., Crusto, C., Wandersman, A., Kumpfer, K.L., Seybolt, D., Morrissey-Kane, E., & Davino, K. (2003). What works in prevention: Principles of effective prevention programs. *American Psychologist, 58*, 449-456.

National Association for Sport and Physical Education. (2006). Recess for elementary school students [Position statement]. Reston, VA: Author. www.aahperd.org/naspe/standards/upload/Recess-for-Elementary-School-Students-2006.pdf.

National Center for Complementary and Alternative Medicine. (2010a). Meditation. http://nccam.nih.gov/health/meditation/.

National Institutes of Health. (2004). First National Sleep Conference March 29-30 explores sleep's role in public health [Press release]. www.nih.gov/news/pr/mar2004/nhlbi-25.htm.

National Sleep Foundation (2010). Children and sleep. www.sleepfoundation.org/article/sleep-topics/children-and-sleep.

National Wellness Institute. (2010). Six dimensional model of wellness. www.nationalwellness.org/index.php?id_tier=2&id_c=25.

National Youth Risk Behavior Survey Overview. (2009). www.cdc.gov/HealthyYouth/yrbs/pdf/us_overview_yrbs.pdf.

Niebuhr, Reinhold. (n.d.). Serenity prayer. http://en.wikipedia.org/wiki/Serenity_Prayer.

Northeast Foundation for Children. (2010). Responsive classroom. www.responsiveclassroom.org/about/aboutrc.html.

Office of the Surgeon General. (1999). Stressful life events. In *Mental Health: A report of the Surgeon General—Executive summary*. Rockville, MD: U.S. Department of Health and Human Services. www.surgeongeneral.gov/library/mentalhealth/chapter4/sec1_1.html.

Oken, B. (2008) Placebo effects; clinical aspects and neurobiology. *Brain, 131*, 2812-2823.

Ornish, D. (n.d.) Dean Ornish, MD. Preventive Medicine Research Institute. www.pmri.org/dean_ornish.html.

Ornish, D., Scherwitz, L., Billings, J., Gould, L., Merritt, T., Sparler, S., Armstrong, W., Ports, T., Kirkeeide, R., Hogeboom, C. & Brand, R. (1998). Intensive lifestyle changes for reversal of coronary heart disease. *Journal of the American Medical Association, 230*(23), 2001-2007.

Partnership for 21st Century Skills. (2009). Framework definitions. www.p21.org/documents/P21_Framework.pdf.

Pastor, P.N., & Reuben, C.A. (2008). Diagnosed attention deficit hyperactivity disorder and learning disability: United States, 2004-2006. *Vital Health Statistics 10*(237).

Pay It Forward Movement. (n.d.). www.payitforwardmovement.org/.

Pierce, L.H., & Shields, N. (1998). The "Be a Star" community-based after-school program: Developing resiliency factors in high risk preadolescent youth. *Journal of Community Psychology, 26*(2) 175-183.

Preventive Medicine Research Institute. www.pmri.org/.

Ratey, J. (2008). *Spark: The revolutionary new science of exercise and the brain*. New York: Little, Brown.

Reivich, K., & Shatté, A. (2002). *The resilience factor and keys to finding your inner strength and overcoming life's hurdles*. New York: Broadway Books.

Rice, M., Kang, D.H., Weaver, M., & Howell, C.C. (2008). Relationship of anger, stress, and coping with school connectedness in fourth-grade children. *Journal of School Health. 78*, 149-156.

Rollin, S.A., Arnold, A.R., Solomon, S., Rubin, R.I., & Holland, J.L. (2003). A stress management curriculum for at-risk youth. *Journal of Humanistic Counseling, Education and Development, 42*, 79-90.

Rutter, M. (1983). Stress, coping, and development: Some issues and some questions (pp. 1-42). In N. Garmezy & M. Rutter (Eds.), *Stress, coping, and development in children*. New York: McGraw-Hill.

Saltzman A. (2010). Conference proceedings. Mindfulness as a Foundation for Teaching and Learning Conference. Lesley University, Cambridge MA, March 2010.

Saltzman. A. & Goldin, P (2008). Mindfulness-based stress reduction for school-aged children (pp. 139-161). In *Acceptance & mindfulness treatment for children & adolescents*. Greco, L., & Hayes, S. (Eds). Oakland, CA: New Harbinger Publications.

Schoeberlein, D. (2009). *Mindful teaching and teaching mindfulness. A guide for anyone who teaches anything*. Boston: Wisdom.

Schuster, M.A., Stein, B.D., Jaycox, L.H., Collins, R.L., Marshall, G.N., Elliott, M.N., Zhou, A.J., Kanouse, D.E., Morrison, J.L., & Berry, S.H. (2001). A national survey of stress reactions after the September 11, 2001, terrorist attacks. *New England Journal of Medicine, 345*(20), 1507-1512.

Sears, S.J., & Milburn, J. (1990). School-age stress (pp. 223-243). In L.E. Arnold (Ed.), *Childhood stress*. New York: Wiley.

Seaward, B.L. (2002). *Managing stress: A relaxation CD*. Sudbury, MA: Jones and Bartlett.

Seaward, B.L. (2006). *Managing stress: Principles and strategies for health and well-being* (5th ed.). Sudbury, MA: Jones and Bartlett.

Seligman, M., Reivich, K., Jaycox, L., & Gillham, J. (2007). The optimistic child: A proven program to safeguard children against depression and build lifelong resilience. New York: Houghton Mifflin.

Selye, H. (1970). The evolution of the stress concept: Stress and cardiovascular disease. *The American Journal of Cardiology, 26*(3), 289-299.

Selye, H. (1974). *Stress without distress*. New York, NY: McGraw Hill.

Sharrer, V.M., & Ryan-Wenger, N. (2002). School-age children's self-reported stress symptoms. *Pediatric Nursing, 28*(1), 21-27.

Sheely, A., & Bratton, S. (2010). A strengths-based parenting intervention with low-income African American families. *Professional School Counseling, 13*(3), 175-183.

Siegel, D. (2007). *The mindful brain*. New York: Norton.

Siegel, D. (2010). *Mindsight: The new science of personal transformation*. New York: Bantam Books.

Spiegel, A. (2008). Creative play makes for kids in control. National Public Radio *Morning Edition* interview with Dr. Adele Diamond. Aired Feb. 28, 2008. www.npr.org/templates/story/story.php?storyId=76838288.

Stalvey, S., & Brasell, H. (2006). Using stress balls to focus the attention of sixth-grade learners. *The Journal of At-Risk Issues, 12*(2), 7-16.

Stamps, L. (2003). Bibliotherapy: How books can help students cope with concerns and conflicts. *The Delta Kappa Gamma Bulletin, 70*(1), 25-29.

Stukin, S. (2001, November). Om schooling. *Yoga Journal*, 89-93, 151-153.

Sumar, S. (1998). *Yoga for the special child: A therapeutic approach for infants and children with Down syndrome, cerebral palsy, and learning disabilities*. Buckingham, VT: Special Yoga Publications; Route 1.

Tacker, K.A., & Dobie, S. (2008). MasterMind: Empower yourself with mental health: A program for adolescents. *Journal of School Health, 78*(1), 54-57.

Taxis, C.J., Rew, L,, Jackson, K., & Kouzekanani, K. (2004). Protective resources and perceptions of stress in a multi-ethnic sample of school-age children. *Pediatric Nursing*. Nov-Dec. 2004, 30 (6).

Taylor, J.V., & Trice-Black, S. (2007). *Girls in real-life situations: Group counseling activities for enhancing social and emotional development*. Champaign, IL: Research Press.

Trad, P.V., & Greenblatt, E. (1990). Psychological aspects of child stress: Development and the spectrum of coping responses (pp. 23-44). In L.E. Arnold (Ed.), *Childhood stress*. New York: Wiley.

Tummers, N. (2009). *Teaching yoga for life: Preparing children and teens for healthy, balanced living*. Champaign, IL: Human Kinetics.

Understanding Youth Violence. (2010). www.cdc.gov/violenceprevention/pdf/YV-FactSheet-a.pdf.

University of Pennsylvania Positive Psychology. (n.d.). Resiliency Research in Children. The Penn Resiliency Project. www.ppc.sas.upenn.edu/prpsum.htm.

U.S Department of Health and Human Services. (2000). *Healthy people 2010* (2nd ed.). With Understanding and Improving Health and Objectives for Improving Health. 2 vols. Washington, DC: U.S. Government Printing Office.

Viadero, D. (2007). Social skills programs found to yield gains in academic subjects. *Education Week, 27*(16), 1-15.

Wang, J., Iannotti, R., & Nansel, T. (2009). School bullying among adolescents in the United States: Physical, verbal, relational, and cyber. *Journal of Adolescent Health, 45*(4), 368-375.

Weil, A. (n.d.). www.drweil.com/.

Winner, J. (2008). *Take the stress out of your life*. Philadelphia: First Da Capo Press.

Woolfolk, R., Lehrer, P. & Allen, L. (2007). Conceptual issues underlying stress management. (pp. 1-15) In *Principles and practice stress management* (3rd ed.). Lehrer, P, Woolfolk, R & Sime, W. Eds. New York, NY: Guilford Press.

Zipkin, D. (1985). Relaxation techniques for handicapped children. *The Journal of Special Education, 19*(3), 283-289.

Resources

Covey, S. (2004). The seven habits of highly effective people (Rev. ed.). New York: Fireside Books.

National Association of School Psychologists. (2008). Helping children cope in unsettling times: The economic crisis: Tips for parents and teachers. Bethesda, MD: www.nasponline.org/families/unsettlingtimes.pdf.

National Center for Complementary and Alternative Medicine. (2010). Clinical trials. http://nccam.nih.gov/research/clinicaltrials/.

Thornton, T.N., Craft, C.A., Dahlberg, L.L., Lynch, B.S., & Baer, K. (2002). Best practices of youth violence prevention: A sourcebook for community action (Rev. ed.). Atlanta: Centers for Disease Control and Prevention. www.cdc.gov/ncipc/dvp/bestpractices/Introduction.pdf.

About the Author

Nanette E. Tummers, EdD, is a professor of health and physical education at Eastern Connecticut State University in Willimantic, Connecticut. Since 1995 she has been teaching stress management skills and providing people with the tools they need to cope with stress. Her audiences have run the gamut from preschool through college students and youth and adults in recovery programs.

Dr. Tummers conducted her doctoral and postdoctoral research on stress management tools and has carried out service projects involving at-risk students and other groups. She has also been a reviewer for books and journals on material relating to stress management.

In her spare time, Dr. Tummers enjoys hiking with her dogs, landscaping, being outdoors, and volunteering in her community.